RAND NATIONAL SECURITY RESEARCH DIVISION

D1527061

Rolling Back the Islamic State

Seth G. Jones, James Dobbins, Daniel Byman, Christopher S. Chivvis, Ben Connable, Jeffrey Martini, Eric Robinson, Nathan Chandler

For more information on this publication, visit www.rand.org/t/RR1912

Library of Congress Cataloging-in-Publication Data is available for this publication.
ISBN: 978-0-8330-9756-9

Published by the RAND Corporation, Santa Monica, Calif.
© Copyright 2017 RAND Corporation
RAND® is a registered trademark.

Cover: *Iraqi forces advance against Islamic State militants in Mosul (Suhaib Salem, Reuters).*

www.rand.org

Preface

In 2014, the Islamic State conducted a blitzkrieg into Iraqi cities, such as Mosul, and seized significant chunks of territory in Syria and Iraq. Its leader, Abu Bakr al-Baghdadi, declared a pan-Islamic caliphate and eventually expanded the group to include eight formal provinces; more than a dozen informal provinces; and tens of thousands of inspired individuals across Asia, the Middle East, Africa, Europe, and North America. This report examines the Islamic State and offers a global strategy to roll the group and its movement back. It assesses key countries where the Islamic State has controlled territory: Iraq, Syria, Libya, Nigeria, Egypt, and Afghanistan. It also analyzes the group's global efforts to spread its ideology; move money, material, and people; secure resources; and conduct attacks. The report should be of interest to policymakers, academics, and general audiences that want to learn more about the Islamic State and strategies to counter the group.

This research was sponsored by a generous grant from the Smith Richardson Foundation and conducted within the International Security and Defense Policy Center of the RAND National Security Research Division (NSRD). NSRD conducts research and analysis on defense and national security topics for the U.S. and allied defense, foreign policy, homeland security, and intelligence communities and foundations and other nongovernmental organizations that support defense and national security analysis. For more information on the International Security and Defense Policy Center, see www.rand.org/nsrd/ndri/centers/isdp or contact the director (contact information is provided on the web page).

Contents

Figures and Tables

Figures

Tables

Summary

From its peak in late 2014, the Islamic State has steadily lost territory. As an actual, if unrecognized, state, it is on a path to collapse. In Syria and Iraq, the Islamic State controlled approximately 45,377 km² and roughly 2.5 million people by early 2017, according to RAND Corporation estimates compiled in this report. These numbers represented a 56-percent decline in population for Syria and an 83-percent decline in population for Iraq from fall 2014 levels. In Egypt, Libya, Afghanistan, and Nigeria, the Islamic State controlled a combined 7,323 km² and 497,420 people by early 2017. These estimates represented a 75-percent drop in population for Nigeria, nearly 100 percent for Libya, and 87 percent in Afghanistan. In Egypt, the Islamic State operated in only a tiny stretch of the Sinai. Polling data also indicated declining support across the Muslim world for the Islamic State and its ideology.

Yet even as its core caliphate contracted, the Islamic States established affiliates in the Middle East, Africa, and Asia while, at the same time, directing and inspiring attacks even further afield. The destruction of the Islamic State's territorial base in Iraq and Syria is likely to diminish the group's wider appeal. Yet it remains possible that the Islamic State, like al-Qa'ida before it, will continue to metastasize and spread its influence even once it loses its home base. The group's global footprint includes eight formal provinces outside Iraq and Syria; more than a dozen informal provinces; and tens of thousands of inspired individuals across the world. A *sine qua non* of the Islamic State's strategy is pan-Islamic expansion across multiple continents. The data compiled and analyzed in this report suggest that the Islamic State has begun to move from an insurgent group that controls territory to a clandestine terrorist group that conducts attacks against government officials and noncombatants. The group is likely to persist for some time in Iraq and Syria with other nodes across the globe, even after it loses most of its territory and its claim to an actual caliphate.

Fully eliminating the threat the Islamic State poses will require continued American leadership for years to come. The group's persistence suggests that the United States will need an effective global strategy to counter it. Much depends on how the group reacts to and evolves after the eventual loss of its core caliphate in Iraq and Syria. In the short and perhaps medium terms, this contraction in territorial control may actually lead to more terrorist attacks across the globe. But over time, the group's capacity to recruit, fund, organize, and inspire such attacks will likely diminish, and its brand may lose its allure if the Islamic State no longer controls territory in Iraq and Syria.

This report proposes that the United States adopt a *rollback strategy* to weaken and ultimately eliminate the Islamic State as a serious threat.

The Rise and Decline of the Islamic State

The Islamic State is a byproduct of the American intervention in Iraq and of the subsequent American departure. The 2003 intervention shifted the political balance in the country away from the formerly dominant Sunni minority toward the Shi'a majority, leaving Sunnis disgruntled, adrift, and divided. Militant Sunni extremists made common cause with tribal leaders and former regime elements to resist the American occupation and then the successor Shi'a-led government. Abu Musab al-Zarqawi, a Jordanian by birth and jihadist by profession, emerged as the most brutal and successful leader of this movement. In 2002, Zarqawi settled in Iraq and became an active leader in the insurgency against U.S. forces, formally allying himself with al-Qa'ida in 2004. This connection to Osama Bin Laden gave Zarqawi, who was killed by U.S. forces in 2006, immediate credibility with international Salafi-jihadists and elevated his stature to de facto chief of the otherwise fractured Sunni Arab Iraqi insurgent movement.

The year 2011 saw the withdrawal of American forces from Iraq and the beginning of a civil war in neighboring Syria. With the advent of the Syrian civil war, al-Qa'ida in Iraq's new leader, Abu Bakr al-Baghdadi, shifted the organization's center of gravity across the border into Syria. Following a failed attempt to assert his leadership over another already present al-Qa'ida affiliate, Baghdadi broke with the parent organization in 2014 and established the Islamic State as a new claimant to global leadership of the Salafi-jihadist movement.

The American withdrawal from Iraq removed a counterweight to Iranian influence, halted professionalization of the Iraqi Army, and reduced American visibility into these forces as they were progressively weakened by the Shi'a dominated regime in Baghdad. The Islamic State columns that advanced out of Syria and rapidly made their way to the very outskirts of Baghdad in early 2014 took Washington by surprise. Iraqi forces finally rallied with the assistance of the United States and Iran, the former advising the Army and police services, the latter bolstering Shi'a militia groups. Baghdad did not fall. The campaign to retake the Sunni heartland of Iraq was begun.

We assess that, at its peak in late 2014, the Islamic State controlled more than 100,000 km^2 of territory containing more than 11 million people, mostly in Iraq and Syria. Over the next year, the Islamic State co-opted local militant networks and added new provinces, or *wilayats*, in Libya, Egypt, Nigeria, and Afghanistan. The Islamic State also proclaimed provinces in Saudi Arabia, Algeria, and the Caucasus, but these controlled no territory. Preexisting Salafi-jihadist groups in Somalia, the Philippines, Turkey, Bangladesh, Indonesia, Mali, and Tunisia pledged their loyalty to the Islamic State and lobbied for provincial status. Tens of thousands of individual recruits from all over the world, including the United States and Europe, swelled the Islamic State's ranks. The group secured this control and spread its appeal by utilizing brutal violence and co-opting local disaffected individuals and groups.

Beginning in 2015, the Islamic State began to lose territory as it faced increasingly effective resistance from local government forces, U.S. and other outside powers, and nonstate armed groups. Figure S.1 highlights changes in Islamic State territorial control in Iraq and Syria between fall 2014 and winter 2016–2017.

Figure S.1
Islamic State Control of Territory in Iraq and Syria, Winter 2016–2017

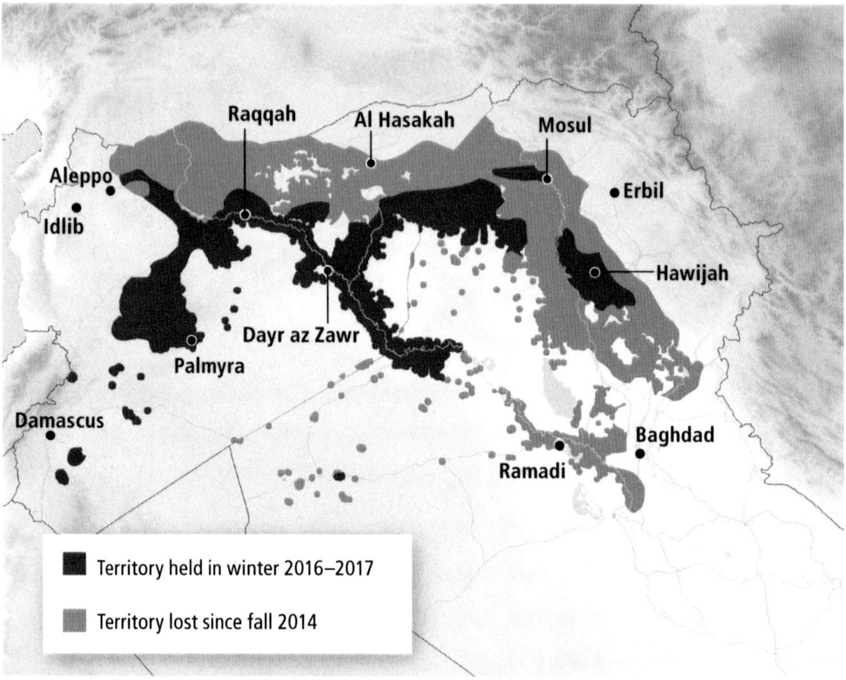

SOURCES: Fall 2014 estimates are based on U.S. Department of Defense, "Iraq and Syria: ISIL's Areas of Influence, August 2014 Through April 2016," Washington, D.C., 2016a. Winter 2016–2017 estimates are based on authors' estimates of changes in control.
RAND RR1912-S.1

The loss of territory and popular support are significant challenges for the Islamic State. At the same time, the Islamic State continues to conduct and inspire attacks abroad in an effort to exact revenge on its enemies, coerce the withdrawal of foreign forces, and bait foreign governments into overreacting in hopes of expanding the reach of its radical ideology. This violence persisted, as indicated in Figure S.2, even as the group began to lose much of its territory.

Figure S.2
Islamic State Global Attacks, 2014–January 2017

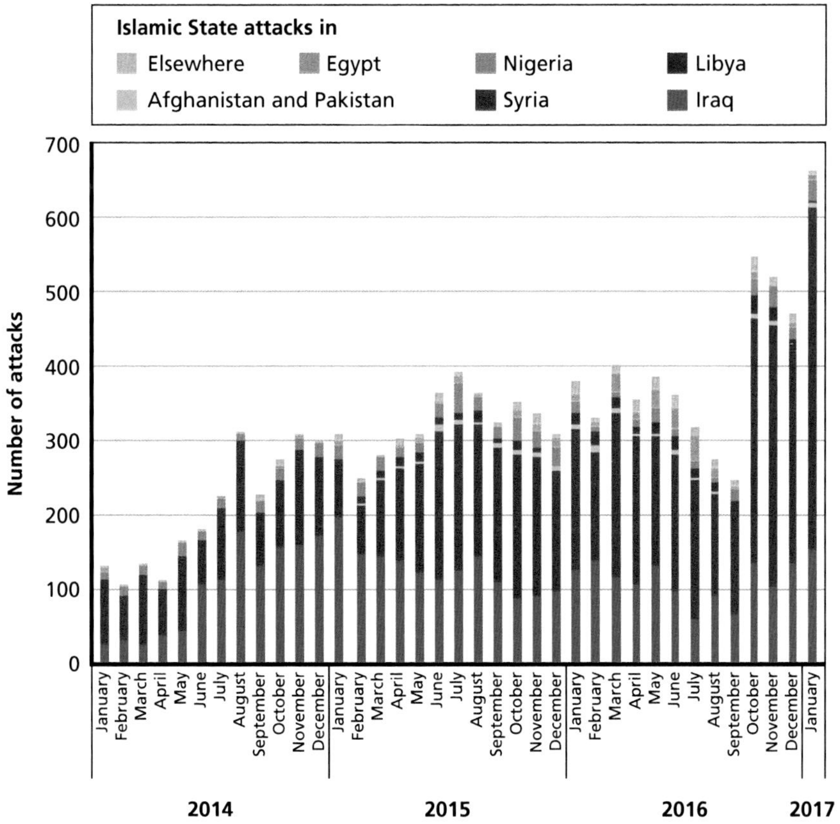

SOURCE: IHS Janes, 2017.
NOTES: "Elsewhere" includes attacks in the Middle East and North Africa (Algeria,
Israel, Kuwait, Lebanon, the Palestinian Territories, Saudi Arabia, Tunisia, and Turkey),
in Southeast Asia (Bangladesh, Indonesia, and Pakistan), and in Western or European
countries (Australia, Belgium, Bosnia and Herzegovina, Canada, Denmark, France,
Germany, Russia, the United Kingdom, and the United States).
RAND RR1912-S.2

Alternative American Strategies

This report examines four possible American strategies for dealing with
the Islamic State: disengagement, containment, rollback "light" (with a
reliance on local forces backed by U.S. special operations forces, Cen-

tral Intelligence Agency and other intelligence assets, and airpower), and rollback "heavy" (adding the employment of American conventional forces in ground combat).

The advocates of disengagement and containment have argued that the Islamic State will eventually burn itself out, having by now gravely antagonized every state and nearly every other insurgent group in the Middle East. This might be true. But the end is uncertain, and the defeat of the Islamic State would be at best distant. While the employment of large numbers of American conventional troops in ground combat might accelerate the recapture of Islamic State territory, such a large American presence could give rise to additional local resistance and would likely leave the United States principally responsible for the aftermath.

We conclude that the United States should pursue a light rollback strategy. Key components are the use of American airpower, special operations forces, and intelligence units to enable local partners to liberate territory and populations currently held by the Islamic State. Rollback also involves working to improve the capacity of local governments and to help address the underlying grievances that the Islamic State has leveraged to secure a foothold in Iraq and Syria and its other, more-distant provinces. Finally, rollback includes conducting an aggressive ideological campaign to counter the Islamic State's messaging and to shut down its easy access to media platforms.

The Obama administration's approach to countering the Islamic State and its predecessor organization, al-Qa'ida in Iraq, shifted over time. The administration initially pursued a disengagement approach and pulled U.S. military forces out of Iraq in 2011, although al-Qa'ida in Iraq continued to conduct attacks in Iraq over the next several years. Following the Islamic State's offensives in spring and summer 2014 in such areas as Anbar Province and Mosul, the United States sought to contain the threat, help defend Baghdad, and then support local forces in taking back Islamic State–controlled territory in Syria and Iraq. Over time, that administration expanded the use of U.S. special operations forces, intelligence units, and airpower to counter Islamic State gains in Libya, Nigeria, and Afghanistan.

We believe that these efforts can be further accelerated while preserving the advantages of the light U.S. footprint by intensifying military efforts in Syria, loosening some current restrictions on military operations, increasing basing access in Africa, expanding efforts to counter Islamic State propaganda and online recruitment, improving the capacity of local authorities to secure and administer territory and population liberated from the Islamic State, and intensifying efforts to ameliorate the local grievances that generate support for violent extremism.

Intensify Military Efforts in Syria

The lack of an acceptable local government partner in Syria has complicated American efforts to roll back the Islamic State without the introduction of conventional American ground forces. The deterioration in U.S. relations with Syria and Russia after the Assad regime's use of chemical weapons in April 2017, as well as the U.S. military strikes against Shayrat air base, also complicated U.S. actions in Syria. Washington has found an effective partner in the mixed Kurdish and Sunni Arab Syrian Defence Forces (SDF), which is dominated by a Syrian Kurdish faction closely linked to a violent separatist movement in Turkey in conflict with the Turkish state. This force has isolated Raqqa and is poised for an assault on the city, but lacks the weaponry that may be necessary for success. Turkey is strongly opposed to any further extension of Kurdish control within Syria and equally opposed to any American effort to arm the SDF. Washington must therefore choose whether to ignore Turkish objections and arm the SDF, seek direct Turkish army participation in the assault as a substitute, or add some American units to the assault force. Waiting for the Turkish army and its Syrian allies to arrive will require postponing the operation several months, with an uncertain end result. Arming the Kurdish-dominated SDF and introducing additional American forces into Syria, beyond the special operations troops already there, may be the fastest and surest way of retaking Raqqa and other Islamic State territory.

Delegate Authority Downward

The Presidential Policy Guidance document titled "Procedures for Approving Direct Action Outside the United States and Areas of Active Hostilities," outlined the Obama administration's policy toward strikes outside areas of active hostilities, which included Afghanistan, Iraq and Syria.[1] Deputies Committee meetings were often necessary to secure approval for strikes. Instead, the White House should push authority to conduct direct action further down the chain of command in a wider range of active war zones, starting with Libya and probably including Yemen and Somalia, where al-Qa'ida affiliates are the target. When American ambassadors and commanders cannot agree, disputes should be referred to Washington. But otherwise, there should be more discretion for action at the local level on the basis of clearly established guidelines, as is already the case in Afghanistan, Iraq, and Syria.

The administration should make a concerted effort to be transparent about strikes overseas, both in discussing the results of operations and explaining the legal and policy framework for authorizing them. With some types of operations, such as hostage rescue missions and raids, authorizing the deployment of U.S. military boots on the ground should still involve White House–level deliberations because the U.S. foreign policy implications are particularly significant.

Washington should also provide greater leeway to commanders when U.S. advisers and special operations forces accompany local partners into combat. American troops have at times been prevented from moving past the last "cover and conceal" position during operations because of security concerns. As a result, the United States has had to rely on partner forces to conduct a range of high value missions to include capturing terrorist material.

---

[1]   White House, "Procedures for Approving Direct Action Against Terrorist Targets Located Outside the United States and Areas of Active Hostilities," Washington, D.C., May 22, 2013. This redacted and declassified document is available via the website of the Federation of American Scientists.

Expand Basing Access in North and West Africa

The loss of Islamic State territory in Iraq and Syria will initiate a reverse flow of foreign fighters, many of whom are likely to head back to North Africa and in some cases further south. While the United States has bases in East Africa, notably in Djibouti, it has no comparable facilities in North or West Africa. The United States should seek arrangements with one or more countries in the region to base U.S. military forces and fly combat and surveillance aircraft.

Restrict Islamic State Internet Access and Counter Its Message

The United States should take further steps to counter the Islamic State's messaging and close down its access to social media and other Internet platforms. American and allied governments should work with companies to shut down social media accounts linked to the Islamic State. Several social media companies, such as Twitter, became more active in suspending accounts linked to the Islamic State that violated their terms of service. While these efforts can help diminish the Islamic State's social media presence, they can sometimes come at a cost by shutting down important sources of information for law enforcement and intelligence agencies. To grapple with this tension, the United States should work with companies to develop trusted flagging mechanisms, algorithms, and perhaps "robust hashing" techniques developed by such computer scientists as Dartmouth College professor Hany Farid that can identify which accounts present national security threats.

There are other productive avenues of partnership between governments and Internet companies. Google, Facebook, and other major companies track their users for advertising and revenue purposes. The same computerized techniques that enable targeted advertising to everyday users can be repurposed for identifying Internet-use patterns associated with potential Islamic State recruits and serving those users with pinpointed counter-messages and information about "off-ramp" options. The government can encourage broader use of these efforts and further assist companies by compiling useful, shareable analysis about the Islamic State to help give the companies a better understanding of the challenge and further motivate them to take action

Strengthen Partner Capacity to Secure and Govern Liberated Territory

The United States should begin to focus more heavily on preventing a resurgence of the Islamic State or other Salafi-jihadist groups after the Islamic State loses its control of territory. Military force is necessary to target the Islamic State and undermine its control of territory but is not sufficient. Military operations that take territory away from the Islamic State will be transitory unless these areas are effectively secured and administered by local authorities and unless the underlying factors that gave rise to insurgency are addressed more effectively. These general guidelines need to be applied in the specific and varied contexts of the states in which the Islamic State has been able to gain territorial foothold. In each case, individually crafted campaigns need to be implemented involving different international coalitions, local partners of varying capacity, and regional actors with distinct and sometimes conflicting objectives.

Iraq

Sunnis' dissatisfaction with their role and treatment in post-Saddam Iraq gave rise to al-Qa'ida in Iraq and then the Islamic State. If these grievances are not addressed, the Islamic State or an equally dangerous successor will arise from its ashes once the current coalition military campaign in Iraq winds down. The United States will need to stay engaged diplomatically, militarily, and economically at something approaching current levels beyond the liberation of Mosul to counterbalance Iranian influence; continue to professionalize the Iraqi security forces; and broker an enduring accommodation among the countries' Shi'a, Sunni, and Kurdish populations.

Syria

The Syrian civil war gave the region's Salafi-jihadists their second wind, following defeat in Iraq at the end of the last decade. This conflict will keep on providing a recruiting ground and magnet for such terrorists as long as it lasts. Yet the United States cannot afford to wait until the Syrian civil war ends to liberate Raqqa from Islamic State control. Once Raqqa has fallen, the United States should consider offering to put it under an interim international administration. Washington should consider working with Moscow to clear what will then be the last significant stronghold in Syria, the oil rich region around the city of Dier ez Zur. Washington should also reengage diplomatically in efforts to consolidate a long-term cessation of hostilities throughout Syria and support the emergence of a decentralized state based, initially at least, upon agreed zones of control recognized and supported by the major outside parties.

Libya

The Islamic State stronghold in the city of Sirte was largely eliminated in 2016 by local militias with American assistance and air support. But Islamic State fighters have dispersed to other locations in the country, from which they threaten neighboring states, as well as Libya itself. America's Middle Eastern partners are backing contending sides for power in this divided country. The United States must work to bolster international support for an effective national government, help train and equip its security forces, and keep the pressure on remaining Islamic State networks combining direct action strikes with support for local partners. At some stage, assuming the Libyan authorities so request, an international peacekeeping force may be necessary to help oversee the disbandment and incorporation of the country's multiple militia groups into a national security force. Over the long run, more effective governance in Libya is critical to prevent the resurgence of the Islamic State and other Salafi-jihadist groups.

Egypt

Although the Islamic State does not control major population centers in Egypt, it does enjoy considerable freedom of movement in the Sinai. The United States should direct its substantial military assistance to Egypt toward training and equipping the Egyptian forces to conduct more-effective counterterrorism and counterinsurgency operations. The Egyptian authorities should be encouraged to reorient their largely conventional military operations against the Islamic State campaign toward the prioritization of civilian security, the provision of development assistance, and the securing of local tribal support in the affected region. Egypt's Gulf State supporters and Israel should be urged to contribute to the developmental aspects of such a campaign.

Nigeria

Boko Haram is the deadliest of the Islamic State affiliates. It operates not just in Nigeria, its home, but in neighboring Chad, Cameroon, Benin, and Niger. Twenty million people live in the affected area, of whom more than 9 million needed lifesaving assistance in 2016. Nearly 3 million were forced from their homes. New leadership in Nigeria and the formation of a multinational joint task force have, however, deprived Boko Haram of some 75 percent of the territory and population that it controlled at its peak in 2014. The United States should continue to support the task force and help professionalize its component militaries. The United States should also continue to encourage the Nigerian leadership to address the pervasive corruption that has generated popular sympathy for the insurgency.

Afghanistan

The Islamic State's control is confined to a small area in the Afghan province of Nangarhar on the border of Pakistan. It has conducted only a handful of attacks, struggled with poor leadership, and faced determined opposition from the Taliban, as well as U.S. and Afghan forces. The United States should continue to work with Afghan and Pakistani authorities to target the Islamic State's local leadership, undermine its support base, counter its extremist ideology, and improve local governance. An enduring American commitment in Afghanistan at or somewhat above the current level of 8,400 soldiers will likely be needed to prevent the country from once again becoming a staging area for attacks on the U.S. homeland by groups like the Islamic State and al-Qa'ida.

Funding Rollback

Weakening and ultimately eliminating the Islamic State as a serious threat will require an enduring American commitment extending beyond the combat phase to encompass support for the development of effective local governance. We assess that total annual military deployment costs and the security, economic, and humanitarian aid costs could range from between $18 billion and $77 billion. This breakdown includes between $12 billion and $40 billion annually for the deployment of 7,900 to 31,050 U.S. military personnel, respectively; between $4 billion and $16 billion for security assistance to key allies; and between $2 billion and $21 billion for economic and humanitarian assistance to key allies. While these costs may seem large, they are significantly smaller than the cost of the wars in Afghanistan (Operation Enduring Freedom) and Iraq (Operation Iraqi Freedom). These wars cost U.S. taxpayers roughly $1.5 trillion between 2001 and 2013, which translated into $115 billion per year for only two countries: Afghanistan and Iraq.[2]

With the decline of the Islamic State's control of territory, the most significant future challenge will be preventing the return of the Islamic State or the reemergence of another Salafi-jihadist group with global ambitions. The United States has dramatically reduced Islamic State territorial control by acting by, with, and through local actors while limiting the direct involvement of American forces. This needs to continue.

Because the Islamic State relies on an image of success to attract recruits, its leaders will continue to conduct and incite external attacks while they lose territory. Advances against the core group in Iraq and Syria may lead to more terrorism in the West, at least temporarily. In the long term, shrinking and eventually ending the Islamic State's base will have a significant payoff. When considering new arenas into which the Islamic State might expand, the United States should recognize the risk of creating new enemies and of overstretch. Some regions, such as Central Asia, may not reach a threat level worthy of significant U.S. attention. Still, intelligence monitoring and cooperation with regional services is worthwhile as contingency planning should the threat change. Diminishing the Islamic State's global appeal is difficult, demands cooperation with allies and partners, and will require a range of instruments. But a comprehensive rollback strategy that targets both the hard and soft power of the Islamic State can tarnish the group's image, hinder its operations, and contribute to its eventual demise.

---

[2] The data reflect an average per year between 2001 and 2013. See Amy Belasco, *The Cost of Iraq, Afghanistan, and Other Global War on Terror Operations Since 9/11*, Washington, D.C.: Congressional Research Service, RL33110, December 8, 2014.

Acknowledgments

We thank a number of individuals for their extraordinary comments and feedback. David Gompert and Howard Shatz provided comprehensive reviews of the document, which significantly improved the quality of the manuscript. Daniel Egel provided valuable help on the costing details. LTG (ret.) Charlie Cleveland, Michael McNerney, and Sarah Meadows also read the document and offered outstanding comments. We also thank those who took time out of their busy schedules to meet with us, including policymakers from the White House, Department of Defense (such as the Office of the Secretary of Defense, U.S. Special Operations Command, Joint Special Operations Command, U.S. Central Command, and U.S. Africa Command), Department of State, U.S. Agency for International Development, U.S. intelligence community, and allied nations.

Marin Strmecki, Nadia Schadlow, and Allan Song at the Smith Richardson Foundation graciously provided financial support for the report and valuable insights along the way. At RAND, Dori Walker and Eric Robinson did an outstanding job developing the graphics, including the maps of Islamic State territorial and population control. Phyllis Gilmore was superb in editing the document, identifying and fixing several errors, and smoothing out the language. Matthew Byrd and Steve Kistler kept watch over the document throughout the publications process.

Finally, we thank Katrina Griffin-Moore for helping shepherd the document through the review and publication process.

PART I

The Challenge and Approach

CHAPTER ONE

Introduction

This report assesses the threat from the Islamic State to the United States and its allies. It also proposes a rollback strategy to eliminate the Islamic State as a serious threat and prevent its resurgence. Since breaking away from al-Qa'ida in 2014, the Islamic State—also referred to as the Islamic State of Iraq and al-Sham (ISIS), the Islamic State of Iraq and the Levant (ISIL), or Da'ish [*al-Dawla al-Islamiya fi al-Iraq wa al-Sham*]—expanded into roughly a dozen countries across Africa, the Middle East, and Asia. It did so by exploiting local grievances, amassing considerable wealth, doling out aid, co-opting or coercing competing extremist movements, seizing territory, and employing extreme violence to control captive populations. The Islamic State also organized or inspired attacks in such countries as the United States, Belgium, France, Germany, Denmark, Canada, Turkey, Australia, and Indonesia—most of which are far from the nerve center in Syria and Iraq. In addition, numerous unsuccessful terrorist plots across the globe have been linked to the group.

While the Islamic State has lost substantial territory and population since 2014, it has not yet been defeated. The group still retains control of some territory in Iraq and Syria, particularly along the Euphrates River. In addition, the Islamic State has established a growing number of formal and informal provinces (*wilayats*) in such countries as Yemen, Libya, Egypt, Saudi Arabia, Algeria, the Caucasus, Afghanistan, and Nigeria. An escalating number of jihadist networks in the Asia-Pacific region, including in the Philippines and Indonesia, have pledged allegiance to the Islamic State. Perhaps most concerning, the Islamic State aggressively encouraged terrorist attacks in the West.

The American-led effort to beat back the Islamic State has made considerable progress. The Trump administration now needs to develop a strategy to complete the liberation of Islamic State–controlled territory (including in its core caliphate of Iraq and Syria), close down its outlying provinces, dismantle its clandestine networks, and prevent its reemergence. Current American-supported efforts may soon permit local Iraqi and Syrian forces to destroy the so-called caliphate, but stabilizing these volatile regions and preventing their reoccupation by violent extremist groups is likely to prove more difficult. The current U.S. military posture will require further adjustment to effectively counter an adaptive enemy that continues to expand its global reach even as its territorial base shrinks. Closing down the core caliphate in Iraq and Syria may lead to defections among the Islamic State's far-flung provincial franchises, but these groups will likely remain active and may even shift their allegiance to al-Qa'ida. Closing down the core caliphate is also likely to diminish the capacity of the Islamic State to recruit, fund, and organize or inspire far-flung attacks, but this effect will be gradual at best and probably incomplete in the absence of further preventive measures from the United States and its partners.

Research Design

This report addresses four questions. First, what are the Islamic State's ideology, objectives, and global reach? Second, what possible strategies and instruments of power should the United States and its allies employ against the Islamic State? Third, what specific steps should be taken to defeat and prevent the reemergence of the Islamic State in the countries where it controls territory and population, such as Iraq, Syria, Afghanistan, Libya, Egypt, and Nigeria? Fourth, what other steps should be taken around the globe to counter the Islamic State's capacity to recruit fighters, raise funds, orchestrate a propaganda campaign, and inspire and direct attacks. While this report recognizes the importance of securing the U.S. homeland, it focuses on U.S. efforts overseas rather than at home. It does not, for example, assess law enforcement efforts in the United States or offer recommendations to counter violent extremism in U.S. cities and towns.

This research employed a combination of qualitative and quantitative data, including the writings, statements, and internal memorandums of Islamic State leaders derived from such sources as jihadist websites, social media forums, Islamic State publications (such as *Dabiq*), the Harmony Database at the Combatting Terrorism Center at West Point, and SITE Intelligence Group. We interviewed subject-matter experts and officials involved in countering the Islamic State at the White House, U.S. Department of Defense (including U.S. Special Operations Command, Joint Special Operations Command, U.S. Central Command, U.S. Pacific Command, and U.S. Africa Command), U.S. Department of State, U.S. Agency for International Development (USAID), U.S. intelligence community, and allied nations. We reviewed country- and region-specific data and literature on current efforts and challenges to counter the Islamic State in Africa, the Middle East, and Asia.

In addition, we compiled and analyzed a range of quantitative data, including an analysis of historical trends in the numbers and types of Islamic State attacks and resulting casualties. Sources included the IHS Jane's World Insurgency and Terrorism database and the Global Terrorism Database at the University of Maryland. To assess Islamic State control, we employed open-source analysis and media reporting to construct our own maps of Islamic State territorial control. Using these territorial control maps, we measured the total land area (in square kilometers) controlled by the Islamic State. To get a better sense of the number of people living under the Islamic State, we incorporated data from the Gridded Population of the World (GPW) data set.[1] GPW data provide a population estimate for every 1-km grid square in the world using available administrative data. We also reviewed data

---

[1]   NASA Socioeconomic Data and Applications Center (SEDAC), "Gridded Population of the World (GPW), v4," undated.

on how earlier terrorist and insurgent groups ended to identify policy instruments and other variables that contributed to their demise.[2]

Definitions

As we use the term here, *strategy* includes designs for the use of all relevant instruments and methods to achieve a defined objective.[3] Policymakers need to consider how to use their political, military, economic, and other resources to weaken or defeat such groups as the Islamic State. A strategy forces planners to foresee the nature of the conflict. Does the plan of attack—the proposed strategy—promise success at a reasonable cost?[4] Combining military and nonmilitary means, the United States has developed national strategies in the past against specific adversaries, such as the Soviet Union. In the 1980s, for instance, the United States updated its strategy to counter the Soviet Union across the globe. This revised approach was embodied in National Security Decision

---

[2]   See, for example, Audrey Kurth Cronin, *How Terrorism Ends: Understanding the Decline and Demise of Terrorist Campaigns*, Princeton, N.J.: Princeton University Press, 2009; Jason Lyall and Isaiah Wilson III, "Rage Against the Machines: Explaining Outcomes in Counterinsurgency Wars," *International Organization*, No. 63, No. 1, Winter 2009; Monica Duffy Toft, *Securing the Peace: The Durable Settlement of Civil Wars*, Princeton, N.J.: Princeton University Press, 2009; David Mason, Joseph P. Weingarten, Jr., and Patrick J. Fett, "Win, Lose, or Draw: Predicting the Outcome of Civil Wars," *Political Research Quarterly*, Vol. 52, No. 2, June 1999; Patrick T. Brandt, T. David Mason, Mehmet Gurses, Nicolai Petrovsky, and Dagmar Radin, "When and How the Fighting Stops: Explaining the Duration and Outcome of Civil Wars," *Defence and Peace Economics*, Vol. 19, No. 6, December 2008; and Ben Connable and Martin C. Libicki, *How Insurgencies End*, Santa Monica, Calif.: RAND Corporation, MG-965-MCIA, 2010.

[3]   On strategy see, for example, Lawrence Freedman, *Strategy: A History*, New York: Oxford University Press, 2013, pp. ix–xvi.

[4]   On strategy—including against nonstate actors—see, for example, Ivan Arreguín-Toft, *How the Weak Win Wars: A Theory of Asymmetric Conflict*, New York: Cambridge University Press, 2005; Jerry M. Tinker, ed., *Strategies of Revolutionary Warfare*, New Delhi: S. Chand & Co., 1969; and Gérard Chaliand, *Guerrilla Strategies: An Historical Anthology from the Long March to Afghanistan*, Berkeley: University of California Press, 1982; B. H. Liddell Hart, *Strategy: The Indirect Approach,* London: Faber, 1967. Also see John J. Mearsheimer, *Conventional Deterrence*, Ithaca, N.Y.: Cornell University Press, 1983, pp. 2, 28–29

Directive 75.⁵ This directive had its roots in previous strategies to counter the Soviet Union, including National Security Council (NSC) 68, which was promulgated during the Truman administration.⁶

This report frequently employs the terms *insurgency* and *terrorism*. An insurgency is a political and military campaign by a nonstate group (or groups) to overthrow a regime or secede from a country.⁷ This definition includes several components. Insurgent groups are nonstate organizations, although they may receive assistance from states. They use violence—and the threat of violence—to achieve their objectives. Insurgency can be understood, in part, as a process of alternative state-building. Groups often tax populations in areas they control, establish justice systems, and attempt to provide other services.⁸ *Terrorism*, on the other hand, is a tactic that involves the use of politically motivated violence against noncombatants to cause intimidation or fear among a target audience.⁹ Most insurgent groups employ terrorism, but many terrorist groups are not insurgents because they do not control or, in some cases, even aspire to control territory. Consequently, we refer to organizations as *insurgent groups* when they seek to hold and govern territory. Since its emergence, the Islamic State has been an insurgent group dedicated to controlling territory. The Islamic State uses terrorist tactics to help achieve its objectives. It will likely remain a terror-

---

⁵ National Security Decision Directive 75, "U.S. Relations with the USSR," January 17, 1983.

⁶ NSC, "A Report to the National Security Council by the Executive Secretary on United States Objectives and Programs for National Security," NSC-68, April 14, 1950.

⁷ See, for example, the definition of insurgency in Central Intelligence Agency (CIA), *Guide to the Analysis of Insurgency*, Washington, D.C., 2012, p. 1.

⁸ Stathis N. Kalyvas, *The Logic of Violence in Civil War*, New York: Cambridge University Press, 2006, p. 245.

⁹ There are many definitions of terrorism. See, for example, U.S. Department of State, *Country Reports on Terrorism 2005*, Washington, D.C.: Office of the Coordinator for Counterterrorism, April 2006, p. 9; Bruce Hoffman, *Inside Terrorism*, 2nd ed., New York: Columbia University Press, 2006, pp. 1–41; Robert A. Pape, *Dying to Win: The Strategic Logic of Suicide Terrorism*, New York: Random House, 2005, p. 9; and Audrey Kurth Cronin, "Behind the Curve: Globalization and International Terrorism," *International Security*, Vol. 27, No. 3, Winter 2002/03, p. 33.

ist organization even if it loses territory and ceases to be an insurgent group, but its capacity to do damage may be significantly diminished.

This report focuses on the Islamic State while recognizing that it is but one of several Salafi-jihadist groups. Another is al-Qa'ida, from which the Islamic State sprung.[10] The Islamic State currently poses the most acute threat because of its territorial control, willingness and ability to attack Western countries, global social media prowess, and adroitness to inspire extremists across the globe. As the former U.S. Director of National Intelligence argued:

> The Islamic State of Iraq and the Levant has become the preeminent terrorist threat because of its self-described caliphate in Syria and Iraq, its branches and emerging branches in other countries, and its increasing ability to direct and inspire attacks against a wide range of targets around the world.[11]

Additionally, the Islamic State has a distinct ideology, objectives, and organizational structure, allowing us to focus on a defined enemy. Still, many of our recommendations are applicable to combating al-Qa'ida and similar groups, and many of the steps we recommend will need to be sustained even after the Islamic State is defeated.

We use the term *Salafi-jihadist* numerous times in the document. We use two criteria for describing a group as Salafi-jihadist: First, the group emphasizes the importance of returning to a "pure" Islam, that of the *Salaf,* the pious ancestors. Second, the group believes that violent jihad is *fard 'ayn* [a personal religious duty].[12] Despite a complex

---

[10] Salafi characterizes an adherent of an ideological strain in Sunni Islam that seeks to emulate, as purer, the thinking and practices of Muhammad and the earliest generations of Muslims. Jihadists believe that violent struggle against non-Muslims and Muslims they judge as apostate is an important religious duty.

[11] James R. Clapper, "Statement for the Record: Worldwide Threat Assessment of the US Intelligence Community," testimony before Senate Select Committee on Intelligence, February 9, 2016, p. 4.

[12] See, for example, bin Laden's fatwa published in the London newspaper *Al-Quds al-'Arabi* in February 1998, which noted that "to kill Americans is a personal duty for all Muslims." The text can be found as Osama bin Laden, "Jihad Against Jews and Crusaders," Federation of American Scientists website, February 23, 1998.

debate among scholars going on since the time of the Prophet Muhammad, jihad is not one of the five pillars of Islam; the five pillars actually are *zakat* [almsgiving], *hajj* [the pilgrimage to Mecca], *salat* [daily prayers], *sawm* [fasting during Ramada], and the *shahada* [accepting Muhammad as God's messenger].[13] Jihad is, instead, a collective duty [*fard kifaya*] under certain circumstances. But Salafi-jihadists consider violent jihad a permanent and individual duty.[14] Many Salafists are opposed to armed jihad and advocate the *da'wa* [call] to Islam through proselytizing and preaching. But al-Qa'ida leader Ayman al-Zawahiri, among others, pushed for both Salafism *and* armed jihad.[15]

We have chosen to use the term *Islamic State*, rather than *ISIS*, *ISIL*, or *Da'ish*. The group calls itself the Islamic State [*al-Dawla al-Islamiya*]. Some argue that using *Islamic State* legitimizes the group or could offend Muslim governments and populations because the Islamic State does not represent mainstream Islam or control an internationally recognized state. But analysts and government officials have long referred to insurgent and terrorist groups using their own names—such as Lashkar-e-Taiba [Army of the Righteous], Jaish-e-Muhammad [Army of Muhammad], and Hezbollah [Party of God]—without legitimizing the groups or their goals. In addition, the Islamic State's focus is on more than just Iraq and Syria, which ISIL and ISIS suggest; rather, the group is transnational in nature and global in aspiration.

Finally, we use the term *al-Qa'ida in Iraq* (AQI) to refer to the group from its establishment in 2004 until al-Qa'ida's break with the group in 2014. The group's leaders used this term from 2004 until

---

[13] On Sayyid Qutb's interpretation of armed jihad as a duty, see Sayyid Qutb, *Ma'alim fi al-Tariq* [*Milestones*], reprint, New Delhi: Islamic Book Service, 2007.

[14] Gilles Kepel, *Muslim Extremism in Egypt: The Prophet and the Pharaoh*, trans. John Rothschild, Berkeley: University of California Press, 1993; Olivier Roy, *Globalized Islam: The Search for a New Umma*, New York: Columbia University Press, 2004, p. 41.

[15] On the term Salafi-jihadists see, for example, Assaf Moghadam, "Motives for Martyrdom: Al-Qaida, Salafi Jihad, and the Spread of Suicide Attacks," *International Security*, Vol. 33, No. 3, Winter 2008/09; Moghadam, "The Salafi-Jihad as a Religious Ideology," *CTC Sentinel*, Vol. 1, No. 3, February 2008 Also see Alain Grignard, "La Littérature Politique du GIA, des Origines à Djamal Zitoun—Esquisse d'Une Analyse," in F. Dassetto, ed., *Facettes de l'Islam Belge*, Louvain-la-Neuve: Academia-Bruylant, 2001.

roughly 2006 and then switched to the *Islamic State of Iraq* as they incorporated other Iraqi insurgent groups. For ease of reference, however, we use *AQI* to refer to the group during the entire ten-year period. U.S. policymakers generally used *AQI*. In addition, the group remained an affiliate of al-Qa'ida during this period, and its leaders pledged *bay'ah*, or loyalty, to al-Qa'ida leader Osama bin Laden and, following his death, to Ayman al-Zawahiri.

Outline of This Report

This report is organized into three parts. Part I focuses on the challenge the Islamic State poses and the strategic options available to the United States to counter it globally. Chapter Two examines the ideology and strategic goals of the Islamic State. It assesses key trends over time, including Islamic State efforts to control territory, garner popular support, establish provinces, and conduct attacks. Chapter Three examines strategic options for the United States and outlines instruments necessary to counter the Islamic State. Defeating the Islamic State will require a step-by-step process that begins with weakening the Islamic State from an insurgent group and protostate to a terrorist movement that controls little or no territory, then gradually suppressing that residual movement. This chapter advocates a rollback strategy that relies on U.S. special operations forces, CIA and other intelligence units, airpower, and civilian efforts to weaken and ultimately defeat the Islamic State wherever it has established sanctuaries. Rollback involves efforts to train, advise, assist, and accompany local state and substate security forces in countries threatened by the Islamic State; improve the governance and institutional capacity of local allies; and aggressively target the Islamic State's global networks and its core caliphate areas of Iraq and Syria.

Part II focuses on the implementation of rollback. Chapters Four through Nine outline campaigns in countries in which the Islamic State has controlled territory: Iraq (Chapter Four), Syria (Chapter Five), Libya (Chapter Six), Nigeria (Chapter Seven), Egypt (Chapter Eight), and Afghanistan (Chapter Nine). We have not included separate case studies for countries in which the Islamic State has a presence but controls no territory, such as Saudi Arabia, Tunisia, or Pakistan. However, these countries are treated in various places throughout the document. We organized each of the country chapters similarly, charting the rise of the Islamic State in the country, positing a desired end state, elaborating the components of a rollback campaign (political and governance, security, and economic and humanitarian), and discussing the regional dimension.

Part III turns to broader steps. Chapter Ten outlines steps needed to counter the Islamic State throughout the world. It examines the components of the Islamic State's message, how the Islamic State promotes this message to influence potential adherents, and options the United States has to counter these efforts. Chapter Eleven summarizes the main findings and policy recommendations.

CHAPTER TWO

The Rise and Decline of the Islamic State

There has been considerable debate in the United States about the strengths and weaknesses of the Islamic State. A few argue that it poses little or no threat to the United States.[1] Ohio State political scientist John Mueller, for example, maintained: "Its numbers are small, and it has differentiated itself from al-Qaeda in that it does not seek primarily to target the 'far enemy,' preferring instead to carve out a state in the Middle East for itself, mostly killing fellow Muslims who stand in its way."[2] In a separate piece, Mueller contended that the annual risk of dying in a terrorist attack in the United States between 1970 and 2007 was one in 3.5 million, much lower than a litany of other incidents, such as traffic accidents, more-routine homicides, natural disasters, industrial accidents, and even drowning in a bathtub.[3] Others have argued that because the Islamic State is weak and because terrorism poses little threat to the United States, it should focus on other challenges: great-power competitors, such as Russia and China; unstable regimes, such as nuclear North Korea; would-be regional hegemons,

---

[1] See, for example, John Mueller and Mark G. Stewart, *Terror, Security, and Money: Balancing the Risks, Benefits, and Costs of Homeland Security*, New York: Oxford University Press, 2011, and John J. Mearsheimer, "America Unhinged," *National Interest*, January–February 2014.

[2] John Mueller, "Why the Islamic State Threat Is Totally Overblown," *The Week*, July 23, 2015.

[3] John Mueller and Mark G. Stewart, "Hardly Existential: Thinking Rationally About Terrorism," *Foreign Affairs*, April 2, 2010.

such as Iran; climate change; cyberattacks; and the stability of the international financial system.[4]

Others, of course, have alleged that the threat from the Islamic State is significant. William McCants, for example, argued that the Islamic State is one of the most lethal and successful Salafi-jihadist groups in modern history, surpassing even al-Qa'ida.[5] David Kilcullen maintained that, with the Islamic State and al-Qa'ida, the West faced "a larger, more unified, capable, experienced and savage enemy, in a less stable, more fragmented region, with a far higher level of geopolitical competition, and a much more severe risk of great-power conflict, than at any time since 9/11."[6]

Primary source documents indicate that a *sine qua non* of the Islamic State's strategy is expansion to establish a pan-Islamic caliphate. The Islamic State has no intention of containing itself within certain countries or even regions. Despite its desire to expand, however, the group has faced significant roadblocks. The data compiled and analyzed in this chapter suggest that the Islamic State has begun to move from an insurgent group that controls territory to a clandestine terrorist group that attacks government officials and noncombatants. Between 2014 and 2017, the Islamic State's control of territory declined in Iraq, Syria, Afghanistan, Libya, and Nigeria as it faced increasingly effective resistance from local government forces, U.S. and other outside powers, and nonstate armed groups. In addition, polling data indicate that support for the Islamic State and its ideology is declining across the Muslim world, as highlighted later in this chapter. The loss of ter-

---

[4]   On the debate about the Islamic State and the threat of terrorism more broadly see Marc Sageman, "The Stagnation of Research on Terrorism," *Chronicle of Higher Education*, April 30, 2013; John Horgan and Jessica Stern, "Terrorism Research Has Not Stagnated," *Chronicle of Higher Education*, May 8, 2013; Mearsheimer, 2014, p. 12; Brian Michael Jenkins, *Stray Dogs and Virtual Armies: Radicalization and Recruitment to Jihadist Terrorism in the United States Since 9/11*, Santa Monica, Calif.: RAND Corporation, OP-343-RC, 2011.

[5]   William McCants, *The ISIS Apocalypse: The History, Strategy, and Doomsday Vision of the Islamic State*, New York: St. Martin's Press, 2015.

[6]   David Kilcullen, *Blood Year: The Unraveling of Western Counterterrorism*, New York: Oxford University Press, 2016, p. 197.

ritory and popular support are significant challenges for insurgents, though less so for terrorist groups.

Ideology and Strategic Goals

Pan-Islamic expansion has long been a *raison d'être* of the organization, making it essential to counter the organization globally. At the same time, its heartland is in Iraq and Syria, putting a priority on efforts to shut down the core caliphate, which is a principal source of the Islamic State's wider appeal.

The Islamic State's behavior is shaped by religious fervor, strategic calculation, and apocalyptic prophesy. After breaking away from al-Qa'ida, Islamic State leaders have sought to establish a pan-Islamic caliphate that extends from Africa through the Middle East, South Asia, and parts of the Pacific. "Rush O Muslims to your state. Yes, it is your state," said Abu Bakr al-Baghdadi. "We make a special call to the scholars, *fuqaha'* [experts in Islamic jurisprudence], and callers, especially the judges, as well as people with military, administrative, and service expertise, and medical doctors and engineers of all different specializations and fields."[7] After overrunning Mosul, the second-largest city in Iraq, in summer 2014, an Islamic State spokesman issued a proclamation outlining the importance of a pan-Islamic caliphate:

> The sun of jihad has risen, and the glad tidings of goodness have shone forth. Triumph looms on the horizon, and the signs of victory have appeared.
>
> Here, the flag of the Islamic State, the flag of monotheism, rises and flutters. Its shade covers land from Aleppo to Diyala. Beneath it the walls of the tyrants have been demolished, their flags have fallen, and their borders have been destroyed . . . .

---

[7] Abu Bakr Al-Baghdadi, "A Message to the Mujahideen and the Muslim Ummah in the Month of Ramadan," Fursan Al-Balagh Media, July 1, 2014b.

It is a dream that lives in the depths of every Muslim believer. It is a hope that flutters in the heart of every mujahid monotheist. It is the caliphate. It is the caliphate—the abandoned obligation of the era . . . .

Now the caliphate has returned. We ask God the exalted to make it in accordance with the prophetic method.[8]

Baghdadi adopted the name and title of Caliph Ibrahim al-Baghdadi, and the Islamic State focused its strategic goals on expanding its control of territory. Holding territory is imperative to the Islamic State's larger ideological vision. It seeks to control local populations, establish an extreme version of sharia (Islamic law), and finance itself through the local economy. In addition, the Islamic State has been among the most virulently anti-Shi'a of any Salafi-jihadist group. Baghdadi denounced Shi'a as apostates and encouraged violent jihad against them: "I direct my call to all the Muslim youth and men all over the world, and call them to make Hijrah to us to consolidate the pillars of the State of Islam and perform Jihad against the Safavid Rafida—the Magian Shiites."[9]

Figure 2.1 illustrates the Islamic State's hierarchical organizational structure, which includes a senior shura and statelike structures of *diwans* (ministries), committees and offices, and *wilayats* (provinces). The Islamic State's diwans issue directives and are organized into functional areas, such as education, finances, health, media, public services, and tribal outreach. The finance diwan, for example, oversees

---

[8] Abu Muhammad al-Adnani, "Hadha wa'd Allah," Al-Battar Media Foundation, June 29, 2014.

[9] Abu Bakr Al-Baghdadi, "Allah Will Not Allow Except that His Light Should Be Perfected," Fursan Al-Balagh Media, July 2012. *Rafida* roughly translates as deserters or defectors and is a derogatory reference to Shi'a Muslims, who do not recognize Abu Bakr and his successors as having been legitimate rulers [*Rashidun*] of the early Muslim community. *Safavid* is a reference to the Safavid dynasty (1501–1722), which controlled Persia and parts of South Asia, Central Asia, the Caucasus during its peak. *Magian* is a derogatory reference to Shi'a as disbelievers, although the term specifically refers to Zoroastrians. Islamic State leaders going back to Abu Mus'ab al-Zarqawi vehemently disagreed with Shi'a doctrine that the Prophet Muhammad's son-in-law and some of his male descendants were infallible and the only legitimate political and religious leaders of the early Muslim community.

Figure 2.1
Islamic State Organizational Structure

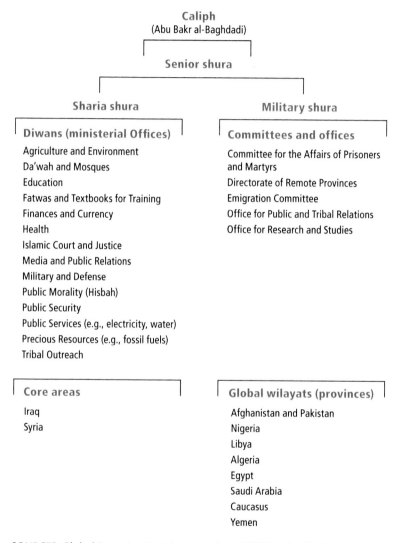

Caliph
(Abu Bakr al-Baghdadi)

Senior shura

Sharia shura

Diwans (ministerial Offices)

Agriculture and Environment
Da'wah and Mosques
Education
Fatwas and Textbooks for Training
Finances and Currency
Health
Islamic Court and Justice
Media and Public Relations
Military and Defense
Public Morality (Hisbah)
Public Security
Public Services (e.g., electricity, water)
Precious Resources (e.g., fossil fuels)
Tribal Outreach

Military shura

Committees and offices

Committee for the Affairs of Prisoners
and Martyrs
Directorate of Remote Provinces
Emigration Committee
Office for Public and Tribal Relations
Office for Research and Studies

Core areas

Iraq
Syria

Global wilayats (provinces)

Afghanistan and Pakistan
Nigeria
Libya
Algeria
Egypt
Saudi Arabia
Caucasus
Yemen

SOURCES: Global Terrorism Database, undated; IHS Jane's, 2016; Aymenn
al-Tamimi, "The Evolution in Islamic State Administration: The Documentary
Evidence," *Perspectives on Terrorism*, Vol. 9, No. 4, 2015; Aidan Lewis, "Islamic
State: How It Is Run," British Broadcasting Corporation, May 22, 2015; Christoph
Reuter, "Secret Files Reveal the Structure of the Islamic State," *Der Spiegel*,
April 18, 2015; authors' estimates.
RAND *RR1912-2.1*

fundraising from producing and selling oil, extorting and taxing local populations, kidnapping for ransom, and seizing bank accounts—all of which require territorial control to remain viable. The committees include such functions as the Directorate of Remote Provinces, which has responsibility for relations with Islamic State provinces overseas. Finally, the Islamic State has an administrative structure for its operations in the core areas of Iraq and Syria and in such global wilayats as Afghanistan, Nigeria, Libya, Algeria, Egypt, Saudi Arabia, Caucasus, and Yemen.

Global Reach

The Islamic State's strategic goals and desire to control territory are consistent with the objectives of insurgent groups, if more expansive than most.[10] The Islamic State is not the only insurgent group to operate in recent history; there have been nearly 200 insurgencies since World War II.[11] What sets the Islamic State apart from these groups is its interest in controlling a wide swath of territory that spans multiple states in Africa, the Middle East, and Asia and in securing the allegiance of Muslims everywhere.[12]

How effective has the Islamic State been in expanding its reach? This section examines four criteria: control of territory and populations, popular support, acquisition of overseas provinces, and levels of violence. To establish a pan-Islamic caliphate, the group needs to con-

---

[10] Audrey Kurth Cronin has argued that the group's complexity suggests that it is a "pseudo-state led by a conventional army" and not a purely terrorist group. Audrey Kurth Cronin, "ISIS Is Not a Terrorist Group," *Foreign Affairs,* March/April 2015a.

[11] Seth G. Jones, *Waging Insurgent Warfare*, New York: Oxford University Press, 2016.

[12] For more detail on Islamic State emergence and ideology, see Brian H. Fishman, *The Master Plan: ISIS, al-Qaeda, and the Jihadi Strategy for Final Victory*, New Haven, Conn.: Yale University Press, 2016; McCants, 2015; Michael Weiss and Hassan Hassan, *ISIS: Inside the Army of Terror,* New York: Regan Arts, 2015; Joby Warrick, *Black Flags: The Rise of the Islamic State*, New York: Doubleday, 2015; Daniel Byman, *Al-Qaeda, the Islamic State, and the Global Jihadist Movement: What Everyone Needs to Know*, New York: Oxford University Press, 2015; and Jessica Stern and J. M. Berger, *ISIS: The State of Terror*, New York: Harper-Collins, 2015; Kilcullen, 2016.

trol territory, mobilize local populations, use violence (and the threat of violence), and expand its global footprint. We measure each of these four criteria and assess trends over time.

Territorial Control

Control can be defined and measured empirically using various indicators, such as the level and presence of forces in a given place and time.[13] Groups do not always fully control an area but may nevertheless exercise significant influence over local populations. We define Islamic State territorial control in terms of freedom of movement. In controlled areas, the Islamic State can garrison fighters in or near villages and cities and can operate freely during most times of day and night. The Islamic State also holds some measure of sway over local populations in these areas, is often the dominant actor, and can establish its governance and security apparatus.[14]

To assess Islamic State control, we analyzed data from the countries in which the Islamic State possesses some territory: Syria, Iraq, Afghanistan, Egypt, Libya, and Nigeria. For Syria and Iraq, areas that Islamic State leaders consider to be their core territory, we used control maps prepared by the U.S. government detailing changes in the Islamic State's holdings since August 2014. We then supplemented with our own assessments of territorial control through winter 2016–2017. For Afghanistan, Egypt, Libya, and Nigeria, we used open-source analysis and media reporting to construct our own maps of Islamic State territorial control in each region, as presented below. Using these territorial control maps for each country, we measured the total land area (in square kilometers) the Islamic State controlled in each country. To estimate the number of people living under Islamic State control, we incorporated data from the GPW data set.[15] GPW data provide a pop-

---

[13] Kalyvas, 2006, p. 210.

[14] Some have referred to these areas as Islamic State "dominant" areas. See, for example, U.S. Department of Defense, "Iraq and Syria: ISIL's Areas of Influence, August 2014 through April 2016," Washington, D.C., 2016a.

[15] SEDAC, undated. The data we used were as of May 2016.

ulation estimate for every 1-km grid square in the world using available administrative data.[16]

Figure S.1 in the Summary showed the Islamic State's decline of territorial control in Iraq and Syria. In Iraq, the Islamic State's control peaked in fall 2014 at an estimated 6.3 million people (19 percent of the population) covering approximately 58,372 km² (13 percent of Iraq's territory). Most of this was in Anbar, Ninawa, Kirkuk, and Salah ad Din provinces, including such cities as Ramadi, Fallujah, Mosul, Tikrit, Bayji, and Sinjar. By winter 2016–2017, however, the Islamic State's territorial reach declined to 15,682 km² (4 percent of the territory) and 1.1 million people (3 percent of the Iraqi population). The Islamic State lost significant territory in the vicinity of Mosul and in such cities as Sinjar, Bayji, Tikrit, and Ramadi to a combination of U.S. and allied strikes; Iraqi Security Force ground assaults; and Sunni, Shi'a, and Kurdish militia forces. There was a similar trajectory in Syria, with the Islamic State controlling an estimated 3.3 million people (14 percent of the population) in fall 2014 covering an area of roughly 47,497 km² (25 percent of the territory). By winter 2016-2017, however, Islamic State control declined to 1.5 million people (6 percent of the population) and 29,695 km² (16 percent of the territory). Most of this lost territory was in the northern and eastern Syrian provinces of Hasakah, Raqqa, and Aleppo.

In Afghanistan, Islamic State governance peaked in spring 2015, when it controlled an estimated 511,777 people (1.9 percent of the population) and roughly 2,919 km² (less than 1 percent of the territory). Most of this control was in the southwestern province of Farah and the eastern province of Nangarhar, with additional Islamic State pockets in and around Kajaki District in the southern Helmand Province. By winter 2016–2017, however, the Islamic State's control decreased to only 64,406 people (an 87-percent drop) and 372 km² (also an 87-percent

---

[16] We acknowledge the fact that historical administrative census data for Iraq, Syria, Afghanistan, Libya, Egypt, and Nigeria are likely biased relative to current population figures, in that they do not adequately account for ongoing conflicts and movements of internally displaced persons (IDPs) within each country. We accept this limitation, and offer these population estimates as the best-available measure of people living under Islamic State control worldwide.

drop) from 2015 levels. In Helmand and Farah provinces, the Islamic State lost all its territory and suffered heavy losses—including the death of deputy leader Abdul Raziq Mehdi—during clashes with the Taliban and periodic strikes from U.S. and Afghan forces. In such districts as Achin in Nangarhar Province, the Islamic State lost some control of territory following aggressive U.S. and Afghan operations.

In Nigeria, the Islamic State lost considerable ground between 2014 and 2017. Its predecessor, Boko Haram, controlled 1,330,115 people (0.7 percent of the population) and 18,019 km² (2 percent of the territory) in fall 2014. Most of this was in the northeastern and eastern areas of Borno, as well as in Adamawa and Yobe. By winter 2016–2017, however, the Islamic State's control had overwhelmingly receded to only 332,841 people (a 75-percent drop from 2014) and 6,041 km² (a 67-percent drop). Starting in late January 2015, a coalition of military forces from Nigeria, Chad, Cameroon, and Niger began a military campaign against Boko Haram strongholds. In March 2015, Boko Haram lost control of the northern Nigerian towns of Bama and Gwoza to the Nigerian army. Nigerian authorities reported that they had taken back 11 of the 14 districts previously controlled by Boko Haram. In April, four Boko Haram camps in the Sambisa Forest were overrun by the Nigerian military, which freed nearly 300 females. Boko Haram forces retreated to the Mandara Mountains along the Nigeria-Cameroon border. Although the Nigerian government claimed the group held little to no territory inside its borders by early 2016, official reports from U.S. Africa Command suggested otherwise; Boko Haram had successfully captured several villages near a district capital, Maiduguri, in northeastern Boro State in May 2016.[17] Ultimately, the group's forces were pushed back to Maiduguri.

The Islamic State's most significant area of control in Libya, the city of Sirte, was eliminated, with small pockets of control remaining in Az Zawiyah, Al Khums, Misratah, Benghazi, Kufrah, Sabha, and Darnah. In Egypt, the Islamic State operated along a small stretch

---

[17] Ladi Olorunyomi, "U.S. General Counters Buhari, Says Boko Haram Still Holds Territory in Nigeria," *Premium Times Nigeria*, March 10, 2016; "Boko Haram Attacks Jere, Borno State," NTA News (Nigeria), May 27, 2016.

in the Sinai between Arish (a district center in northern Sinai) and Rafah (the border crossing between Egypt and the Gaza Strip) and south toward the United Nations (UN) Multinational Observer Force base in Sinai. This area covers roughly 910 km^2 and has approximately 100,000 residents, less than 0.1 percent of Egypt's territory and population. The Islamic State's efforts at control have centered on the small village of Sheikh Zuweid, with few efforts to expand beyond this narrow corridor. Initial control in the area was established in early 2015 and had not expanded through early 2017.

Overall, these numbers represented a significant decline in Islamic State control of population between 2014 and winter 2016–2017: a 56-percent drop in Syria, 83 percent in Iraq, 75 percent in Nigeria, nearly 100 percent in Libya, and 87 percent in Afghanistan. The Islamic State province in Egypt did not lose substantial territory, although it operated in only a tiny segment of territory in the Sinai to begin with.

Popular Support

Gaining support from and coercing local populations are common features of all insurgencies. But popular support is a means to an end—usually territorial and population control—and not an end in itself. Support is translated into concrete assistance—money, logistics, recruits, sanctuary, intelligence, and other aid—from the local population. As Mao Tse-Tung argued in one of the most common axioms of insurgent warfare, a primary feature of insurgent operations is "their dependence upon the people themselves."[18] Mao likened the local population to water and insurgents to fish that need water to survive.[19]

Opinion polling provides one indicator of support for the Islamic State beyond its areas of actual control, albeit with some limitations.[20]

---

[18] Mao Tse-Tung, *On Guerrilla Warfare* Urbana and Chicago: University of Illinois Press, [1937] 2000, p. 51.

[19] Mao, 2000, p. 93.

[20] The data come from ASDA'A Burson-Marsteller, "Inside the Hearts and Minds of Arab Youth: Arab Youth Survey 2016," Dubai, 2016; Joby Warrick, "New Poll Finds Young Arabs Are Less Swayed by the Islamic State," *Washington Post*, April 12, 2016a; Jacob Poushter, "In Nations with Significant Muslim Populations, Much Disdain for ISIS," Washington, D.C.: Pew Research Center, November 17, 2015; David Pollock, "ISIS Has Almost No Support in

First, there are few to no publicly available polling data from several key countries in which the Islamic State operates, such as Syria and Libya. Second, obtaining reliable survey data in combat zones often presents methodological challenges. In some cases, survey teams may be unable or unwilling to poll individuals in combat areas because of security concerns. In other cases, those interviewed may not be entirely truthful if they fear for their safety. Third, most polls do not include time-series data that allow researchers to gauge trends over time. Fourth, most polls do not provide microlevel data that show polling results at the provincial, district, city, or even neighborhood level. Consequently, it is often difficult or impossible to identify variation in Islamic State support by geographic area over time. Still, the limited data available provide a useful lens to examine macrolevel attitudes toward the Islamic State in some countries in which the group operates or might influence local populations. Some organizations, such as Pew Research Center, have track records of reliable polling with transparent estimates of confidence levels and reasonable margins of error. We used these data to examine popular support for the Islamic State globally.

Perhaps the most important conclusion from the available polling data is the overwhelmingly negative views of the Islamic State in the Arab world. According to an April 2016 poll by ASDA'A Burson-Marsteller, a public relations firm that tracked young Arabs' views,

> tacit support for the militant group is declining with nearly four in five (78 per cent) rejecting the group outright even if it were to change its tactics –13 per cent of young Arabs agree they could see themselves supporting Daesh if it did not use so much violence (compared to 19 per cent last year).[21]

Egypt, Saudi Arabia, or Lebanon—But America Has Little More," *Fikra Forum*, October 14, 2015; Munqith M. Dagher, "Public Opinion Towards Terrorist Organizations in Iraq, Syria, Yemen, and Libya: A Special Focus on Dai'sh in Iraq," briefing presented at the Center for Strategic and International Studies (CSIS), Washington, D.C., March 4, 2015; Zogby Research Services, "Today's Middle East: Pressures and Challenges," November 2014; and Arab Center for Research and Policy Studies, *The Military Campaign Against the Islamic State in Iraq and the Levant: Arab Public Opinion*, Doha, November 26, 2014.

[21] ASDA'A Burson-Marsteller, 2016, p. 11.

According to data that the Pew Research Center collected in 11 countries with significant Muslim populations, locals from Nigeria and Jordan to Indonesia overwhelmingly expressed negative views of the Islamic State. One exception was Pakistan, where a majority offered no definite opinion of the Islamic State. In no country surveyed did more than 15 percent of the population show favorable attitudes toward the Islamic State.[22]

In Lebanon, almost every person surveyed who provided an opinion had an unfavorable view of the Islamic State. An overwhelming 99 percent of those respondents expressed a very unfavorable opinion of the group. Distaste toward the Islamic State was shared by Lebanese Sunni Muslims (98 percent unfavorable) and 100 percent of Shi'a Muslims and Lebanese Christians. Israelis (97 percent) and Jordanians (94 percent) were also strongly opposed to the Islamic State, including 91 percent of Israeli Arabs. And 84 percent in the Palestinian territories had a negative view of the Islamic State, both in the Gaza Strip (92 percent) and the West Bank (79 percent). Six in ten or more had unfavorable opinions of the Islamic State in a diverse group of nations, including Indonesia, Turkey, Nigeria, Burkina Faso, Malaysia, and Senegal.[23] In Nigeria, there was somewhat more support for the Islamic State, with some 20 percent of the Muslim population expressing a favorable view. Ten percent of Pakistanis did the same.[24]

While these figures illustrate the limited prospects for the Islamic State as a popularly based insurgency, they suggest more than enough support to allow it to persist as a terrorist threat. It will be important to determine whether this support erodes further as the Islamic State loses its territorial base and its so-called caliphate.

Public opinion polling on the Islamic State is only one measure of popular support for the group. Most of these polls gauge support for the group in theory, or based on assessments of the group's favorability as a general construct. Given the constraints on conducting public opinion surveys in hostile or denied areas, little survey research has

---

[22] Poushter, 2015.

[23] Poushter, 2015.

[24] Poushter, 2015.

gauged attitudes toward the Islamic State among the people actually living under its control. Support for the Islamic State in Iraq and Syria has been driven largely by underlying grievances related to the under-representation of Sunni political interests by the majority Shi'a government in Baghdad and by the Alawite Assad regime in Damascus. To this extent, popular support may not mean that locals view the Islamic State as "favorable" in the same way that a public opinion poll would capture, but rather that they view the Islamic State as the least bad option in a theater full of rival groups. In Syria, some media reporting noted that residents in Raqqa supported the Islamic State for the relative stability brought about despite the group's heavy-handed rule, particularly relative to the lawlessness of other areas controlled by rebel groups.[25] In Iraq, the Islamic State benefitted in some areas from the belief that Baghdad would likely rely on hardline Iranian-backed Shi'a militias to retake Islamic State territory. Sunni tribal support for the Islamic State, whether coerced or actual, afforded the group opportunities to build local legitimacy.

Anecdotal evidence suggests that the Islamic State has governed areas under its control poorly, relying largely on various forms of compulsion to secure local support. As further and larger population centers are liberated, it may become possible to form a more comprehensive picture of the quality of Islamic State governance of its core caliphate. Beyond support from locals within the territory it controls, the Islamic State has been able to generate support abroad for its cause through online propaganda and messaging operations. Internet-based propaganda and tailored social media provide ways for the Islamic State to communicate with current and future adherents and inspire them to mount attacks, conduct information operations, send money, travel to an existing Islamic State province as a foreign fighter, or otherwise support the organization. These propaganda tools provide the group with a source of global legitimacy, a steady flow of foreign fighters, and the ability to develop nascent networks of inspired individuals who will conduct attacks in areas outside the Islamic State's current territory.

---

[25] Ruth Sherlock, "Why Business Is Booming Under the Islamic State One Year On," *Telegraph*, June 8, 2015.

The Islamic State has drawn on a variety of social networking applications to promote its cause, such as Facebook, Instagram, Tumbler, Telegram, Ask.fm, and Twitter. For example, it used Twitter to disseminate slick propaganda videos, promote its religious ideology and state-building efforts, and make one-on-one connections with prospective recruits. It also benefited from small cells of influencers or "disseminators" that played an outsized role in providing encouragement, justification, and religious legitimacy.[26] Figure 2.2 uses Twitter data to reveal levels of global Islamic State support in 2014 and 2015.[27] The figure highlights the number of pro–Islamic State Twitter users based on the geographic locations of the tweets. The data suggest that Islamic State enjoyed a global interactive audience of Twitter supporters—numbering over 75,000 users—based in such areas as the Middle East, Africa, North America, and sections of Asia and Latin America.

Expansion of Provinces

Following its break from al-Qa'ida in January 2014, the Islamic State expanded to include four components: a core area in Iraq and Syria, roughly eight formal provinces outside Iraq and Syria, a set of aspiring provinces and networks, and a large number of inspired individuals. To begin with, the Islamic State established a *core area* in Iraq and Syria. While Islamic State leaders seek a pan-Islamic caliphate, Iraq and Syria are its heartland. Sunni prophecies attributed to Muhammad praise the region of al-Sham. "O youth of Islam!" declared Abu Bakr al-Baghdadi, "Go forth to the blessed land of Sham!"[28]

In addition, the Islamic State also established a number of *formal provinces*—in Yemen (2014), Libya (2014), Egypt (2014), Saudi Arabia (2014), Algeria (2014), the Caucasus (2015), Afghanistan (2015), and

---

[26] Joseph Carter, Shiraz Maher, and Peter Neumann, "#Greenbirds: Measuring Importance and Influence in Syrian Foreign Fighter Networks," London: International Centre for the Study of Radicalization and Political Violence, 2014.

[27] The data include 4.5 million pro-Islamic State tweets and 75,946 user accounts between July 1, 2014, and April 30, 2015, based on how Twitter users refer to the Islamic State. The Islamic State requested that its followers refer to it as الدولة الإسلامية, [the Islamic State], while group detractors often used the Arabic initials, شعاد, [Da'ish].

[28] Abu Bakr al-Baghdadi, "Baqiya fi al-'Iraq wa-l-Sham," audio recording, June 2014a.

Figure 2.2
Location of Islamic State Twitter Supporters

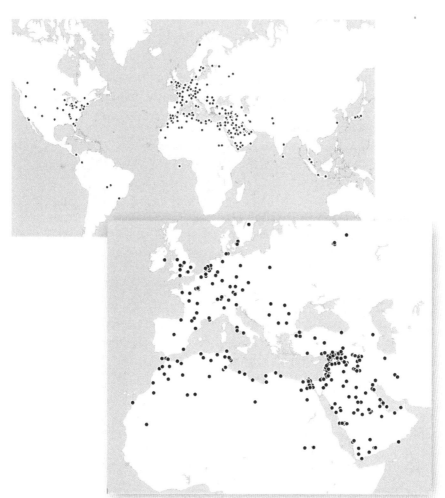

SOURCES: Twitter data from July 2014 to May 2015 and Elizabeth Bodine-Baron, Todd Helmus, Madeline Magnuson, and Zev Winkelman, *Examining ISIS Support and Opposition Networks on Twitter*, Santa Monica, Calif.: RAND Corporation, RR-1328-RC, 2016. Map credit: © OpenStreetMap contributors © CartoDB.
RAND RR1912-2.2

Nigeria (2015)—which pledged *bay'ah* to Islamic State leader Bagh-dadi. And Baghdadi, in turn, formally accepted their pledges. The provinces in Yemen, Libya, Egypt, Saudi Arabia, and Algeria were formed by co-opting existing militant networks. In Egypt, for example, the Islamic State co-opted the Salafi-jihadist group Ansar Bayt al-Maqdis [Supporters of Jerusalem], which had been involved in a campaign of violence against Egyptian and Israeli targets. In Algeria, the Islamic State co-opted the group Jund al-Khilafah [Soldiers of the Caliphate], which had previously been allied with al-Qa'ida in the Islamic Maghreb. In the fifth issue of its magazine, *Dabiq*, the Islamic State outlined these expansions. "Glad tidings, O Muslims," exclaimed Baghdadi,

> for we give you good news by announcing the expansion of the Islamic State to new lands, to the lands of al-Haramayn and Yemen. . . to Egypt, Libya, and Algeria. We announce the acceptance of the bay'ah of those who gave us bay'ah in those lands, the nullification of the groups therein, the announcement of new wilayat for the Islamic State, and the appointment of wulat [governors] for them.[29]

In January 2015, the Islamic State added a province in Afghanistan. It co-opted disaffected members of the Afghan Taliban, Tehreek-e-Taliban Pakistan (TTP), Islamic Movement of Uzbekistan, and other militant groups. This province was initially led by Hafiz Saeed Khan, and referred to as Wilayat Khorasan (or the Islamic State–Khorasan Province). In March 2015 and June 2015, the Islamic State approved provinces in Nigeria and the Caucasus, respectively. The Nigerian province was particularly noteworthy since the Islamic State had successfully co-opted the Salafi-jihadist group Boko Haram, which changed its name to Wilayat Gharb Ifriqiyyah (Islamic State West Africa Province).

There were also a number of *aspiring provinces and networks*. These networks pledged *bay'ah* to Baghdadi, but the Islamic State did not yet formally accept their pledges. Examples included groups in Somalia, the Philippines, Turkey, Bangladesh, Indonesia, Mali, and Tunisia. As with its formal provinces, the Islamic State attempted to co-opt indi-

---

[29] "Remaining and Expanding," *Dabiq*, No. 5, 1436 Muharram [2014], p. 22.

viduals from existing groups, such as al-Shaba'ab in Somalia and the Abu Sayyaf Group in the Philippines.

The Islamic State has also inspired individuals and established clandestine cells around the globe, as highlighted in the Twitter data in Figure 2.2. These individuals were not all formal members of the Islamic State. But they were inspired by the organization's ideology, its claim to have resurrected the caliphate, and its actions and propaganda campaign on the Internet and social media and conducted attacks or provided other types of assistance in support of the Islamic State and its cause. Figure 2.3 highlights the expansion of the Islamic State and its formal and informal provinces outside Iraq and Syria. These provinces are located in areas where the Islamic State desired to create its pan-Islamic caliphate.

In creating a web of formal and aspiring provinces, the Islamic State's Directorate of Remote Provinces brokered deals with a variety of local groups. Beginning around spring 2014, while the Islamic State was busy consolidating its hold on the Syrian city of Raqqa and expanding back into Anbar Province in Iraq, its leaders communicated with militant groups in Libya, Egypt, Nigeria, Yemen, Algeria, Afghanistan, and Pakistan. Their goal was to increase the Islamic State's influence and recruit fighters in several ways.

First, the Islamic State attempted to exploit local grievances and leverage established militant networks. In Afghanistan and Pakistan, for example, the Islamic State leaders reached out to disaffected TTP and Afghan Taliban commanders. Following the death of several TTP leaders, Hafiz Saeed Khan became increasingly disenchanted with TTP. Saeed had apparently been one of the main contenders for the TTP's top spot but was passed over. This discontent provided an opening for the Islamic State, which began to woo Khan and his network in Pakistan's Federally Administered Tribal Areas (FATA) and neighboring Afghanistan. The Islamic State used a similar strategy with disaffected Afghan Taliban in such provinces as Helmand and Farah.[30]

---

[30] See, for example, Seth G. Jones, "Expanding the Caliphate: ISIS' South Asia Strategy," *Foreign Affairs*, June 11, 2015.

Figure 2.3
Examples of Formal and Informal Islamic State Provinces

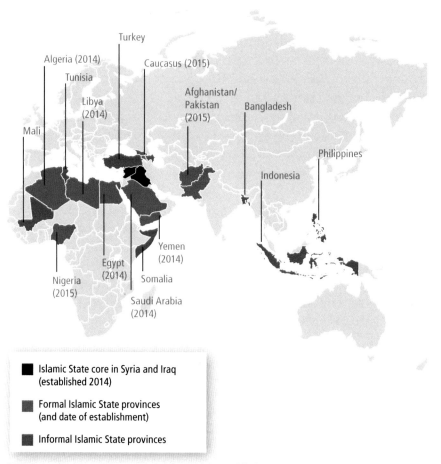

NOTE: Authors' estimates. Map adapted from dikobraziy/GettyImages.
RAND *RR1912-2.3*

Second, the Islamic State then doled out some money to prospective allies. The group accrued substantial financial resources in Iraq and Syria from selling oil, taxation, extortion using mafia-style rackets, kidnapping for ransom, and seizing bank holdings. For instance, this allowed the Islamic State to provide money and other aid to Boko

Haram in Nigeria after it had suffered military setbacks at the hands of the Nigerian and neighboring government forces.

Third, the Islamic State's initial military conquests in Iraq and Syria, which were broadcast through an effective social media strategy, attracted many sympathizers. The creation of a core caliphate set the Islamic State apart from existing Salafi-jihadist networks. In Libya, for example, the Islamic State sent emissaries in late 2014 to meet with extremist groups, such as Ansar al-Sharia, in an effort to establish a formal relationship. In Egypt, leaders from the group Ansar Bayt al-Maqdis, based in the Sinai, pledged their loyalty to Baghdadi. Taken together, Islamic State leaders used a multipronged strategy to expand its base from Iraq and Syria to a broad system of formal provinces, aspiring provinces and networks, and informal individuals and cells connected through an innovative use of social media.

Patterns of Violence

The Islamic State's primary means to expand its control is the use of violence. We used data from IHS Jane's World Insurgency and Terrorism Database to track levels of attacks initiated by the Islamic State and its affiliates globally since 2014. The data, collected from news and social media reporting worldwide, capture details of attacks conducted by nonstate armed groups, including the method of attack, intended targets, known casualties, and city-level latitude and longitude location information.

The Islamic State's employment of violence is consistent with the behavior of most insurgent groups. When the Islamic State has faced a much stronger government adversary or attempted to establish a foothold in a new country, it has often adopted classic guerrilla tactics. Guerrilla warfare involves the use of military and political resources to mobilize a local population, conduct hit-and-run raids (rather than face the enemy directly on the battlefield), and undermine the government's will to fight.[31] A guerrilla strategy is attractive to groups that are

---

[31] Arreguín-Toft, 2005, pp. 32–33.

significantly weaker than government security forces, which is why a guerrilla campaign is sometimes likened to a "war of the flea."[32]

But when facing a weak government or feeble nonstate adversaries, the Islamic State often adopts a conventional military strategy that involves efforts to capture or destroy its adversary's forces.[33] The goal has been to win a decisive engagement or a series of battles, thereby destroying the adversary's physical capacity to resist.[34] The principal military objective in conventional campaigns is to overcome the adversary's main forces; the principal political aim is the displacement of the governing authorities.[35] In conventional operations, military confrontation is direct, either across well-defined front lines or between armed columns. Clashes often take the form of set battles, trench warfare, and town sieges.[36] This is the type of warfare the Islamic State utilized in early 2014 when its fighters from Syria surged across the border into Iraq's Anbar province in large conventional columns of mechanized, even some armored, vehicles, joining operatives that had already been active in Fallujah and Ramadi. As one account explained, the Islamic State

> was acting more like a conventional army than a guerrilla organization: instead of operating in small, clandestine cells, in plain clothes, by night, with civilian vehicles and light weapons, the Islamic State was running columns comprising dozens of technical trucks, artillery pieces, and captured armored vehicles.[37]

---

[32] Robert Taber, *War of the Flea: The Classic Study of Guerrilla Warfare*, Washington, D.C.: Potomac Books, 2002.

[33] Craig Andrew Whiteside, "The Smiling, Scented Men: The Political Worldview of the Islamic State of Iraq, 2003–2013," dissertation, Pullman: Washington State University, December 2014.

[34] Arreguín-Toft, 2005, pp. 30–31.

[35] Bard E. O'Neill, "Insurgency and Terrorism: From Revolution to Apocalypse, 2nd ed. rev., Washington, D.C.: Potomac Books, 2005 p. 50.

[36] Stathis N. Kalyvas and Laia Balcells, "International System and Technologies of Rebellion: How the End of the Cold War Shaped Internal Conflict," *American Political Science Review*, Vol. 104, No. 3, August 2010.

[37] Kilcullen, 2016, p. 85.

The data suggest that violence by the Islamic State core and its formal provinces involved direct combat (49 percent), bombings (26 percent), assassinations (14 percent), sabotage and raids (7 percent), and kidnappings (4 percent). The Islamic State fighters in Iraq, Syria, Libya, and Afghanistan all used similarly high percentages of direct combat tactics—which involved assaults against adversary positions and conventional engagements against often ineffectual resistance—reflecting their desire to control territory.[38] The other provinces used much higher percentages of unconventional attacks—such as bombings, sabotage, and assassination—which are more common in guerrilla campaigns when weak insurgent groups face a much stronger government adversary. The Islamic State's operations in Iraq—but not yet Syria—have increasingly relied on unconventional attacks.

Islamic State attacks within Iraq, Syria, and the provinces rose sharply from 2014 through early summer 2016; declined during summer 2016; and then significantly increased in early 2017 (Figure 2.4). Most of this surge in late 2016 and early 2017 was in Iraq and Syria, where the Islamic State conducted an aggressive campaign of bombings and assassinations as they lost territory. Combined attacks by the Islamic State provinces outside of Iraq and Syria increased through mid-2016 and then began to fall. Islamic State attacks in Nigeria increased in frequency, declined somewhat in Egypt and Afghanistan, and remained relatively steady in Libya between 2014 and early 2017.

The data also indicate an expansion in the geographic scope of violence by the Islamic State over time. In 2014, Islamic State violence was almost solely concentrated in Iraq and Syria, with a few attacks in such countries as Algeria, Libya, Egypt, Turkey, and Saudi Arabia. There were also a small number of Islamic State–inspired attacks in the West. In October 2014, for example, Michael Zehaf-Bibeau was involved in an Islamic State–inspired attack in Canada, killing one soldier at a war memorial in Ottawa and wounding two others at Parliament building. In December 2014, Man Haron Monis killed two Australians in Sydney during a siege at the Lindt Chocolate Café at

---

[38] The Islamic State devoted 53 percent of its violence to direct combat in Iraq and Syria combined, 40 percent in Libya, and 63 percent in Afghanistan.

Figure 2.4
Number of Islamic State Attacks

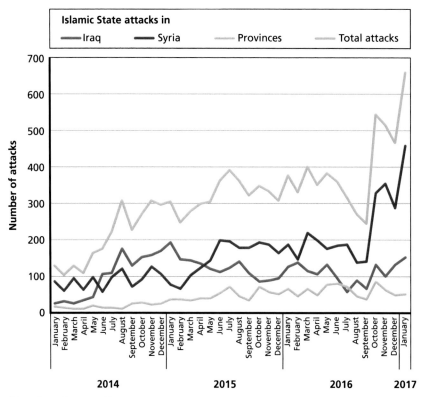

SOURCE: IHS Janes, 2017.
RAND RR1912-2.4

Martin Place. But 2015 was a banner year for the Islamic State. The number of attacks attributed to the Islamic State exploded in Nigeria as Boko Haram joined the Islamic State. Other Islamic State provinces in Afghanistan, Egypt, and Libya also conducted attacks. In the West, there were the Islamic State–organized or –inspired attacks in France, Denmark, Turkey, the United States, and Australia. Among the most high-profile attacks outside the areas of active hostilities were the December 2015 San Bernardino, California, attacks by Syed Rizwan Farook and Tashfeen Malik, which killed 14 people and wounded another 21 people, and the November 2015 Paris attacks that killed 130 people and wounded another 368 people.

In 2016, Islamic State violence continued to expand into Western countries including Belgium, where Islamic State–linked operatives killed 32 people in coordinated bombings at Zaventem Airport and on a subway train. Other attacks included the July 2016 cargo truck attack in Nice, France, which killed 86 people and injured more than 400 others, and the June 2016 attack in Orlando that killed 49 people. On December 19, 2016, a 24-year-old Tunisian immigrant hijacked a truck in Berlin and drove into a Christmas marked, killing 12 people. In addition, Islamic State attacks spread into the Asia-Pacific region. In January 2016, for example, Dian Joni Kurnaiadi, Muhammad Ali, Arif Sunakim, and Ahmad Muhazan bin Saron killed four civilians in a coordinated bombing and firearms attack in Jakarta, Indonesia.

These attacks continued into 2017. In January, at least 39 people were killed and nearly 70 wounded in Istanbul, Turkey, after a gunman opened fire at a nightclub in an attack claimed by the Islamic State. Khalid Masood, who had radicalized in part because of Islamic State and other Salafi-jihadist propaganda, killed four people and wounded another 50 in London. Figure 2.5 highlights the spread of Islamic State attacks globally.

Conclusion

Since its establishment, a core objective of the Islamic State's strategy has been the creation and expansion of a pan-Islamic caliphate. While Syria and Iraq remain the ideological heartland of the Islamic State, its leaders seek enlargement of their caliphate into Africa, the Middle East, and Asia. In addition, Islamic State leaders increasingly emphasized directed or inspired attacks in North America, Europe, Australia, and elsewhere against Western governments and populations.

But the group has faced significant hurdles in realizing this vision. The Islamic State experienced an initial surge in 2014 and 2015 by seizing territory in Iraq and Syria, then expanding into Libya, Egypt, Afghanistan, and Nigeria by co-opting local groups. But the group's

Figure 2.5
Global Islamic State Attacks, 2014–2016

Number of attacks

- 0
- 1–10
- 11–50
- 51–200
- 201–500
- 500+

SOURCE: IHS Janes, 2016. Map adapted from dikobraziy/Getty Images.
RAND RR1912-2.5

control of territory and populations subsequently declined as it faced resistance from government forces and nonstate armed groups in all these areas. Polling data indicate that the Islamic State and its ideology enjoy limited and declining support across the Muslim world. Yet the group has continued to inspire terrorist attacks.

The Islamic State's appeal to Muslim populations beyond its immediate control likely rests in large measure on its success in establishing a functioning protostate and emergent caliphate. Its capacity to inspire, support, and direct attacks outside its areas of control may thus ultimately diminish as that control declines, although there may be some lag time between the elimination of its territorial control and the decline in attacks. Without territory, the Islamic State may have a more difficult time recruiting and indoctrinating additional foreign fighters.

Many of the thousands of foreign fighters it already has will seek to return home, and some may seek to conduct attacks there. The loss of the core caliphate may also lead several of its outlying provinces to redirect their allegiance, perhaps to al-Qa'ida, or perhaps to continue operating independently. Unless liberated territory is effectively governed, however, the Islamic State or a violent successor is likely to rise again.

CHAPTER THREE

U.S. Strategy

In this chapter, we evaluate four strategies for dealing with the Islamic State: disengagement, containment, light rollback, and heavy rollback. These strategies represent the four main options that policymakers and analysts have advocated to deal with the Islamic State. The four strategies differ in their objectives, employment of American military forces, geographic scope, and underlying assumptions about such issues as the terrorist threat to the United States. We elaborate further on the strategy that we assess will be most effective, setting out its political, military, economic, and ideological components. Table 3.1 lays out the essential elements of these four strategies. Common to all of them is a robust defense of the homeland and close collaboration with partners around the world in the diplomatic, intelligence, military, and law-enforcement spheres.

We distinguish the alternatives in four ways. First, we examine the objectives of each strategy. They range from disengagement to preventing further expansion of the Islamic State to weakening and ultimately defeating the group. Second, we summarize the major components of each strategy. They vary in scope from focusing primarily on protecting the U.S. homeland to conducting global operations against the Islamic State. Third, we qualitatively assess the costs and benefits of the strategies, such as U.S. financial and human costs, the potential for blowback, and the U.S. role in directly targeting the Islamic State. Fourth, we outline the risks of each strategy. After describing each strategy along these four dimensions, we provide a short critique,

Table 3.1
A Summary of Strategic Options

Strategy	Objectives	Geographic Scope	Benefits	Risks
Disengagement	End most U.S. military operations overseas against the Islamic State and support partners instead	• Focus on homeland security • Expend limited U.S. resources to build capacity of local partners	• Minimizes U.S. financial and human costs • Lowers the potential for blowback resulting from the presence of U.S. forces	• Gives the United States little ability overseas to counter the Islamic State • Assumes that partners have the capability and will to weaken or defeat the Islamic State • Assumes the Islamic State threat is low and will decrease with U.S. retrenchment
Containment	Prevent further expansion of the Islamic State and contain the group in Iraq and Syria	• Utilize limited U.S. military and civilian resources to prevent Islamic State expansion • Build capacity of partners	• Retains some U.S. influence through presence • Decreases likelihood of blowback • Keeps financial and human costs relatively low	• Assumes Islamic State will eventually collapse from its own internal problems • Assumes low terrorist threat from the Islamic State • Assumes Islamic State global expansion can be contained with limited resources • Assumes that partners have the capability and will to weaken or defeat the Islamic State

Table 3.1—Continued

Strategy	Objectives	Geographic Scope	Benefits	Risks
Rollback (light)	Weaken and ultimately defeat the Islamic State	• Use U.S. SOF, air-power, and intel-ligence units working with local partners • Build capacity of local partners	• Allows the United States to directly counter the Islamic State • Limits delegation of U.S. security to others • Keeps U.S. pres-ence limited to SOF, air, and intel-ligence units	• Risks inflaming the local popula-tion and bolstering the Islamic State narrative • Slower than heavy rollback in decreasing Islamic State control • Assumes that partners have the capability and will to weaken or defeat the Islamic State with U.S. help • Assumes others will do bulk of stabilization and reconstruction
Rollback (heavy)	Weaken and ultimately defeat the Islamic State	• Employ U.S. con-ventional forces in ground combat to defeat Islamic State • Supplement with SOF and airpower • Build capacity of local partners	• May accelerate liberation of key territory • Provides greater control over pace and direction of campaign	• Increases the possibility of inflaming the local population and triggering blowback • Entails high financial and human costs • Leaves the United States heav-ily responsible for holding and rebuilding liberated areas and coping with residual resistance

weigh the risks and benefits, and make a recommendation on the optimal strategy.[1]

The Obama administration's approach to countering the Islamic State and its predecessor organization, AQI, shifted over time. The administration initially pursued a disengagement approach and pulled U.S. military forces out of Iraq in 2011, while AQI continued to conduct attacks over the next several years. Following the Islamic State's offensives in spring and summer 2014 in such areas as Anbar Province and Mosul, the United States briefly focused on containing the threat and helping defend Baghdad, then shifted to support efforts to take back Islamic State–controlled territory in Syria and Iraq. As the White House explained, the U.S. effort was on blunting "ISIL's momentum on the battlefield *in Iraq and Syria*, which is a source of recruitment and strength."[2] U.S.-led military operations began in summer 2014 as the United States established Operation Inherent Resolve (OIR), a military mission to degrade and defeat the Islamic State.[3] A three-star general coordinated OIR and led the organizational structure, Combined Joint Task Force OIR, under U.S. Central Command. Combined Joint Task Force OIR's mission was to leverage the Iraqis, Syrian resistance, and other partners to "militarily defeat Daesh in the Combined Joint Operations Area [Iraq and Syria] in order to enable whole-of-coalition governmental actions to increase regional stability."[4]

Over time, the United States expanded the use of U.S. military, intelligence units, and airpower to such countries as Libya and Nigeria, where U.S. military forces conducted strikes against Islamic State operatives and trained, advised, and assisted local partners. The United States also established a global coalition task force to counter the Islamic State, which was led by a special presidential envoy that

---

[1]   For a similar qualitative methodology to assess strategies, see Barry R. Posen and Andrew L. Ross, "Competing Visions for U.S. Grand Strategy," *International Security*, Vol. 21, No. 3, Winter 1996/1997.

[2]   White House, "Our Strategy to Defeat and Ultimately Destroy ISIL," strategy pocket card, November 20, 2015. Emphasis added.

[3]   See the OIR website for details.

[4]   Combined Joint Task Force, "Operation Inherent Resolve Fact Sheet," undated.

reported to the U.S. Secretary of State. The 66 countries that made up the coalition sought to "degrade, and ultimately destroy, ISIL through a comprehensive and sustained counterterrorism strategy."[5] The United States used a range of instruments, such as building partner capacity, enhancing intelligence collection, disrupting the Islamic State's finances, and providing humanitarian assistance.

Various U.S. government documents outlined these instruments. They described nine "lines of effort," including supporting effective governance; five lines of effort, including impeding the flow of foreign fighters; four "pillars," including increased support to forces fighting the Islamic State on the ground; then eight "things" the U.S. did to defeat the Islamic State, including seeking a diplomatic solution in Syria.[6]

Strategic Options

Disengagement

This strategy would rely almost entirely on other countries to provide the military component of an anti-Islamic State coalition. Proponents of this strategy argue variously that it is not essential to U.S. security that the Islamic State be defeated; that American military participation in such an effort may actually be counterproductive; and that, in any case, the Islamic State is likely to be defeated by its regional enemies.[7] Some also argue that the Islamic State would have little reason to target the United States and its citizens, either abroad or at home, were the

---

[5] See the Global Coalition to Counter ISIL website for details (U.S. Department of State, "Global Coalition to Counter ISIL," webpage, undated).

[6] See White House, "The Administration's Strategy to Counter the Islamic State of Iraq and the Levant (ISIL) and the Updated FY 2015 Overseas Contingency Operations Request," fact sheet, November 7, 2014; U.S. Department of State, undated; and Tanya Somanader, "President Obama Provides an Update on Our Strategy to Degrade and Destroy ISIL, July 6, 2015.

[7] On disengagement and related strategies, such as neoisolationism, see Posen and Ross, 1996/1997.

United States to refrain from military engagement in Iraq, Syria, and other Middle Eastern countries.[8] As one assessment noted:

> Without the American presence, extremists would no longer be able to position themselves as the Islamic defenders against Western crusaders. Moreover, if the Islamic State really is the existential threat to the region that the bipartisan Washington war chorus says it is, then, if left to themselves, the Sunnis and Shiites, Turks and Kurds, Iranians and Saudis would be compelled for their own survival to join together to take it down.[9]

Disengagement advocates generally ask whether the Islamic State threatens the sovereignty of the United States or its territorial integrity. They assess that it does not. As one proponent noted, the Islamic State's "numbers are small, and it has differentiated itself from al-Qa'ida in that it does not seek primarily to target the 'far enemy,' preferring instead to carve out a state in the Middle East for itself, mostly killing fellow Muslims who stand in its way."[10] Some have argued that the annual risk of dying in a terrorist attack in the United States is lower than a litany of other incidents, such as traffic accidents, more-routine homicides, natural disasters, and home and industrial accidents.[11] Some also assert that the threat from terrorist groups, including the Islamic State, is lower today than in some past eras. "Terrorism," one assessment concludes, "most of it arising from domestic groups—was a much bigger problem in the United States during the 1970s than it has been since the Twin Towers were toppled."[12]

A disengagement strategy involves concentrating on homeland security while encouraging other countries to fight the Islamic State.

---

[8]   See, for example, John Mueller and Mark G. Stewart, *Chasing Ghosts: The Policing of Terrorism*, New York: Oxford University Press, 2015; Mueller and Stewart, 2011; Mearsheimer, 2014; Sageman, 2013; and Posen and Ross, 1996/1997, p. 11.

[9]   Jeff Faux, Muhammad Idrees Ahmad, Phyllis Bennis, and Sherle R. Schwenniger, "Is it Time for the U.S. to Pull out of Iraq and Syria?" *Nation*, January 14, 2016.

[10]   Mueller, 2015.

[11]   Mueller and Stewart, 2010.

[12]   Mearsheimer, 2014, p. 12. Also see, for example, Jenkins, 2011.

As U.S. presidential candidate Bernie Sanders summarized: "It is my firm belief . . . that the war against ISIS will never be won unless nations in the Middle East step up their military efforts and take more responsibility for the security and stability of their region."[13] Sanders continued: "It is worth remembering that Saudi Arabia, for example, is a nation controlled by one of the wealthiest families in the world and has the fourth largest military budget of any nation. This is a war for the soul of Islam and Muslim nations must become more heavily engaged."[14] Some proponents of disengagement support limited U.S. involvement, such as air strikes against Islamic State targets or diplomatic action with local actors. But most advocate handing over all—or almost all—of the fighting to locals.

Disengagement has several potential benefits. It minimizes U.S. financial and human costs by shifting these to local U.S. allies. As Bernie Sanders remarked about the U.S. wars in Iraq and Afghanistan: "Today, after 13 years in Afghanistan and 12 years in Iraq, after the loss of almost 7,000 troops and the expenditure of trillions of dollars, I very much fear U.S. involvement in an expanding and never-ending quagmire in that region of the world."[15] It is also less likely than other strategies to inflame anti-Americanism among local populations in ways that might increase terrorist recruitment. Some proponents contend that one of the most important inflection points was the first Gulf War, when America's decision to deploy combat forces to the Arabian Peninsula became the chief rallying cry for Osama bin Laden against the United States and its allies.[16]

But disengagement also carries several risks, which makes it a poor choice. First, the Islamic State, like several other terrorist organizations, such as al-Qa'ida in the Arabian Peninsula, continues to plot and inspire attacks against the United States at home and over-

---

[13] Bernie Sanders, "Bernie Sanders on ISIS," February 2015.

[14] Sanders, 2015.

[15] Sanders, 2015.

[16] Robert A. Pape and James K. Feldman, *Cutting the Fuse: The Explosion of Global Suicide Terrorism and How to Stop It*, Chicago: University of Chicago Press, 2010, p. 12.

seas.[17] The director of the National Counterterrorism Center warned that "the pool of potential [homegrown violent extremists (HVEs)] has expanded" and "the FBI has investigations on around 1,000 potential HVEs across all 50 states."[18] Disengagement advocates tend to understate the terrorism threat, including the U.S. public's concerns about terrorism. A January 2017 Pew Research Center poll found that most Americans viewed the Islamic State as the most significant threat to the country, followed by cyberattacks, North Korea, Russian influence, and climate change.[19] These findings were similar to a 2016 poll that also showed that Americans saw the Islamic State as the top global threat to the United States.[20]

Second, disengagement severely limits U.S. influence over developments in the Middle East by outsourcing the campaign against the Islamic State entirely to other state and nonstate actors, many of which are more interested in fighting each other than the Islamic State. Regional governments can be fickle, uncooperative, and fragile. Some, including Russia and Iran, may have interests that compete against those of the United States. While every regime in the Middle East opposes the Islamic State, virtually none of them, with the exception of Iraq, rate it as their principal enemy.

Third, it is also risky to assume that the Islamic State would cease to target the United States and its citizens, abroad and at home, if the United States disengaged from Iraq, Syria, and other affected countries. The Islamic State actively encourages attacks in Western countries for ideological reasons, regardless of their deployment of military forces overseas.

---

[17] See, for example, Clapper, 2016, and Nicholas J. Rasmussen, "Worldwide Threats to the Homeland: the Islamic State and the New Wave of Terror," testimony before the House Homeland Security Committee, July 14, 2016.

[18] N. Rasmussen, 2016.

[19] Pew Research Center, "The World Facing Trump: Public Sees ISIS, Cyberattacks, North Korea as Top Threats," Washington, D.C., January 12, 2017.

[20] Bruce Drake and Carroll Doherty, *Key Findings on How Americans View the U.S. Role in the World*, Washington, D.C.: Pew Research Center, May 5, 2016.

Fourth, disengagement has a poor track record and has produced unintended and unfortunate consequences over the past several decades. The U.S. neglect of Afghanistan throughout the 1990s opened the country to the Taliban and al-Qa'ida, resulting in the attacks of September 11, 2001. The U.S. withdrawal from Iraq in 2011 contributed to a resurgence of AQI, its subsequent transformation into the Islamic State, and its spread across the region.[21] Following the Obama administration's 2014 announcement that the U.S. "combat mission in Afghanistan is ending, and the longest war in American history is coming to a responsible conclusion," the Islamic State subsequently established a sanctuary in the country.[22] Other American disengagements, from Lebanon in 1984 and Somalia in 1994, have been less obviously disastrous, although both societies descended further into civil war after American forces withdrew.

Containment

This strategy would employ American military assets as part of a broader effort to prevent any further expansion of the Islamic State's territorial control while leaving to others the reduction of its current strongholds.[23] As the name implies, containment involves thwarting a state or nonstate actor from *expanding* its influence, not seeking to

---

[21] Daniel Byman, "Six Bad Options for Syria," *Washington Quarterly*, Vol. 38, No. 4, Winter 2016a.

[22] Barack Obama, "Statement by the President on the End of the Combat Mission in Afghanistan," Washington, D.C.: The White House, December 28, 2014.

[23] See, for example, Stephen Biddle and Jacob Shapiro, "The Problem with Vows to 'Defeat' the Islamic State," *Atlantic*, August 21, 2016b; Barry R. Posen, "Contain ISIS," *Atlantic*, November 20, 2015; James Fromson and Steven Simon, "ISIS: The Dubious Paradis of Apocalypse Now," *Survival*, Vol. 57, No. 3, June–July 2015; Stephen Biddle and Jacob Shapiro, "America Can't Do Much About ISIS," *Atlantic*, April 20, 2016a; Dov S. Zakheim, "The Only the Islamic State Strategy Left for America: Containment," *National Interest*, May 23, 2015; Stephen M. Walt, "ISIS as a Revolutionary State," *Foreign Affairs*, Vol. 94, No. 6, November/December 2015b; Jessica Stern, "Containing ISIS: What Would George Kennan Do?" *Atlantic*, December 9, 2015; Marc Lynch, *The Tourniquet: A Strategy for Defeating the Islamic State and Saving Iraq and Syria*, Washington, D.C.: Center for a New American Security, 2014; Jenna Jordan and Lawrence Rubin, "An ISIS Containment Doctrine," *National Interest*, June 14, 2016; Audrey Kurth Cronin, "Why Counterterrorism Won't Stop the Latest Jihadist Threat," *Foreign Affairs*, March/April 2015b; and Clint Watts, "Let Them

eliminate that influence. During the Cold War, the U.S. containment strategy involved preventing Soviet expansionism around the globe. It took inspiration from George Kennan's writings from the 1940s and was initially implemented by the Truman administration.[24] The strategy evolved with the publication of NSC-68, which was put into effect between 1950 and 1953.[25] The United States provided military and economic aid to Greece and Turkey and designed the Marshall Plan to thwart Soviet expansion. The goal was not to overthrow the Soviet Union or liberate Eastern Europe but rather, as Cold War historian John Lewis Gaddis summarized, "to limit Soviet expansionism" on the grounds that "communism posed a threat only to the extent that it was the instrument of that expansion."[26]

Successive U.S. administrations sought to maintain a balance of power with the Soviets in the expectation, or at least the hope, that the Communist system would ultimately collapse because of its contradictions and inefficiencies.[27] George Kennan anticipated that the territorial acquisition and spheres of influence the Soviet Union had obtained would ultimately become a source of insecurity, because resistance to Moscow's control might grow in Eastern Europe and even in the Soviet Union itself.[28] "Soviet power, like the capitalist world of its own conception, bears within it the seeds of its own decay," Kennan wrote in 1947, adding that "the sprouting of those seeds is well advanced."[29]

Proponents of modern-day containment argue that it is not practical or feasible for the United States to *defeat* the Islamic State. The Soviet empire, ideology, and state ultimately did collapse. Some of

---

Rot: The Challenges and Opportunities of Containing rather than Countering the Islamic State," *Perspectives on Terrorism*, Vol. 9, No. 4, August 2015.

[24] X, "The Sources of Soviet Conduct," *Foreign Affairs*, Vol. 25, No. 4, 1947, pp. 566–582.

[25] NSC, 1950.

[26] John Lewis Gaddis, *Strategies of Containment: A Critical Appraisal of Postwar American National Security Policy*, New York: Oxford University Press, 1982, p. 34.

[27] John Lewis Gaddis, *We Now Know: Rethinking Cold War History,* New York: Oxford University Press, 1997, p. 39.

[28] Gaddis, 1997, p. 37.

[29] X, "1947.

those who argue for containing the Islamic State believe that it too will ultimately disintegrate or be eliminated by its many local adversaries.[30] For others, the West may have to live with Islamic State control in some areas.[31] One proponent argued that "fortunately, history suggests that if ISIS survives, it will become a more normal state over time."[32] Still others note that unlike such states as China or Russia, which have substantial economic and military resources, the Islamic State is not a powerful global or even regional actor.[33] The Islamic State's potential support base is relatively small, and it has neither the military nor the economic means to greatly expand its power. The threat it poses to the United States may be manageable, they argue, as long as its territorial and population control is not extended further.

Limited U.S. military efforts, proponents argue, may be adequate to contain the Islamic State in Syria, Iraq, and the few other states where it has gained a foothold. As one analyst put it, "the sobering fact is that the United States has no good military options in its fight against ISIS."[34] Further, postconflict stabilization and reconstruction of liberated areas would likely be very difficult and resource intensive. Consequently, a

> smart containment strategy should include serious efforts to assist regional powers in coping with the humanitarian fallout of Syrian and Iraq violence, to limit the risk that neighboring states suffer those countries' fate, and to encourage long-run political settlements where possible.[35]

Containment proponents warn that deploying large numbers of U.S. forces to dislodge the Islamic State is unlikely to succeed and will

---

[30] Biddle and Shapiro, 2016b.

[31] On living with the Islamic State see, for example, John McLaughlin, "How the Islamic State Could Win," *Washington Post*, May 17, 2015; Stephen M. Walt, "What Should We Do if the Islamic State Wins? Live with It," *Foreign Policy*, June 10, 2015a.

[32] Walt, 2015b, p. 49.

[33] See, for example, Walt, 2015a.

[34] Cronin, 2015a, p. 97.

[35] Biddle and Shapiro, 2016a.

inflame local anti-American sentiments. They also note that there is neither the political will in Washington nor the domestic appetite in the United States to expend American blood and treasure on the scale needed to defeat the Islamic State.[36]

Containment has several potential benefits. It limits U.S. financial and human costs by shifting them to local allies, although not as much as disengagement does. It also eschews nation-building and so does not open the prospect of a major American role in the long and potentially expensive effort that will be needed to rebuild war-torn countries. Unlike disengagement, however, containment involves some U.S. military operations against the Islamic State. It also assumes that the fight will be a long one and does not promise a quick resolution.

But containment has several risks that make it a suboptimal choice. First, it is unclear, perhaps even unlikely, that the Islamic State will collapse or be defeated anytime soon without outside support. The Islamic State has expanded its global network and continued to conduct attacks overseas even after its control of territory has shrunk. In Iraq, the Islamic State only began to lose territory *after* the United States began its bombing campaign and deployed military advisers to the country. In addition, without dealing more effectively with governance problems, such as Sunni disenfranchisement, that allowed the Islamic State to develop a sanctuary, it is unlikely that the Islamic State—or another Salafi-jihadist group in its place—will self-destruct. In addition, containing the Islamic State on the Internet and in social media may be even more difficult because of its demonstrated ability to leverage forums, such as Twitter and Facebook.[37]

Second, delaying the Islamic State's demise does little to impede the number and frequency of these attacks and rising numbers of refugees and IDPs. Even if the Islamic State eventually collapses, it has space *now* to cause damage. As long as it has a base from which to operate—whether it is in Syria, Iraq, Libya, or elsewhere—the Islamic State can conduct operations, infiltrate, subvert, and destabilize.

---

[36] Zakheim, 2015.

[37] Jordan and Rubin, 2016.

Third, the U.S. public is more concerned about terrorism than containment advocates acknowledge. While the Islamic State does not possess the military and economic resources of a great power, its ability to conduct or inspire attacks in the United States—along with France, Belgium, Germany, Canada, Turkey, and other Western countries—has triggered serious concerns among the U.S. population. In a 2017 Pew Research Center poll, nearly 80 percent of Americans said the Islamic State posed a "major threat" to the well-being of the United States.[38] In addition, Americans were significantly more concerned about the threat from the Islamic State than from Russia and China because of the Islamic State's willingness and ability to conduct attacks in the U.S. homeland. In 2016, 73 percent of Americans believed the Islamic State was a "very serious" threat to the United States, compared to only 24 percent for China and 21 percent for Russia.[39]

Fourth, some containment arguments have developed straw man alternatives, claiming that the only activist option is deploying large numbers of U.S. conventional forces and promising a quick and decisive victory.[40] As one proponent argued, containment is a better option because it is

> hard to see how Western ground forces can liberate the areas of Iraq and Syria currently held by ISIS, and sit on that territory for as long as it takes to ensure that ISIS is no more and that yet another terrorist organization does not rise from its ashes, with fewer numbers and less bloodshed than the original invasion and subsequent counterinsurgency in Iraq entailed.[41]

The light rollback approach explained later offers an activist U.S. option that would not involve large numbers of U.S. ground forces. In short, containment was a sensible approach during the Cold War because the Soviet Union was a nuclear-armed power and because direct confronta-

---

[38] Pew Research Center, 2017.

[39] CNN/ORC International, poll, May 5, 2016.

[40] See, for example, Biddle and Shapiro, 2016b; Watts, 2015; Stern, 2015.

[41] Posen, 2015.

tion with Moscow—including a rollback strategy—risked escalation to nuclear war. No such danger exists with the Islamic State.

Heavy Rollback

A heavy rollback strategy focuses on reversing Islamic State gains in countries where it has a sanctuary by employing U.S. conventional forces in ground combat.[42] Proponents of a conventional ground combat element to the strategy argue that local forces in such countries as Iraq and Syria are generally too weak, divided, or poorly motivated to defeat Islamic State fighters even when assisted by American airpower. One advocate argued that, for removing the Islamic State from Iraq, "The surest means of attaining this strategic objective is with the introduction of U.S. ground combat forces and the necessary sustainment packages to support them."[43] Unlike a containment strategy, which would focus on preventing further Islamic State expansion, heavy rollback involves weakening and ultimately defeating Islamic State forces wherever they establish safe havens. And unlike disengagement, which would involve ending U.S. involvement overseas and instead supporting allies against the Islamic State, heavy rollback involves direct U.S. political, military, and other activism.

During the Cold War, the notion of rollback surfaced in the late 1940s but gained wider currency just after the outbreak of the Korean War in 1950.[44] The U.S. government considered authorizing direct action against the Soviet Union.[45] In the end, the United States declined to pursue a rollback strategy. U.S. officials concluded that aggressive designs to roll back communism—particularly using force against the Soviet Union—were far too dangerous and counterproductive. Since the Soviet Union was a nuclear power, attempting to defeat

---

[42] Kimberly Kagan, Frederick W. Kagan, and Jessica D. Lewis, *A Strategy to Defeat the Islamic State*, Washington, D.C.: Institute for the Study of War, September 2014.

[43] David E. Johnson, "Fighting the 'Islamic State': The Case for US Ground Forces," *Parameters*, Vol. 45, No. 1, Spring 2015, p. 14.

[44] NSC, 1950.

[45] Peter Grose, *Operation Rollback: America's Secret war Behind the Iron Curtain*, New York: Houghton Mifflin Co., 2000, pp. 7–8.

the Soviets or undermine their influence in Eastern Europe could lead to nuclear war. Eisenhower's secretary of state, John Foster Dulles, believed that attempts to undermine Soviet satellites in Eastern Europe would increase the risk of general war and, in the end, would do little to alter the central balance of power. Furthermore, aggressive action might imperil the Western coalition and would destroy any chances of reaching agreement with the Soviet Union. Containment was a less risky strategy. The retreat from rollback was reaffirmed in 1953, when the administration adopted NSC-174, which described the restoration of East European independence as only a long-term U.S. aim.[46] Care had to be taken not to incite "premature" rebellion.[47]

A potential advantage of heavy rollback is that it promises the fastest and surest way to close down the core caliphate in Iraq and Syria. But there are substantial risks with dependence on such a heavy military footprint. First, while American troops might be able to more quickly clear Raqqa, Mosul, and other Islamic State territory, using American troops to hold, stabilize, and reconstruct these areas could quickly become a financial and bloody burden. But rapidly withdrawing American troops could leave a vacuum filled by a resurgent Islamic State, other Salafi-jihadist groups, or Iran and its proxy organizations. Unless local forces can secure these areas, and local governments effectively administer them, any victory could be short lived while American forces were tied down for an extended period.

Second, most recent successful campaigns against terrorist groups that involved foreign soldiers were conducted by small numbers of elite forces, intelligence units, and airpower.[48] Examples range from the effective U.S. operations in the Philippines and Colombia to the

---

[46] NSC, "United States Policy Toward the Soviet Satellites in Eastern Europe," Washington, D.C., NSC 174, December 11, 1953.

[47] László Borhi, "Containment, Rollback, Liberation or Inaction? The United States and Hungary in the 1950s," *Journal of Cold War Studies*, Vol. 1, No. 3, 1999.

[48] Daniel Byman, "ISIS Goes Global: Fight the Islamic State by Targeting Its Affiliates," *Foreign Affairs*, Vol. 95, No. 2, March/April 2016b.

French campaign in Mali.[49] American conventional forces were able to quickly overrun Saddam's Iraq but proved unable to stabilize either that country or Afghanistan. Perhaps larger, better-prepared stabilization forces would have produced better results, but only at a considerable cost over an extended period. Significant numbers of U.S. forces in Muslim countries have tended to inspire terrorist attacks locally and in the homeland. Many of the terrorists involved in U.S. homeland plots on and after 9/11—such as José Padilla's plan to blow up apartment buildings in the United States, Nidal Hassan's mass shooting at Fort Hood, and Najibullah Zazi and Faisal Shahzad's respective plots to conduct terrorist attacks in New York City—were motivated, in part, by objections to the deployment of U.S. combat troops in Muslim countries and by a conviction, however erroneous, that Muslims were America's victims.[50]

Light Rollback

This version of rollback would employ American airpower; intelligence units; and, predominantly, special operations forces in support of regional allies to target the Islamic State. Unlike heavy rollback, light rollback would not involve large numbers of U.S. conventional combat forces against the Islamic State. It would also entail the use of political and economic, as well as military, instruments to defeat the Islamic State and to strengthen local governments.[51]

---

[49] See, for example, Linda Robinson, Patrick B. Johnston, and Gillian S. Oak, *U.S. Special Operations Forces in the Philippines, 2001–2014*, Santa Monica, Calif.: RAND Corporation, RR-1236-OSD, 2016, and Christopher S. Chivvis, *The French War on Al Qa'ida in Africa*, New York: Cambridge University Press, 2015.

[50] Seth G. Jones, *Hunting in the Shadows: The Pursuit of Al-Qa'ida Since 9/11*, New York: W.W. Norton, 2012.

[51] See, for example, Hal Brands and Peter Feaver, "Trump and Terrorism: U.S. Strategy After ISIS," *Foreign Affairs*, Vol. 96, No. 2, March/April 2017; Michèle Flournoy and Richard Fontaine, *An Intensified Approach to Combating the Islamic State*, Washington, D.C.: Center for a New American Security, 2015a; Samuel R. Berger, Stephen J. Hadley, James F. Jeffrey, Dennis Ross, and Robert Satloff, *Key Elements of a Strategy for the United States in the Middle East*, Washington, D.C.: Washington Institute for Near East Policy, 2015; Dennis Ross, "A Strategy for Beating the Islamic State," *Politico*, September 2, 2014;

This strategy would employ unconventional warfare, foreign internal defense, and direct action to weaken the Islamic State and improve the capacity of local governments. Unconventional warfare includes activities to enable a resistance movement to "coerce, disrupt, or overthrow a government or occupying power by operating through or with an underground, auxiliary, and guerrilla force in a denied area."[52] Examples include working with Libyan militias or with Kurdish forces in Syria and Iraq against the Islamic State. Foreign internal defense consists of a variety of actions by civilian and military agencies to improve the capacity of a foreign government to "protect its society from subversion, lawlessness, insurgency, terrorism, and other threats to its security."[53] Examples range from improving the border security capabilities of Tunisian forces to improving the surveillance and reconnaissance capabilities of the Iraqi security forces. Direct action includes strikes and other small-scale offensive actions to seize, destroy, capture, exploit, recover, or damage designated targets.[54] Examples are drone strikes or raids against the Islamic State.

A light rollback strategy has risks. First, direct U.S. engagement could add credence to the narrative of the Islamic State and other extremist groups, which will invariably attempt to portray the conflict as one between Islam and Western countries. However, this concern is much less significant than with a heavy rollback strategy and the deployment of large numbers of conventional U.S. forces. Even covert U.S. activities will likely become public, putting pressure on local governments from publics opposed to Western involvement. After the 2009 U.S. killing of TTP leader Baitullah Mehsud, Faisal Shahzad attempted to detonate a car bomb in New York City after receiving training from TTP operatives in Pakistan. While the United States should be mindful of local sensitivities and minimize civilian casual-

---

Byman, 2016b; and Michèle Flournoy and Richard Fontaine, "To Defeat the Islamic State, the U.S. Will Have to Go Big," *Washington Post*, June 24, 2015b.

[52] Joint Publication (JP) 1-02, *Department of Defense Dictionary of Military and Associated Terms*, Washington, D.C.: Joint Staff, February 15, 2016, p. 249.

[53] JP 1-02, 2016, p. 92.

[54] JP 1-02, 2016, pp. 68–69.

ties, the Islamic State will likely continue to plot and inspire attacks against the United States and other Western countries regardless of U.S. engagement.

Second, the financial and human costs are greater with roll-back than with disengagement or containment. The strategy also puts American soldiers, diplomats, and intelligence operatives at greater risk. Some will die as a result.

Third, there is a potential for mission creep if small numbers of U.S. forces are insufficient or if the Islamic State abandons its efforts at territorial control in favor of guerilla tactics, potentially leading some U.S. policymakers to call for larger numbers of U.S. soldiers. After all, light rollback assumes that others will do the bulk of stabilization and reconstruction once the Islamic State loses its territory. U.S. policy-makers will need to carefully weigh the pros and cons of larger U.S. deployments and be mindful of the risks outlined with heavy rollback.

Fourth, light rollback hinges on the capabilities and interests of local partners, much as disengagement and containment do. The reliance on partners means that this approach may be slower than heavy rollback to dislodge the Islamic State from territory it controls. Locals can be fickle, poorly trained, ineffective, corrupt, and undemocratic. They can also lose power. In Yemen, the United States lost a valuable partner in its fight against al-Qa'ida in the Arabian Peninsula when the Houthis overthrew the government of Abd Rabo Mansur Hadi. Weak and ineffective partners can be improved with a long-term, well-designed training and advisory mission, although there are limits to what U.S. assistance can do.[55]

Recommendation: Light Rollback

We conclude that light rollback offers the best combination of timely and assured success with acceptable cost and contained risk. The basic

---

[55] Daniel L. Byman, "Friends Like These: Counterinsurgency and the War on Terrorism," *International Security*, Vol. 31, No. 2, Fall 2006; Daniel L. Byman, *Going to War with the Allies You Have: Allies, Counterinsurgency, and the War on Terrorism*, Carlisle, Pa.: U.S. Army War College, November 2005.

problem with disengagement and containment is that their outcomes are too uncertain. Whatever degradation of the Islamic State results could come too slowly, and there are substantial risks with the Islamic State controlling territory for any amount of time. The heavy rollback strategy offers the prospect of a quicker overthrow of the Islamic State, but the costs and ancillary risks are also higher.

Acting by, with, and through local partners, the United States has made substantial progress toward closing down the core caliphate in Iraq and Syria and diminishing the control of affiliated groups in Libya, Nigeria, and Afghanistan. We have suggested ways the Obama administration's efforts can be extended and intensified without introducing American forces in a conventional ground combat role. We also conclude that local forces and local authorities will be more likely to secure and effectively govern these areas when they have played the leading role in their liberation. This is not to suggest that the American mission will be completed when the Islamic State has been driven underground. Previous experience has shown that the troop and other resource commitments need to stabilize postconflict societies and consolidate the peace sometimes exceed those needed to win the war. Even if local partners remain in the lead and provide the conventional ground element, the United States may need to remain engaged at or above current levels in the immediate postconventional combat phase.

It is important to deny the Islamic State its territorial base and to do so soon, before further attacks on the American homeland and those of its allies leads to dangerous overreactions. While one can make a statistically valid case that such attacks rank well below the other risks Americans face in their daily lives, American voters do not agree.[56] In France, this anxiety has led to the suspension of some civil liberties and bans against Muslim clothing, such as the burkini, the full-body swimwear. Further attacks on the scale of those that have hit Paris, Berlin, or Orlando, let alone another attack on the scale of 9/11, could precipitate a reaction less measured and more costly to civil liberties and democratic values.

---

[56] Pew Research Center, 2017; CNN/ORC International, 2016.

Depriving the Islamic State of a territorial base will not end the threat but will greatly diminish that group's capacity to organize large-scale, complex attacks and to inspire imitators. Suppressing the Islamic State once it has been dispossessed of its actual caliphate may be the work of years, much as has been the case with al-Qa'ida. But forcing this group underground is a necessary first step and one we believe to be sufficiently urgent to justify the employment of American military force in the measured manner we propose.

Policy Instruments of Rollback

The Islamic State has embedded itself in a number of societies, co-opting local insurgencies and drawing support from local grievances. Defeating the Islamic State will therefore require context-specific country campaigns, which we provide in the following chapters. In the remainder of this chapter, we review elements that will be common to these campaigns.

Political

The military theorist Carl von Clausewitz argued that the "political object . . . will be the standard for determining the aim of the military force and also the amount of effort to be made," which is just as relevant for operations against the Islamic State and other insurgent groups as it is for conventional warfare.[57] The United States should integrate politics into virtually every aspect of its campaigns against the Islamic State, including building coalitions, helping negotiate ceasefires and peace settlements, providing aid to improve governance and better address the grievances that give rise to insurgency, and utilizing information campaigns that maximize support for local allies and undermine that for the Islamic State.

In most countries in which the Islamic State has a sanctuary, local governance needs improvement. As used here, *governance* is defined as the set of institutions by which legitimate authority in a country is

---

[57] Carl von Clausewitz, *On War*, New York: Penguin, 1968, p. 109.

exercised.[58] It consists of the ability to establish law and order, effectively manage resources, and implement sound policies. German sociologist Max Weber defined the state as "a human community that (successfully) claims the monopoly of the legitimate use of physical force within a given territory."[59] When state institutions are weak, opportunistic elements in society are able to take advantage.[60] State weakness is particularly likely in remote areas, where insurgent and terrorist groups can establish rural strongholds.[61] The more extreme the decline or absence of authority in a region, the more the population becomes "virgin territory" for those who would become an alternative government.[62] Weak governance fuels alternative power centers, and warlords often flourish.[63] Poor governance also increases the likelihood of insurgency and terrorism because the state's security forces are weak and lack popular legitimacy. These forces may be badly financed and equipped, organizationally inept, corrupt, politically divided, and poorly informed about events at the local level.[64]

A large body of quantitative evidence suggests that weak and ineffective governance is critical to the onset of insurgencies. This is certainly the case with the rise of the Islamic State. One study analyzed 161 cases over a 54-year period and found that financially, organizationally,

---

[58] World Bank, *Governance Matters 2006: Worldwide Governance Indicators*, Washington, D.C.: World Bank, 2006, p. 2.

[59] Max Weber, "Politics as a Vocation," in H.H. Gerth and C. Wright Mills, eds., *From Max Weber: Essays in Sociology*, New York: Oxford University Press, 1958, p. 78.

[60] World Bank, *Reforming Public Institutions and Strengthening Governance*, Washington D.C., 2000; Jessica Einhorn, "The World Bank's Mission Creep," *Foreign Affairs*, Vol. 80, No. 5, 2001.

[61] Ann Hironaka, *Neverending Wars: The International Community, Weak States, and the Perpetuation of Civil War*, Cambridge, Mass.: Harvard University Press, 2008, pp. 42–46.

[62] Kalyvas, 2006, p. 216; Timothy P. Wickham-Crowley, *Guerrillas and Revolution in Latin America: A Comparative Study of Insurgents and Regimes Since 1956*, Princeton, N.J.: Princeton University Press, 1992, p. 35.

[63] Jane Stromseth, David Wippman, and Rosa Brooks, *Can Might Make Rights? Building the Rule of Law after Military Interventions*, New York: Cambridge University Press, 2006, pp. 137–140.

[64] Byman, 2006; Byman, 2005.

and politically weak central governments render insurgencies more feasible and attractive because of weak local policing or inept counterinsurgency practices.[65] The reverse is also true: Effective governance decreases the probability of insurgency. In looking at 151 cases over a 54-year period, one study found that governance is critical to prevent insurgencies, arguing that success requires the "provision of temporary security, the building of new institutions capable of resolving future conflicts peaceably, and an economy capable of offering civilian employment to former soldiers and material progress to future citizens."[66] In addition, governmental capacity is a negative and significant predictor of civil war, and between 1816 and 1997, "effective bureaucratic and political systems reduced the rate of civil war activity."[67]

Governance had declined in every country in which the Islamic State subsequently became embedded. According to World Bank data, for example, rule of law decreased from 2009 to 2014—the year that the Islamic State became an independent organization—in Egypt, Libya, Nigeria, and Syria. In several other countries, such as Somalia, Iraq, and Afghanistan, the rule of law was already among the lowest in the world.[68] In addition, insurgencies are caused, in part, by grievances of the sort that motivate such groups as the Islamic State and those it has co-opted. Charismatic leaders, such as Abu Bakr al-Baghdadi, use religious, hypernationalist, or other types of rhetoric to mobilize individuals and organize rebellion.[69] Insurgent leaders employ grievances instrumentally to persuade individuals to join and to retain loyalists who already support the cause. Insurgents generally view themselves as agents of change. As Che Guevara wrote, "We must come to the inevitable conclusion that the guerrilla fighter is a social reformer . . .

---

[65] James D. Fearon and David D. Laitin, "Ethnicity, Insurgency, and Civil War," American Political Science Review, Vol. 97, No. 1, February 2003, pp. 75–76.

[66] Michael W. Doyle and Nicholas Sambanis, *Making War and Building Peace* Princeton, N.J.: Princeton University Press, 2006, p. 5.

[67] Hironaka, 2008, p. 45.

[68] World Bank, Worldwide Governance Indicators, database, 2017.

[69] On mobilization see Ted Robert Gurr, *Peoples Versus States: Minorities at Risk in the New Century*, Washington, D.C.: U.S. Institute of Peace, 2000.

and that he fights in order to change the social system that keeps all his unarmed brothers in ignominy and misery."[70] To do this, the Islamic State employs an effective political campaign to highlight grievances and a narrative to convince locals to participate in the struggle. This campaign requires denouncing local governments, providing a counternarrative, and explaining how the group will govern when they come to power.

The counterinsurgent's challenge is to understand what grievances actually increase the probability of an insurgency. In Iraq, for example, Sunni Arabs had substantial complaints about the Iraq government, which had replaced Sunni officials with loyal but often venal and incompetent Shi'a, used the courts and security forces to harass and pursue Sunni Arab politicians, and violently suppressed peaceful Sunni protests. In Syria, the Alawi Arabs, a minority religious sect and identity group that had had little influence or authority through the mid-20th century, emerged as the dominant force within the military and security services. Alawi Ba'athists dominated the Syrian government at the expense of other ethnosectarian groups, notably Sunni Arabs. In Libya, the Islamic State benefited from multiple political divisions, with a UN-backed government in Tripoli, a competing government in Tobruk, and any number of autonomous militias.

Consequently, rollback needs to involve efforts to improve governance, help local authorities deal with grievances leveraged by the Islamic State, and effectively administer areas liberated from it.

Military

Rollback requires helping local governments, substate actors, and regional partners drive out Islamic State fighters and secure liberated populations. The American goal should be to build the capacity of local actors, not to battle the Islamic State for them, over the long run. For the United States, such assistance should come primarily from special operations forces, intelligence operatives, and airpower—although conventional forces can also provide training and fire support

---

[70] Ernesto "Che" Guevara, *Guerrilla Warfare*, Lincoln, Neb.: University of Nebraska Press, 1998, p. 9.

to local forces. At the core of this strategy is the use of such practices as unconventional warfare, foreign internal defense, and direct action to strengthen local partners. A light rollback strategy is limited in the sense that American forces would not generally engage in ground combat but, rather, would act as advisers and enablers. The effectiveness of U.S. efforts depends, in part, on the competence of indigenous forces. Examples of U.S. support include

- providing operational planning and advice to foreign headquarters down to the division, brigade, battalion, and even company levels
- conducting civil affairs operations, such as assessments; community outreach; water, education, and health projects; and construction of roads, bridges, and airstrips
- conducting information, psychological, and cyber operations
- conducting intelligence support operations, including the creation and running of fusion centers
- providing logistics and other forms of institutional advice and support
- providing medical evacuation, emergency medical care, quick reaction, and combat search and rescue via air and maritime mobility platforms
- training conventional, special operations forces, and other ground units in a wide variety of operational and tactical skills, from sniper tactics to countering improvised explosive devices (IEDs)
- training air crews in night-vision capability, forward air control, close air support, and casualty and medical evacuation
- training maritime forces in interdiction and other operations
- training police forces
- providing precision air strikes from drones, fixed-wing aircraft, or helicopters
- conducting raids to capture or kill capture or kill terrorists or insurgents, free hostages, seize their supplies for intelligence collection and exploitation, or target their finances.[71]

---

[71] We thank Linda Robinson for helping us identify key tasks.

The United States has established a number of programs to improve military and law-enforcement partner capacity:

- International Military Education and Training trains future leaders, creates a better understanding of the United States, establishes rapport between the U.S. military and a country's military to build alliances for the future, enhances interoperability and capabilities for joint operations, and focuses on professional military education.
- U.S. Code, Title 10, §2282 grants the U.S. Secretary of Defense authority to train and equip foreign military forces and foreign maritime security forces to perform counterterrorism operations and to participate in or to support military and stability operations in which U.S. military forces are participating.
- The Combating Terrorism Fellowship Program provides funding to educate and train mid- and senior-level defense and security officials.
- U.S. Department of Defense institution-building programs that have been designed to help partner nations build more effective, transparent, and accountable defense institutions, including the following:
  - Defense Institution Reform Initiative
  - ministry of defense advisors
  - Wales Initiative Fund
  - U.S. Department of Defense regional centers
  - partner outreach and collaboration support.
- The U.S. Department of State conducts a number of programs intended to strengthen local partnerships, improve civilian capacity, and share information to counter the Islamic State and other terrorist groups.[72]

---

[72] These programs include the Antiterrorism Assistance Program, Countering Violent Extremism, Countering the Financing of Terrorism Finance, Counterterrorism Partnerships Fund, Foreign Emergency Support Team, Global Counterterrorism Forum, International Security Events Group, Regional Strategic Initiative, Technical Support Working Group, Terrorist Screening and Interdiction Programs, Trans-Sahara Counterterrorism Partnership, and Partnership for Regional East African Counterterrorism.

The United States can also transfer defense articles and services through sales, leases, or grants. Examples include Foreign Military Sales and other programs designed to address and expedite international partners' requirements or capability. In addition to aiding local forces in each of the societies in which the Islamic State has become embedded, the United States should seek to sever links between the core part of the Islamic State in Syria and Iraq and its global provinces. To that end, the United States and its allies should target provincial command-and-control centers and local leaders who have personal relationships with top Islamic State leaders in Iraq and Syria.[73]

We believe more can be done than the Obama administration did to sustain and accelerate progress while retaining the essential features of this approach. For example, Obama officials established a flexible, adaptive policy for drone strikes against imminent threats in so-called "areas of active hostilities," such as Iraq, Afghanistan, and Syria.[74] In these areas, the decision to conduct strikes was pushed down to local U.S. commanders and did not require White House–level approval. Outside these countries, the Obama administration's PPG outlined that the use of lethal force required interagency review of operational plans and approval by senior official from across the government.[75] But the Islamic State is a different organization today from what it was in 2013, when the PPG was written. And effectively targeting an increasingly decentralized set of terrorists requires aggressive network-based approaches that can rapidly target leaders and their successors.[76] These changes require a review of current targeting procedures, as described in Chapter Eleven. We also urge giving further consideration to expanding basing options in North and West Africa. The attack on the American diplomatic facility in Benghazi illustrated the difficulty

---

[73] Byman, 2016b.

[74] White House, "Procedures for Approving Direct Action Against Terrorist Targets Located Outside the United States and Areas of Active Hostilities," Washington, D.C., May 22, 2013. This redacted and declassified document, also known as Presidential planning guidance (PPG), is available via the website of the Federation of American Scientists.

[75] White House, 2013.

[76] Luke Hartig, "U.S. at Crossroads on Drone Ops," CNN, August 21, 2016.

of protecting American personnel and responding rapidly to challenges in these regions when the nearest rapid-reaction forces may be located as far away as Europe. Securing agreements for the use of facilities in these areas will improve reach and reaction times, allowing U.S. forces to provide intelligence and other support to local partners more effectively.

Financial

The Islamic State has benefited from two main sources of revenue: oil and taxation, the latter of which often takes the form of extortion. Its overall revenues have been estimated to range from about $1 billion to $2.4 billion.[77] A significant portion of the money raised by the Islamic State came from the group's capture of key oil fields and refineries in northeastern Syria and in parts of Northern Iraq between June 2014 and September 2014, in addition to its control of key arterial roads and other centers of commerce.[78] The majority of oil revenues were from local sales, which were taxed multiple times along the supply chain from oilfield to refinery to local markets.[79]

The Islamic State demands between 2.5 and 20 percent of revenue from businesses in its territories and operates other "mafia-style" rackets to earn money. These levies included fines collected by the Islamic State al-Hisbah [morality police].[80] The Islamic State couches its extortion-related activities in terms of *zakat*, the traditional Muslim tax on capital or wealth, and *jizya*, which is traditionally a tax paid by non-

---

[77] Daniel L. Glaser, "Testimony of A\S for Terrorist Financing Daniel L. Glaser Before the House Committee on Foreign Affair's Subcommittee on Terrorism, Nonproliferation, and Trade, and House Committee on Armed Services' Subcommittee on Emerging Threats and Capabilities," June 9, 2016; Center for the Analysis of Terrorism, *ISIS Financing 2015*, Paris, May 2016.

[78] Tom Keatinge, "How the Islamic State Sustains Itself: The Importance of the War Economy in Syria and Iraq," London: Royal United Services Institute, August 29, 2014.

[79] Yeganeh Torbati, "Islamic State Yearly Oil Revenue Halved to $250 million: U.S. Official," Reuters, May 11, 2016; Benoit Faucon and Margaret Coker, "The Rise and Deadly Fall of Islamic State's Oil Tycoon," *Wall Street Journal*, April 24, 2016.

[80] Patrick Johnston, "Islamic State's Money Problems," *USA Today*, March 4, 2016.

Muslims living in Muslim lands. These efforts are similar in effect to "revolutionary" taxes collected by a number of other insurgent groups.[81]

Countering the Islamic State's finances is critical. Under the auspices of Operation Tidal Wave II, coalition airstrikes have reduced the Islamic State oil revenues.[82] The United States and its allies have directly targeted the Islamic State's oil and gas supply chain, including airstrikes against oil fields, refineries, and tanker trucks. Separate lines of effort have included attacking cash storage sites, and eliminating high-value targets critical to the Islamic State's financial and logistical operations. Territorial losses have been important because less territory means fewer people and businesses that can be taxed. Turkey also increased its efforts to stop the flow of individuals and materiel crossing its borders, thereby restricting the Islamic State's access to supplies, volunteers, and the black market for sale of its oil.[83] In contrast, the Assad regime purchased oil and gas from the Islamic State.[84] By early 2017, U.S. and European officials assessed that oil and gas sales to Assad's regime were the Islamic State's largest source of funds, replacing such sources as revenue from tolls on the transit of goods and taxes on wages within its territory.[85] Securing borders is a challenging task, but one that Turkey seems more firmly committed to in the wake of recent terrorist attacks in some of their major cities. While the Turkish-Syrian border will likely never be fully blocked, earnest efforts to deploy military and police have made it more difficult for smugglers to move contraband back and forth.

In addition to attacking the Islamic State's oil and natural gas supply chain, airstrikes have also targeted sites in Iraq where the Islamic

---

[81] Michael Jonsson, "Following the Money: Financing the Territorial Expansion of Islamist Insurgents in Syria," Swedish Defense Research Agency, FOI Memo #4947, May 2014.

[82] Johnston, 2016.

[83] Ayla Albayrak and Dana Ballout, "U.S., Turkey Step Up Border Campaign Against Islamic State," *Wall Street Journal*, April 26, 2016.

[84] See, for example, U.S. Department of Treasury, "Treasury Sanctions Networks Providing Support to the Government of Syria, including for Facilitating Syrian Government Oil Purchases from ISIL," Washington, D.C., November 25, 2015.

[85] Benoit Faucon and Ahmed Al Omran, "Terror Group Boosts Sales of Oil, Gas to Assad Regime," *Wall Street Journal*, January 20, 2017.

State stores its cash. Two airstrikes in January 2016 in Mosul destroyed money, while four more airstrikes in February hit cash storage and distribution facilities. Estimates ranged from tens of millions to more than $100 million.[86] Airstrikes have also successfully targeted important individuals, killing a number of high-ranking financial officials, including two of the group's finance ministers, Abu Saleh in November 2015 and Haji Imam in March 2016.

Other measures are decreasing liquidity in Islamic State–held territory. By summer 2015, the government of Iraq banned and held in escrow the distribution of government salaries in the Islamic State held territories; the Islamic State had been taxing these salaries as a source of revenue.[87] Iraq began to prohibit bank branches in cities and towns held by the Islamic State from making international transfers, instead ordering all requests to be routed through the central bank in Baghdad, where they can, in theory, be intercepted and stopped. The U.S. Department of the Treasury, in cooperation with the Central Bank of Iraq, has worked to prevent the Islamic State from accessing the international financial system. Ninety bank branches within the Islamic State held territory were cut off from both the international and Iraqi banking systems, and 150 exchange houses were "named and shamed" and banned from participation in the Central Bank of Iraq's dollar auctions. As long as the Islamic State remains unable to access the banking system both locally and regionally, it will have to continue to store its cash in locations that are increasingly vulnerable to coalition airstrikes.[88] Furthermore, blocking the Islamic State from accessing exchange houses and currency auctions will likely limit its ability to procure U.S. dollars. These actions, in turn, may deny the group rev-

---

[86] See Adam Szubin, "Remarks of Acting Under Secretary Adam Szubin on Countering the Financing of Terrorism at the Paul H. Nitze School of Advanced International Studies," October 20, 2016.

[87] Daniel L. Glaser, "Remarks by Assistant Secretary for Terrorist Financing Daniel Glaser at Chatham House," U.S. Department of the Treasury, February 8, 2016.

[88] Jim Michaels, "Air Campaign Shifts to the Islamic State's Cash and Oil," *USA Today*, April 17, 2016.

enue it could potentially earn from exchange-rate arbitrage and limit its ability to pay its members and buy weapons and ammunition.

The Counter ISIL Finance Group (CIFG)—led by Italy, Saudi Arabia, and the United States and currently comprising 37 member states and organizations—should continue preventing the Islamic State from using the international financial system, including unregulated money remitters, denying the Islamic State external funding, and preventing the Islamic State from providing financial or material support to foreign affiliates.[89] The Financial Action Task Force is the intergovernmental standard-setting body for anti–money laundering and countering the financing of terrorism and should continue working with the CIFG to strengthen the international financial system to combat the threats the Islamic State and terrorist financing more broadly pose.[90]

As the Islamic State loses further territory and population, international cooperation to cut off exogenous sources of funding will become ever more important.

Ideological

The Islamic State relies heavily on foreign fighters drawn from around the world to seize and hold territory. One report found that more than 80 countries supplied recruits.[91] Even as it pulls Muslims to its heartland, the group also pushes violence and radical ideas outward from this base. The Islamic State has shown an ability to expand rapidly outside its core areas through a variety of strategies: sending and infiltrating its operatives around the world to conduct attacks, inspiring local Muslims to commit terrorism as part of local cells, and co-opting a range of existing jihadist groups.

---

[89] U.S. Department of State, "Establishment of the Counter-ISIL Finance Group in Rome, Italy," media note, Washington, D.C.: Office of the Spokesperson, March 20, 2015b.

[90] Financial Action Task Force, "FATF-CIFG Communiqué," February 2016.

[91] Seamus Hughes, "Countering the Virtual Caliphate," testimony before the House Committee on Foreign Affairs, June 23, 2016; Soufan Group, *Foreign Fighters: An Updated Assessment of the Flow of Foreign Fighters into Syria and Iraq*, New York, December 2015.

Central to this global operation is the Islamic State's messaging. The group's ideology is often incoherent or shallow from a theological point of view, and its volunteers are often remarkably ignorant of their faith. But its brand—and its means of disseminating its ideas— is strong among many Muslim communities. As with other successful terrorist groups, the Islamic State does not have one message, but many. Its propaganda stresses the group's successes, the heroic nature of its violence, and the need to defend Sunni Muslims from perceived oppressors. Strains of apocalypticism also are pronounced, and the group's "heroic" brand offers criminals, alienated Muslims, and even misguided idealists some sense of legitimacy and purpose. It also provides a powerful brand to local fighting groups that are unpopular or that otherwise seek to change their image. These ideas are disseminated in part through a vast array of media operations.

The Islamic State has proven particularly adept at using social media, spawning a massive propaganda machine to attract and inspire recruits. Some of this propaganda is a top-down, directed operation, while other messaging is generated by low-level supporters communicating within their immediate social circles. An array of preachers and other ideologues, often operating from outside Islamic State territory, promote a message of sectarianism and violence in the name of Islam. To translate these messages into action, however, human contact is often vital. Social media and propaganda are commonly the first step in moving individuals to join a terrorist group, but facilitators' and recruiters' personal touches often are what make the difference between vague support of and actually joining a terrorist group.

The most distinctive feature of the Islamic State's self-marketing has been its emphasis on the existence of the core caliphate in Iraq and Syria. Eliminating that accomplishment may be the single most important means of damaging the brand. There are also a number of other steps the United States and its partners can take to counter Islamic State propaganda. Islamic State social media sites should be shut down. Disinformation can also be inserted into these sites. Recruiters and propagandists must be targeted everywhere, both kinetically in war zones and through aggressive police and intelligence efforts elsewhere. These individuals are often more dangerous than fighters. To prevent recruits from joining the Islamic State and to dissuade returning fighters from using violence, community action and social integration programs should be embraced, including ones involving prisons. The United States and its allies should also push other partners, such as Saudi Arabia, to stop the spread of sectarianism and other ideas on which the Islamic State feeds. The United States must also work with allies to integrate and care for refugees. If they are not successfully integrated, however, alienation within Muslim communities in the West could breed violent extremism. Chapter Ten develops the ideological and informational aspects of the global fight against the Islamic State further.

In Chapters Four through Nine, we apply these general guidelines to individual campaigns designed to roll back the Islamic State. As noted earlier, we focus on the countries in which the Islamic State has controlled territory: Iraq, Syria, Libya, Nigeria, Egypt, and Afghanistan. We have not included separate chapters for countries in which the Islamic State has failed to control territory, such as Saudi Arabia, Tunisia, and Pakistan. But these countries are treated in various places throughout the document. The most critical of these campaigns are in Iraq and Syria, the core caliphate, where the bulk of the Islamic State's leadership territory and population is located. Once these areas are reclaimed, the Islamic State will likely lose its distinguishing characteristic and most powerful appeal: its so-called caliphate. One or more of the insurgent groups in Nigeria, Egypt, Libya, and Afghanistan that have allied themselves with the Islamic State and pledged obedience to its leadership may choose new affiliations or become independent.

PART II

Country Campaigns

CHAPTER FOUR

Iraq

In Iraq, as in Syria, the rise of the Islamic State is a product of ongoing Sunni disenfranchisement. The group first emerged in Iraq, is led primarily by Iraqis, and has depended heavily on territorial control in Iraq to sustain its funding and local recruitment. Islamic State leadership declared that it has erased what it calls the Sykes-Picot line between Iraq and Syria by incorporating territory that straddles the internationally recognized border.[1] The loss of territorial control in Iraq will deal a serious blow to the Islamic State's military capacity; finances; organizational credibility; and ability to recruit, organize, and inspire attacks elsewhere. Retaking Iraqi territory from the Islamic State is thus central to any effective rollback strategy.

But the Islamic State may be able to operate within Iraq's borders as long as Sunni Arabs remain disenfranchised and the Iraqi security forces comparatively weak.[2] Where the Islamic State has lost territory, in such cities as Ramadi and Fallujah, its fighters have melted away into

---

[1] There is ongoing debate over the degree to which the current internationally recognized border between Iraq and Syria derived from the Sykes-Picot Accord of 1916. While the Islamic State adopts the simplest interpretation—that Europeans "drew" Iraq's borders during the Sykes-Picot process—deeper analysis suggests these borders predated the accords and were then finalized during conferences and accords that postdated Sykes-Picot. See Sara Pursley, "'Lines Drawn on an Empty Map': Iraq's Borders and the Legend of the Artificial State (Part 1)," *Jadaliyyah*, June 2, 2015, and Al Hayat, "The End of Sykes-Picot," LiveLeak. com, video, Islamic State in Iraq and Syria, undated.

[2] For a detailed explanation of this assessment, see Ben Connable, "Defeating the Islamic State in Iraq," testimony presented before the Senate Foreign Relations Committee, Santa Monica, Calif.: RAND Corporation, CT-418, 2014.

the dense agricultural and desert areas around the urban centers and along the Iraq-Syria border.[3] Operating out of these *jazirah* areas,[4] the Islamic State can replicate the model it perfected, when known as AQI, from 2004 to 2006. It can sustain itself through low-level criminal activity, cache sufficient munitions for extended guerrilla operations, and execute a grueling murder and intimidation campaign against both the Sunni Arab citizens and the Iraqi security forces.

This threat may be extended indefinitely even if the Islamic State is destroyed, splits, or evolves. Precursor groups to the Islamic State underwent multiple name and organizational changes, but the threat from each iteration of the group remained and indeed grew. The Iraqi security forces may gain in strength and exert physical control over the urban areas of the Sunni provinces, they will be subjected to an endless series of terror and guerrilla attacks until the government can convince the Sunni Arab Iraqis of its legitimacy. Ejecting the Islamic State from its remaining strongholds will reduce, but not end, its capacity to destabilize Iraq and threaten other societies, including the United States. This chapter describes the rise of the Islamic State in Iraq against the backdrop of Sunni disenfranchisement, then recommends a strategy designed to weaken and ultimately defeat the Islamic State.

The Rise of the Islamic State in Iraq

As noted in Chapter Two, Abu Musab al-Zarqawi formed the group that would eventually become the Islamic State.[5] Zarqawi's Jama'at

---

[3] See, for example, Hassan Hassan, "Is the Islamic State Unstoppable?" *New York Times*, July 9, 2016; Taylor Luck, "ISIS, Losing Territory in Syria, Signals Strategic Shift," *Christian Science Monitor*, May 27, 2016; and Michael Schmidt and Eric Schmitt, "As the Islamic State Loosens Grip, U.S. and Iraq Prepare for Grinding Insurgency," *New York Times*, July 25, 2016.

[4] *Jazirah* is a transliteration of the Arabic word for island or peninsula. In this case, it refers to islands of isolation outside population centers in Iraq. There are several prominent jazirah areas in Anbar Province.

[5] Zarqawi's actual name was Ahmad Fadeel Nazal Al-Khalayleh. For details of Zarqawi's life and the rise of AQI, see M. J. Kirdar, "Al-Qa'ida in Iraq," Washington, D.C.: Center for

al-Tawhid wal Jihad [Organization of Monotheism and Jihad] worked in parts of northern Iraq beginning in the early 2000s. In summer 2002, Zarqawi settled in northern Iraq with the help of the terrorist group Ansar al-Islam. He was not a member of al-Qa'ida, preferring to run his own group, although he had contacts with several senior al-Qa'ida members. Between 2003 and 2004, Zarqawi's group competed and collaborated with a range of emerging Sunni nationalist insurgent elements, as well as a few groups, such as Ansar al-Islam, that lay claim to a Salafi-jihadi agenda.[6] Jama'at al-Tawhid wal Jihad was able to survive and then thrive in the six provinces with heavy Sunni populations—Anbar, Nineweh, and Salah-al-Din, with smaller percentages in Diyala, northern Babil, and Baghdad—because the invasion had upended nearly half a millennium of Sunni domination in Iraq.[7] As the Shi'a Arab majority in Iraq began to assume control of the state and as the U.S.-led Coalition Provisional Authority implemented de-Ba'athification and the dissolution of the Iraqi Army, many Sunni found themselves mostly unemployed, unemployable, and essentially disenfranchised from the government they once controlled.[8] These conditions fed the rise of the diffuse Sunni insurgency, a de facto sectarian civil war, and the eventual rise of the Islamic State.

Nationalist groups led by former regime officers, Sunni religious figures, and Ba'athists dominated the insurgency through early 2004

Strategic and International Studies, June 2011; Mary Anne Weaver, "The Short, Violent Life of Abu Musab al-Zarqawi," *Atlantic*, July/August 2006; and Gary Gambill, "Abu Musab al-Zarqawi: A Biographical Sketch," *Terrorism Monitor*, Vol. 2, No. 24, December 15, 2004.

[6] There were links between Zarqawi and Ansar al-Islam, later called Ansar al-Sunna (alt. Sunnah), prior to the 2003 invasion; see Weaver, 2006. For a summary of armed insurgent groups in Iraq during this period, see Joint Intelligence Committee (JIC), "Iraq: Sunni Arab Opposition," September 30, 2004a (a declassified intelligence report presented as part of the Government of the UK Iraq Inquiry), and Ahmad S. Hashim, "Iraq's Numerous Insurgent Groups," National Public Radio, June 8, 2006.

[7] Fanar Haddad, "Reinventing Sunni Identity in Iraq After 2003," *Current Trends in Islamist Ideology*, Vol. 17, 2014.

[8] See James Dobbins, Seth G. Jones, Benjamin Runkle, Siddharth Mohandas, *Occupying Iraq: A History of the Coalition Provisional Authority*, Santa Monica, Calif.: RAND Corporation, MG-847-CC, 2009.

up to the first Battle of Fallujah in early April.[9] While Jama'at al-Tawhid wal Jihad was not necessarily the dominant insurgent group between mid-2003 and early 2004, it made a name for itself as the most ruthless and the most focused among its peer competitors. Where other Sunni insurgent groups, such as the 1920 Revolution Brigade and the Islamic Army, primarily sought to expel U.S. military forces and regain lost authority, Zarqawi had a complex local and international strategy that would presage Abu Bakr al-Baghdadi's agenda. He simultaneously sought to eject the U.S. occupation force, turn Sunni Arabs against the government of Iraq, break apart the U.S.-led coalition in Iraq, and foment civil war between Sunni and Shi'a Arabs.[10] The last of these was intended to give Jama'at al-Tawhid wal Jihad the opportunity to position itself as defender of the Sunni faithful, something it was able to accomplish by early 2006, just before Zarqawi's death that summer.

Zarqawi led Jama'at al-Tawhid wal Jihad's ascension in Iraq during summer 2004, after the United States had ceded control of Fallujah to a motley group of Sunni insurgents. Zarqawi leveraged his organization's seemingly limitless brutality to dominate and then subsume cells from non-Salafi insurgent groups.[11] In October 2004, Zarqawi pledged allegiance to al-Qa'ida and changed the name of his organization from Jama'at al-Tawhid wal Jihad to Tandhim Qaidat al-Jihad fi al-Bilad al-Rafidain [Organization of the Base of Jihad in the Land of the Two Rivers], more commonly known as AQI. This formal connection to Osama Bin Laden gave Zarqawi immediate, global credibility with international Salafi-jihadists and elevated his stature to de facto leader of the otherwise fractured Sunni Arab Iraqi insurgent movement. From 2004 through 2006, Zarqawi implemented a ruthless strategy of sui-

---

[9] This battle resulted from the killing and mutilation of four U.S. contractors in Fallujah in late March 2004. The first effort to assert control over Fallujah resulted in the withdrawal of U.S. forces and a deal that ceded control of the city to the so-called Fallujah Brigade, which was really a loose coalition of insurgents. See Rajiv Chandrasekaran, "Key General Criticizes April Attack in Fallujah," *Washington Post*, September 13, 2004.

[10] Gambill, 2004.

[11] The degree to which Zarqawi controlled the Sunni insurgents in Fallujah during this period is debated. For example, see "Two Locals Were Core of Fallujah Insurgency," Associated Press, November 24, 2004.

cide bombings, murder, blackmail, kidnapping, hijacking, and direct military attacks against coalition and Iraqi forces. He targeted both Sunni and Shi'a Iraqis, but he leveraged bombings of Shi'a civilian targets to stoke sectarian resentment.

Zarqawi and his successors, such as Abu Ayyub al-Musri and Abu Umar al-Baghdadi, developed a number of organizational approaches in Iraq from 2003 to 2010 that would reemerge under Abu Bakr al-Baghdadi's leadership. Criminal activity allowed Zarqawi and al-Musri to fund their Iraq operations, which in turn ensured their relative independence from al-Qa'ida leaders, who were appalled by the group's more extreme tactics.[12] AQI made expert use of the media, proliferating videos of attacks, beheadings, and propaganda messages on video disks and the Internet. Zarqawi organized the group hierarchically, designating emirates and emirs across Iraq that could and did operate with semiautonomy.[13] He took control of Iraq's smuggling routes and black market economies, which provided a source of revenue and gave him leverage over local Sunni notables, who were now forced to work with or for AQI.[14] AQI emirs coerced local women to marry their fighters in an effort to reward loyal members and further entangle local tribes with AQI. This forceful, all-encompassing co-opting of the Sunni Arab Iraqis is a hallmark of Islamic State operations.

In late 2005, Sunni Iraqi Arabs made their first real foray into the new electoral process, demonstrating a modicum of trust in the Iraqi government. This was accompanied by a lull in Sunni insurgent violence from late 2005 to early 2006 and the emergence of the Anbar People's

---

[12] See Weaver, 2006, and Benjamin Bahney, Howard J. Shatz, Carroll Ganier, Renny McPherson, and Barbara Sude, *An Economic Analysis of the Financial Records of Al-Qa'ida in Iraq*, Santa Monica, Calif.: RAND Corporation, MG-1026-OSD, 2010.

[13] Bahney et al., 2010.

[14] See Timothy S. McWilliams and Curtis P. Wheeler, eds., *Al-Anbar Awakening*, Vol. I: *American Perspectives, U.S. Marines and Counterinsurgency in Iraq, 2004–2009*, Quantico, Va.: Marine Corps University Press, 2009, and Gary W. Montgomery, and Timothy S. McWilliams, eds., *Al-Anbar Awakening*, Vol. II: *Iraqi Perspectives From Insurgency to Counterinsurgency in Iraq, 2004–2009*, Quantico, Va.: Marine Corps University Press, 2009; and Bahney et al., 2010.

Committee, a precursor to the Anbar Awakening.[15] Zarqawi was losing support from the Sunni Arabs.[16] By mid-January, AQI had murdered key members of the Anbar People's Committee and forced others into hiding.[17] On February 22, 2006, AQI demolished the golden dome of the Shi'a Al-Askeri mosque in Samarra. This attack triggered a massive wave of intersectarian violence that allowed AQI to undertake a self-serving defense of Sunni interests.[18] By mid-2006, intelligence officials in the predominantly Sunni Arab province of Anbar assessed that AQI was the dominant group there, even more powerful and influential than the U.S. military.[19] At the zenith of AQI's success, Zarqawi was killed in a U.S. aerial bombing attack. He was succeeded by al-Musri, who would go on to lead the group along with Abu Omar al-Baghdadi through 2010.[20] Al-Musri and al-Baghdadi would lead AQI to a major strategic defeat in the face of the U.S.-supported Sunni Awakening movement.

The rise and decliine of the so-called Sunni Arab Awakening— *sahwah* in Arabic—holds perhaps the most important lessons for developing a strategy to counter the Islamic State. The Anbar-centric awakening evolved into a widespread Sunni Arab Iraqi revolt against AQI that resulted from a complex range of factors, including ongoing and egregious AQI abuses of the Sunni population, tribal infighting,

---

[15] McWilliams and Wheeler, 2009.

[16] Interviewees in both McWilliams and Wheeler, 2009, and Montgomery and McWilliams, 2009, make this observation from a number of perspectives.

[17] McWilliams and Wheeler, 2009; Michael Gordon and Bernard E. Trainor, *Endgame: The Inside Story of the Struggle for Iraq, from George W. Bush to Barack Obama*, New York: Pantheon Press, 2012.

[18] Michael Crowley, "How the Fate of One Holy Site Could Plunge Iraq Back into Civil War," *Time*, June 26, 2014.

[19] JIC, "Iraq: Insurgency, Sectarianism, and Violence," July 19, 2006b (a declassified intelligence report presented as part of the Government of the UK Iraq Inquiry); JIC, "Iraq: How Is the Sunni Insurgency Evolving?" May 10, 2006a (a declassified intelligence report presented as part of the Government of the UK Iraq Inquiry); Multinational Forces West, *State of the Insurgency in al-Anbar*, Multinational Forces Iraq, August 17, 2006 (declassified December 16, 2010 by the U.S. Department of Defense Office of Security Review).

[20] JIC, 2006b.

criminal disputes, coalition engagement, elite payoffs, and the surge of U.S. military forces.[21] Sunni Arabs joined anti-AQI militia groups and subjected themselves to nominal coalition and Iraq government control. They helped identify AQI leaders for targeting and were crucial to reversing AQI's momentum. Many of those who joined such groups as the Sons of Iraq and Concerned Local Citizens militias were former insurgents. In some cases, sahwah recruitment represented a one-for-one swap from anti- to progovernment armed groups. The results of the awakening were clear: AQI had lost control of the Sunni population and, by 2008, was forced into internal exile in the most remote areas of Iraq.[22]

Between mid-2008 and early 2010 there was a weak but legitimate honeymoon between the Sunni Arabs, U.S.-led coalition, and Iraq government. While Sunni Arab attacks against the government continued, they had significantly abated in comparison to the 2003–2008 period. Prime Minister Nuri al-Maliki impressed the Sunnis with his aggressive military action to bring Shi'a cleric and militia leader Muqtada al-Sadr to heel in Basra, demonstrating his nationalist bona fides.[23] Al-Maliki had an opportunity to build on the Awakening and on Sunni Arab willingness to participate in the government. Instead, the al-Maliki government exercised what analyst Myriam Benraad called a "profound hostility" toward the Sons of Iraq and Concerned Local Citizens members.[24] Even as AQI was being forced into retreat, al-Maliki's government began cutting militia pay, while harassing, disarming, and arresting members. Former members of sahwah militias

---

[21] For better insight into the awakening, see Niel Smith and Sean MacFarland, "Anbar Awakens: The Tipping Point," *Military Review*, August 2008; McWilliams and Wheeler, 2009; Montgomery and McWilliams, 2009; Gordon and Trainor, 2012; and Sterling Jensen, *Iraqi Narratives of the Anbar Awakening*, doctoral thesis, King's College London, 2014.

[22] Jensen, 2014, summarizes some of this debate. Also see Myriam Benraad, "Iraq's Tribal 'Sahwa': Its Rise and Fall," *Middle East Policy Council Journal*, Vol. 18, No. 1, Spring 2011. For a summary of Sons of Iraq and Concerned Local Citizens militias, see Farouk Ahmed, "Sons of Iraq and Awakening Forces," Washington, D.C.: Institute for the Study of War, February 21, 2008.

[23] Richard Iron, "Charge of the Knights," *RUSI Journal*, Vol. 158, No. 1, 2013.

[24] Benraad, 2011.

remember their experience with deep bitterness toward both the Iraq government and the United States.[25]

Whatever good will had been gained from late 2006 to 2008 had been squandered by March 2010, when the al-Maliki government was widely viewed as playing a role in the removal of Sunni Arab candidates from the parliamentary election lists. Whether these removals were legally justifiable under Iraq's de-Ba'athification law, they gave the perception that al-Maliki and his Shi'a Da'wa Party was purposefully disenfranchising Sunni Arabs.[26] Even after apparently losing the election, al-Maliki leveraged a corrupt judiciary to maintain control of the government. With his ambitions laid bare, al-Maliki made little effort to hide what amounted to a four-year targeted campaign to consolidate his hold on power at the expense of Sunni Arabs. He replaced competent Sunni Arab and Kurdish military officers with loyal but often incompetent Shi'a; he used the courts and security forces to harass and pursue Sunni Arab politicians; and most important, his security forces violently suppressed peaceful Sunni protests.[27]

At the same time, al-Maliki moved closer to Iran and allowed the existing Sunni Arab perception that he led an Iranian puppet government to grow. In 2011, he did little to facilitate the retention of U.S. military forces in Iraq. But then, the Obama administration was not keen to have them stay. The last U.S. military unit left Iraq in December of that year.[28] While the United States retained a diplomatic pres-

---

[25] This observation is derived from the chapter author's ongoing interactions and more than 60 long-form interviews with Sunni Arab Iraqis from Anbar and Nineweh Provinces, Iraq, from 2012 to 2016.

[26] See Stephen Wicken, *Iraq's Sunnis in Crisis*, Washington, D.C.: Institute for the Study of War; Reidar Vissar, "Iraq's New Government and the Question of Sunni Inclusion," *CTC Sentinel*, September 29, 2014, and Ali Khedery, "Why We Stuck With Maliki—And Lost Iraq," *Washington Post*, July 3, 2014.

[27] See, for example, Max Boot, "Maliki's Actions, and Obama's Inaction, Threaten an Iraq Democracy," *Los Angeles Times*, May 9, 2010.

[28] Khedery, 2014; Rick Brennan, Jr., Charles P. Ries, Larry Hanauer, Ben Connable, Terrence K. Kelly, Michael J. McNerney, Stephanie Young, Jason H. Campbell, and K. Scott McMahon, *Ending the U.S. War in Iraq: The Final Transition, Operational Maneuver, and Disestablishment of the United States Forces–Iraq*, Santa Monica, Calif.: RAND Corporation, RR-232-USFI, 2013.

ence in Baghdad and in the Kurdistan Regional Government, it no longer had direct influence on the growth and quality of the Iraqi security forces. Sunni leaders generally perceived the U.S. withdrawal as an abdication to Iran and as a signal of Iran's growing primacy in Iraq. Physical suppression of Sunni Arabs in Hawijah, Ramadi, and other areas destroyed the last vestiges of Sunni Arab support for al-Maliki.[29] By the time Islamic State forces rolled into the city of Fallujah in January 2014, the Sunni Arabs of Iraq were in de facto revolt against their government.

The Islamic State's rise in Iraq followed its reemergence in Syria, as outlined in Chapter Five. The group continued to conduct attacks in Iraq between the end of the awakening period in 2008 and 2014 but at relatively low levels that did not attract significant attention.[30] During this period, the group infiltrated agents into Iraqi cities, co-opted local leaders, cut deals with nationalist and Ba'athist insurgents, and set the stage for a full-scale military assault into Iraq.[31] In January 2014, the Islamic State launched a column of armed trucks and fighters across the Syria-Iraq border, down the western Euphrates River Valley, and into Fallujah.[32] In collusion with nationalist insurgents, the Islamic State took control of Fallujah and established a base of operations in the heart of Sunni Arab Iraq, less than 60 km from downtown Baghdad.[33] This surprise attack left the Iraqi government reeling. Iraqi Army units that the United States had trained earlier either collapsed or withdrew to their bases, unwilling to face the Islamic State on the battlefield. Police units fled or were overrun. Prime Minister al-Maliki responded with

---

[29] Vissar, 2014; "Iraqi Sunni Protest Clashes in Hawija Leave Many Dead," British Broadcasting Corporation, April 23, 2013; Tim Arango, "Dozens Killed in Battles Across Iraq as Sunnis Escalate Protests Against Government," *New York Times*, April 23, 2013.

[30] Jessica Lewis, "Al-Qa'ida in Iraq Resurgent: Breaking the Walls Campaign, Part 1," Washington, D.C.: Institute for the Study of War, September 2013.

[31] Dexter Filkins, "The Fight of Their Lives," *New Yorker*, September 29, 2014.

[32] Yasir Ghazi and Tim Arango, "Iraq Fighters, Qaeda Allies, Claim Falluja as New State," *New York Times*, January 3, 2014.

[33] This distance can be measured in many different ways. We used city centroids in the Google Map application.

force in an effort to address the immediate threat, ignoring the broader implications of the reemergence of what was, essentially, the successor to AQI.[34] While it may have been too late in early 2014 to sufficiently address Sunni grievances and stem the Islamic State advance, no efforts were made to do so.

In June 2014, the Islamic State made another major advance, this time seizing Iraq's second largest city, Mosul. In the course of this offensive, the group murdered more than 1,500 Iraqi security force recruits in Tikrit, in what would be known as the Speicher Massacre. This type of extreme violence would become the hallmark of Islamic State operations.[35] The Islamic State soon had control of most major urban areas in Sunni provinces, as well as oil fields, military bases, police stations, and the critical Bayji refinery. It took control of the Syria-Iraq border crossings. The group was reportedly able to capture hundreds of millions of dollars in cash even as it co-opted and increased black market oil trade, greatly increasing its ability to self-finance.[36] U.S.-led coalition military operations to counter the Islamic State began in summer 2014, and in October 2014 the U.S. established OIR, the military mission to counter the Islamic State.[37] At the same time, the U.S. established a global coalition task force for the same purpose.[38]

Initially, the Iraqi security forces proved incapable of defending Iraqi territory. As the Islamic State reached the outskirts of Baghdad in 2014, Shi'a Grand Ayatollah Ali al-Sistani issued a general call for Shi'a to organize and join militia forces to defend Baghdad and Shi'a areas.[39] This call resulted in the explosive growth of Shi'a militia groups, all

---

[34] Rod Nordland, "Iraqi Premier Places Unity Second to Fighting the Islamic State," *New York Times*, July 2, 2014.

[35] Camp Speicher Massacre Trial Begins in Iraq," Al Jazeera, December 27, 2015.

[36] Howard J. Shatz and Erin-Elizabeth Johnson, *The Islamic State We Knew: Insights Before the Resurgence and Their Implications*, Santa Monica, Calif.: RAND Corporation, RR-1257-OSD, 2015.

[37] See the OIR website for details.

[38] See the Global Coalition to Defeat ISIL website for details (U.S. Department of State, undated).

[39] "Iraq Cleric Issues Call to Arms Against ISIL," Al Jazeera, June 13, 2014.

beholden to different and sometimes competing leaders. The strongest groups, such as Badr Corps, Asa'ib Ahl al-Haq, and Katibat al-Hezbollah, had strong ties to Iran. These militia groups, known as *hashed al-shabi* [people's militias], helped stem the Islamic State's advance while becoming as powerful—or, in some areas, more powerful—than the Iraqi army and police. Also in 2014, the Iranian Revolutionary Guard Corps expanded its presence in Iraq, entering into direct conflict with the Islamic State and supporting both the hashed groups and the Iraqi security forces. Collectively, this direct Iranian involvement, the Iranian backing of some hashed groups, and the presence of senior Iranian military leaders reinforced Sunni perceptions that Iran had taken control of the Iraq government.[40] Meanwhile, the United States provided direct support to Kurdish elements fighting the Islamic State in the north of the country but only limited and indirect support, to fledgling Sunni militias delivered via the Iraqi government, Sunni efforts to obtain support directly from the United States were rebuffed in deference to Baghdad's concerns. Sunni efforts to pass a national guard law that would have allowed Sunnis to organize their own defense were also blocked by Baghdad.[41]

Beginning in 2014, the Islamic State's control of Iraqi territory expanded dramatically but then began to contract. It threatened the Kurdistan Regional Government capital of Erbil and seized Anbar's provincial capital, Ramadi. By late 2015, the Islamic State had suffered some setbacks but retained control of large portions of Iraq.[42] By 2016, the Iraqi security forces had become more effective—aided by U.S. airstrikes—and the Islamic State had lost significant territory, including the cities of Ramadi and Fallujah.[43] In October 2016, the Iraqi security

[40] See, for example, Jim Muir, "Fears of Shia Muscle in Iraq's Sunni Heartland," British Broadcasting Corporation, May 18, 2015.

[41] Tamer al-Ghobashy, "U.S.-Backed Plan for Iraqi National Guard Falters," *Wall Street Journal*, October 16, 2014.

[42] Kathy Gilsinan, "How ISIS Territory Has Changed Since the U.S. Bombing Campaign Began," *Atlantic*, September 11, 2015.

[43] Caitlin Forrest, "ISIS Sanctuary Map: July 1, 2016," Washington, D.C.: Institute for the Study of War, July 1, 2016.

forces, Kurdish Peshmerga, and other militias launched coordinated operations to recapture Mosul with support from the United States. Iraq's security forces were excessively dependent on the small, elite Counter Terror Service to conduct offensive operations. The employment of Shia militia in dominantly Sunni areas provoked resentment and concern over Iranian influence. Finally, even as the Islamic State's territory contracted in Iraq, the group began to disperse into the population with a view to conducting protracted guerrilla warfare and terrorist campaigns.

As highlighted in Figure 4.1, Islamic State control peaked in fall 2014 at an estimated 6.3 million people, or 19 percent of the population, which covered roughly 58,372 km^2. Most of this territory was in the provinces of Anbar, Ninawa, Kirkuk, and Salah ad Din. By winter

Figure 4.1
Islamic State Control of Territory in Iraq

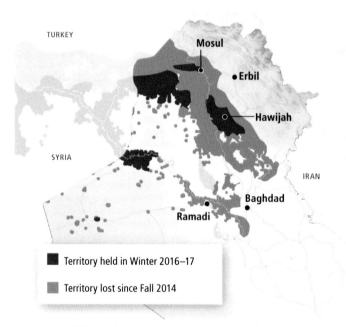

SOURCES: Fall 2014 estimates are based on U.S. Department of Defense, 2016a. Winter 2016–2017 estimates are based on authors' estimates of changes in control.
RAND RR1912-4.1

2016–2017, the Iraqi security forces—aided by Sunni, Shi'a, and Kurdish militia, Iran, the U.S., and other allied forces—took back territory from an overstretched Islamic State in Mosul, Sinjar, Bayji, Tikrit, Ramadi, and other cities. Islamic State territorial control declined to 1.1 million people (an 83-percent drop from 2014) and 15,682 km^2 (a 73-percent decrease from 2014).

Desired End State

The immediate American objective should be to help liberate Mosul and free any remaining population centers from Islamic State control. This victory will be short lived, however, unless Iraqi forces can secure the regained territory, and Iraqi authorities can effectively administer it. The U.S. government has articulated a desired end state for Iraq on several occasions. The first of these appeared in the 2005 *National Strategy for Victory in Iraq*. Written by the U.S. NSC, this document proposed a clear objective for the sovereign state of Iraq: "We will help the Iraqi people build a new Iraq with a constitutional, representative government that respects civil rights and has security forces sufficient to maintain domestic order and keep Iraq from becoming a safe haven for terrorists."[44] This 2005 end state bears remarkable similarity to the set of objectives for the Middle East that the departments of State and Defense presented to Congress in 2016. This "Section 1222 report" envisaged a Middle East made up of sovereign, stable, democratic, and economically prosperous states capable of controlling their own territories and preventing their use for international terrorism.[45]

---

[44] NSC, *National Strategy for Victory in Iraq*, Washington, D.C.: The White House, November 2005, p. 1.

[45] Ashton B. Carter and John F. Kerry, "Section 1222 Report: Strategy for the Middle East and to Counter Violent Extremism," report submitted to Congress in response to NDAA for Fiscal Year 2016 requirement under Section 1222, undated but written and posted in May 2016, p. 1. This end state is:

> The United States' objectives in the Middle East are: that all countries of the region meet their international commitments on non-proliferation; that terrorist groups no longer threaten the United States, our allies, and our interests; that our allies and partners enjoy

For the purposes of defeating the Islamic State in Iraq, we propose a somewhat more limited objective: a sovereign, if more decentralized, Iraqi state; the inclusion of most Sunni Arabs in that state under generally acceptable conditions; equitable sharing of the country's oil wealth; a reduction in the role of Shi'a militias and the influence of Iran; and the strengthening of local and national security forces capable of suppressing residual violent extremism from the Islamic State and comparable groups. Reaching even these more-modest objectives will be difficult and time consuming.

U.S. and Allied Steps

Achieving these end states will require a strategy that integrates political and governance, security, and economic and humanitarian steps and more effectively addresses the Sunni-Shi'a divisions in Iraq.

Political and Governance

The initial political objective should be to promote a comprehensive Iraqi government reconciliation plan that directly addresses collective Sunni Arab grievances, such as prisoner release and fair judicial practices. Simultaneous with Iraqi government implementation, the United States should continue to work with Sunni Arabs and other groups to help coalesce Sunni Arab leadership, with the eventual goal of identifying legitimate interlocutors for more far-reaching negotiations with the Iraqi government.

U.S. officials should conduct a comprehensive review of ongoing Iraqi government reform efforts. The objective should be to build toward an eventual constitutional convention, which will allow all

---

stability, prosperity, and security; that governments in the region have the strength and legitimacy to provide both security and a positive future for their people; that open lines of communication allow critical trade and natural resources to reach the global economy . . . that governments respect the human rights of their people and address societal violence and discrimination; that women and men are able to live free from violence and participate fully in the political and economic development of their countries; that economies are open and realize their full potential.

parties—Sunni, Shi'a, Kurd, and other minorities—to have another opportunity to ensure that their roles and livelihoods are protected. Intensive efforts should be made to move the language of reform away from ethnosectarian divisions toward geographic federalism. U.S. and coalition diplomats should encourage Iraqi government consideration of increased decentralization and perhaps a geographic realignment of provincial and regional boundaries. This should be done with the intent of reducing the ethnosectarian discord that underlies much of the Islamic State's popular support. It is important that Sunni interlocutors participate in the conceptual development of a constitutional convention.

Security

American military assets—including aerial bombing, rotary-wing aviation attacks, frontline advising, and the commitment of intelligence and special operations forces—should continue to assist Iraqi forces to drive the Islamic State out of its remaining strongholds. The United States considers Iraq to be an "area of active hostility," meaning that the U.S. military and other agencies can target Islamic State leaders without going through a range of steps outlined in the Obama administration's PPG.[46] This authority has allowed U.S. forces to conduct an aggressive campaign against an adaptive enemy, helping weaken the Islamic State by targeting its leadership structure.

In addition, the United States should press Iran, the Iraqi government, and Shi'a militia leaders to reduce their presence in Sunni areas. Increased U.S. presence and support for operations to counter the Islamic State should help create a de facto shift in authority away from Shi'a militias in Sunni areas. Lessening the need for militia support will allow the Iraqi government to encourage members to return to Shi'a areas. At the moment, U.S. military posture is sufficiently robust in Iraq. U.S. military forces use a number of bases across the country, such as al Asad Air Base in Anbar Province, to conduct operations against the Islamic State. The United States also has a force presence of more than 5,000 soldiers. These bases can be helpful to support the

---

[46] White House, 2013.

CIA and other intelligence units that play important counterterrorism and counterinsurgency roles.

Once the Islamic State has been removed from Iraq's population centers, the next phase should involve ensuring Iraqi security force primacy. The U.S. military should alter its training of Iraqi military and police forces to concentrate on preparing them for the population-centric aspects of counterinsurgency that are essential to holding and stabilizing Sunni Arab areas once the Islamic State has been driven underground. This can be accomplished by training different types of forces for different activities. Military advising should focus on population-centric activities, such as population engagement, cooperative security, local reconstruction and development, and local grievance resolution. The United States should also provide training and other assistance to key local organizations, such as forces from the Kurdistan Regional Government. The U.S.-led coalition should provide direct funding to Iraqi counterinsurgency efforts. The United States should encourage Iraqi government efforts to reduce the number and size of Shi'a militias to the point that they no longer have the capacity to challenge the authority of the Iraqi state. Ideally, this plan would be backed by Shi'a religious leaders in Najaf and Karbala. Iraqi government and U.S.-supported incentives, including jobs programs and a national program to recognize the bravery of militia fighters, might be used to help ease the transition from militias to either the Iraqi security forces or civilian employment.

Washington should begin planning for a long-term U.S. advising presence in Iraq. An enduring presence will likely require negotiation of a formal status of forces agreement.

Economic and Humanitarian

Both economic and humanitarian efforts should be designed to support reconciliation and Iraqi government reform. As with the governance and security approaches, more direct economic and humanitarian action should be taken in the early phases to ensure that rapid progress is made and stability is achieved. Human security concerns will need to be addressed before the reconciliation and reform efforts will bear fruit. The second purpose of U.S. assistance should be to mitigate the impact on the already unstable Iraqi government budget and to lessen programmatic vulnerability to fluctuations in international oil prices.

Economic efforts in the initial phase should be targeted at both reconciliation and reform, with an emphasis on rapid repair of damaged and destroyed infrastructure in urban centers, such as Mosul, Ramadi, Fallujah, and Bayji. Initial emphasis should be in the Sunni areas most susceptible to Islamic State resurgence or to the rise of new or splinter Sunni Arab insurgent organizations. Direct U.S. investment should be made through an overarching "reconstruction for reconciliation" package. Reconstruction assistance should be openly associated with efforts to move both the Iraqi government and Sunni Arabs closer. Iraqi political leaders should be given credit for supporting the reconstruction projects and should be rewarded with increased control over funding as they leverage reconstruction to further reconciliation. Realistic expectations should be set. As the United States should have learned in previous efforts in Iraq and Afghanistan, whenever investing money in conflict zones, there will be inevitable failures to match funds with outcomes or to complete projects to U.S. standards.

U.S. military assets should be employed to provide direct aid to Iraqi IDPs. The United States should emphasize the positive role the U.S. in mitigating the suffering of IDPs. These efforts should merge with economic reconstruction efforts to encourage the return of IDPs to Iraqi cities. Humanitarian aid should be delivered to urban areas on a consistent basis until the U.S. assesses that the Iraqi government can extend sufficient services to Sunni Arab, Yazidi, Shi'a, and Turkomen areas damaged or destroyed during fighting against the Islamic State.

Washington should sustain a modest assistance program for Iraq in future years. This will provide leverage in coordinating with other bilateral and multinational donors from whom more can be expected and will allow the United States to address some priority areas the Iraqi government is not. Humanitarian aid should focus on repatriation of refugees to Iraq and their resettlement across Iraq.

Regional Dimension

While the situation inside Iraq is complex enough, the addition of
Saudi Arabian, Iranian, Turkish, and other Arab Gulf interests makes
it even more so.[47] Iran has perhaps the greatest interest in Iraq stemming from the Iran-Iraq war, Iraq's large Shi'a population, and Iraq's
geographic proximity to Iran. Iranian leaders are willing to commit
considerable resources to ensure Iraq's government is friendly to Iran's
interests.[48] To maintain its influence, Iran continues to invest in nongovernmental or pseudogovernmental Shi'a militia groups, such as the
Badr Corps and Asa'ib Ahl al-Haq.[49] Over time, the failure to disarm
or incorporate these militias will present a serious threat to Iraq's legitimacy. The Saudi Arabia government or individual Saudi citizens have
reportedly invested in Sunni insurgent groups to hedge against what
they view as encroaching Iranian influence in the Middle East.[50] Iraq
is caught between these two great Middle Eastern powers. At the same
time, the Kurdish Iraqis are caught between Turkish and Iranian interests that threaten to deepen the internal divide between the Kurdistan
Democratic Party and the Patriotic Union of Kurdistan.

Reconciliation between the main Iraqi factions, if achieved, can
help reduce the leverage these external actors enjoy. But Iran in particular has the capacity to block any such reconciliation via of its influence with the Iraqi government and the various Shi'a militias. The
United States will need to work with all Iraq's neighbors, including
Iran, to secure support for a program of national reconciliation. An
oft-threatened Kurdish decision to declare independence can be kept
at bay by making inclusion in a unified Iraq more attractive. A stable

---

[47] See, for example, Ted Galen Carpenter, "How the West Should Respond to a Divided
Iraq—And Not Intervene Again," *Aspenia*, August 27, 2014.

[48] Pierre Razoux, *The Iran-Iraq War*, trans. Nicholas Elliot, Cambridge, Mass.: Harvard
University Press, 2015.

[49] Ranj Alaaldin, "Iran's Weak Grip: How Much Control Does Tehran Have Over Shia
Militias in Iraq?" *Foreign Affairs*, February 11, 2016.

[50] Helene Cooper, "Saudi's Role in Iraq Frustrates U.S. Officials," *New York Times*, July 27,
2007, and Lori Plotkin Boghardt, "Saudi Funding of ISIS," Washington, D.C.: Washington
Institute for Near East Policy, June 23, 2014.

Iraqi government that has at least some basic legitimacy in the eyes of Iraqi Kurds is more likely to deter Turkish and Iranian meddling in the north. An economically robust Iraq that is able to equitably disperse oil revenues to the Kurdistan Regional Government can help resolve the disputes over territories claimed by both Kurds and Arabs.

Stabilizing post–Islamic State Iraq, overcoming its ethnic and sectarian divisions, and securing support from its mutually hostile neighbors will be a formidable task, one that ultimately proved beyond the United States from 2003 to 2011. Yet the failure to persevere in that effort opened the door to the Islamic State, and a failure to resume the effort once the Islamic State is driven underground will likely produce a similar effect.

CHAPTER FIVE
Syria

While the Islamic State originated in Iraq, it locates the capital of its so-called caliphate in Raqqa, Syria—a city of nearly 250,000.[1] The Islamic State has drawn considerable resources from its control of Syrian oil-fields in the east of the country and from taxation of civilians in Raqqa and other cities and towns across the Syrian northeast.[2] A great deal of Islamic State propaganda has focused on selling the caliphate by trying to demonstrate that Raqqa is a safe, stable homeland for Islamic extremists and their families.[3] But the Islamic State is vulnerable in Syria. Expulsion from Raqqa and the few other the population centers it controls there will represent a significant threat to the group. Such a defeat will scatter the Islamic State's leadership, severely undermine its prestige, and call into question its dominance of the loosely associated Salafi-jihadist movement. The Islamic State is likely to survive and con-

---

[1] Graeme Wood, "What ISIS Really Wants," *Atlantic*, March 2015. Assessment for the remainder of this paragraph and for much of this chapter was drawn from Wood, 2015, and Stern and Berger, 2015; Aaron Y. Zelin, "The Islamic State's Territorial Methodology," Washington, D.C.: Washington Institute for Near East Policy, No. 29, January 2016; Bryan Price, Dan Milton, Muhammad al-`Ubaydi, and Nelly Lahoud, *The Group That Calls Itself a State: Understanding the Evolution and Challenges of the Islamic State*, West Point, N.Y.: Combatting Terrorism Center, December 16, 2014; Charles Lister, *Profiling the Islamic State, Profiling the Islamic State*, Washington, D.C.: Brookings Institution, November 2014; Charlie Winter, *Documenting the Virtual Caliphate*, London: Quilliam Foundation, October 2015.

[2] Bahney et al., 2010.

[3] See, for example, Orlando Crowcroft and Arij Liman, "ISIS: Foreign Fighters 'Live Like Kings' in Syrian Raqqa Stronghold of Islamic State," *International Business Times*, March 12, 2015.

duct attacks as a mobile, networked insurgent force in Syria but probably will not pose the same regional and global threat. Defeating the Islamic State in Syria, as in Iraq, must continue to be a central pillar in the overall strategy. Once suppressed, the group must stay so and then be gradually dismantled, lest it rise again.

Much as in Iraq, the Islamic State arose amidst the chaos that resulted from a mostly Sunni Arab revolt, in this case against Bashar al-Assad's government of Syria. The Islamic State may not have great popular support in Syria but can continue to exist there, at least as a clandestine insurgent movement, as long as the country remains in civil war.

This chapter briefly describes and acknowledges the complexity of the Syria problem, placing even more emphasis on regional dynamics than did the chapter on Iraq. In Syria, the Islamic State thrives within a fractured sea of multisectarian, multiethnic violent armed groups; a massive refugee and IDP crisis; widespread material destruction; and an indirect, yet damaging, competition between Russia, Iran, Lebanese Hezbollah, Turkey, and the United States.

The Rise of the Islamic State in Syria

Syria's war, which erupted as part of the broader Arab Spring movement in 2011, created the environment that allowed the Islamic State to reemerge from the remnants of AQI as much more of a potent threat. There is a complex, nuanced legacy of power politics; violent oppression; international influence; and geographic, class, and ethnosectarian division in Syria that cannot be given adequate treatment here. But a brief summary is necessary to explain the proposed rollback strategy.[4] The primarily Alawi (a Shia sect) Arab regime founded by Hafez

---

[4]   For a sampling of relevant historical and topical analyses, see M. E. Yapp, *The Near East Since the First World War: A History to 1995*, London: Addison Wesley Longman, Ltd., 1996; Flynt Leverett, *Inheriting Syria: Bashar's Trial by Fire*, Washington, D.C.: Brookings Institution, 2005; Volker Perthes, *The Political Economy of Syria under Asad*, New York: I.B. Tauris and Company, Ltd., 1995; and Emile Hokayem, *Syria's Uprising and the Fracturing of the Levant*, London: International Institute for Strategic Studies, 2013.

al-Assad, and continued under his son Bashar al-Assad, has oppressed and disenfranchised a significant proportion of Syria's majority population. This long-standing oppression ultimately led to the 2011 revolt, then to the rise of the Islamic State.

Hafez al-Assad rose to power in a coup in 1970, emerging as the president, leader of Syria's Ba'ath Party, and de facto leader of Syria's Alawi community. At this point, Syria had already established a firm diplomatic and military relationship with the Soviet Union. Syria benefitted from Soviet protection against real and perceived threats from Western powers and Israel. The Soviet Union benefitted from direct access to the Middle East and the Mediterranean Sea.[5] Hafez al-Assad did everything possible to strengthen this relationship. Succeeding his father in 2000, Bashar al-Assad inherited close and enduring diplomatic, military, and economic ties between the Alawi regime and post-Soviet Russia. Russia maintains military airfields and port facilities in Syria, which serve as its only substantial forward presence in the Mediterranean basin. Russian leadership views Syria as part of Moscow's traditional sphere of influence and views the stability of the Syrian government as essential to maintaining its network of regional ties.[6]

From the 1970s through the 1990s, Hafez al-Assad also built and cemented a close partnership with Iran. Because Syrian and Iraqi Ba'athists had long since separated under a cloud of distrust and anger, al-Assad found himself in direct opposition to Iraq's Ba'athist government. Further isolated by the 1979 Egypt-Israel peace treaty, al-Assad aligned himself with Iran's new revolutionary Shi'a Islamic government, deepening the divide with the region's Sunni Arab regimes. Iran would leverage its relationship with Syria to influence Lebanese Shi'a and provide direct and indirect support to Lebanese Hezbollah and other militant groups as part of an Iranian-led axis of resistance against Western and Sunni Arab powers. This axis constitutes what some Sunni leaders perceive to be a "Shi'a Crescent," ranging from the Palestinian territories

---

[5] See, for example, Yair Even, "Syria's 1956 Request for Soviet Military Intervention," Washington, D.C.: Wilson Center, February 2, 2016.

[6] David Herszenhorn, "For Syria, Reliant on Russia for Weapons and Food, Old Bonds Run Deep," *New York Times*, February 18, 2012.

to Lebanon through Syria, Iran, and into Persian Gulf states, such as Bahrain. For Tehran, continued pro-Iranian governance in Syria is critical to Iran's ability to counter the influence of hostile Arab states. Many dispute this primordialist view of regional politics, but it is sufficient to say that Iranian leaders view Syria as essential to Iran's ability to influence the Levant and support Lebanese Hezbollah and its networks of agents.[7] In turn, Lebanese Hezbollah views ongoing Syrian government support as essential to its survival and, with Iranian support, it has committed military force to back the Damascus regime.[8]

Alawi Arabs, a minority group in Syria that had little influence or authority through the mid-20th century and who had sometimes suffered under Sunni majority domination, emerged as the dominant class under Hafez al-Assad.[9] Alawi Arab Ba'athists came to dominate the Syrian government at the expense of other ethnosectarian groups, primarily Sunni Arabs. But two dynamics of Alawi domination are important to understand. First, as Emile Hokayem argues, "*asabiyya* (group solidarity or kinship), rather than outright and primal sectarianism, better explains [Alawi] family and regime dynamics and decisionmaking."[10] Syrian government control is thus less about religion than it is about group organization for survival and power dominance. Second, Bashar al-Assad consolidated power even further than his father within his close familial circles. While this helped him retain control of the state throughout the war, it might provide a more limited target for regime change than, by comparison, Iraq's entire ruling and working class of Sunni, Shi'a, and Kurdish Ba'ath Party members under Saddam.

---

[7]   Moshe Ma'oz, *The Shi'a Crescent: Myth and Reality*, Washington, D.C.: Brookings Institution, November 15, 2007.

[8]   Marisa Sullivan, *Hezbollah in Syria*, Washington, D.C.: Institute for the Study of War, April 2014.

[9]   This is not to say that Sunnis, Kurds, and other Syrians had no official role; in fact, Sunnis made up a majority of the army, and many were loyal to the regime. As with assumptions of monolithic Shi'ism, primordialist assumptions about the Sunni in Syria or across the Middle East are erroneous.

[10]   Hokayem, 2013, p. 32.

From the early 1970s through 2000, the Syrian government oppressed Sunni and many Kurdish Syrians, jailing; torturing; and, in the case of the Hama Massacre in 1982, reportedly slaughtering Sunni by the thousands.[11] High hopes for the seemingly moderate Bashar al-Assad were dashed by 2001, when reformers inspired by the death of Hafez al-Assad sought greater freedom in a collective effort known as the Damascus Spring.[12] Within a year, Bashar al-Assad shut down the reforms and began to oppress the reformers. This behavior continued through 2011, although with a glossier veneer of pseudodemocracy than under Hafez al-Assad. At the same time, Bashar al-Assad shifted economic power to urban areas, alienated rural Sunni tribes, and failed to improve the economic or social situations of the average Syrian outside Damascus. What began as a mild protest of intellectuals quickly spread to Dara'a in the south and then to Homs and other cities. By the end of 2011, Syria was in a full-fledged civil war.[13] Bashar al-Assad has remained in power with the support of Russian military forces; Iranian and Lebanese Hezbollah advisors and fighters; and a solid core of loyal Alawi military, political, and civic leaders. Assad intentionally fostered the radicalization of his opposition, deliberately releasing extremist figures. The Islamic State emerged out of this chaos. Syria's Kurds add another complicating factor to a rollback strategy. Located almost entirely in the north of the country, Syrian Kurds have a longstanding history of opposition to the Assad regime. But Syrian Kurdish political and military groups also have close ties with the radical anti-Turkish Kurdistan Workers' Party (Partiya Karkeren Kurdistane, PKK). The main Syrian Kurdish political party, the Democratic Union

---

[11] In 1982, al-Assad faced a Muslim Brotherhood revolt in Hama and sent the military to destroy the group. Casualty estimates of the Hama Massacre are disputed, but the end result was a widespread perception that al-Assad was a ruthless dictator who would not shy away from murdering Sunni Arabs to retain power. See, for example, Deborah Amos, "30 Years Later, Photos Emerge from Killings in Syria," National Public Radio, February 2, 2012, and Bill Rugh, "Syria: The Hama Massacre," Washington, D.C.: Middle East Policy Council, February 26, 2015.

[12] Seth Wikas, *Battling the Lion of Damascus: Syria's Domestic Opposition and the Asad Regime*, Washington, D.C.: Washington Institute for Near East Policy, May 2007.

[13] For a narrative of the 2011 uprising, see Hokayem, 2013.

Party (PYD), was originally an offshoot of the PKK.[14] This places the PYD in opposition to the government of Turkey, which views Kurdish autonomy in northern Syria as a direct threat to Turkey.[15] Yet, since the Syrian Kurds have not taken a strong or militant position against the Syrian government, the regime and its Russian sponsors have not targeted the PYD.[16] The PYD has hedged its bets between the United States and Russia and received American support to fight the Islamic State. But it must fear that the United States will withdraw this support after the defeat of the Islamic State to maintain the U.S. relationship with Turkey. Syrian Kurds have pressed forward against the Islamic State with U.S. military support, and their surging confidence led them to claim an autonomous federated state in the northeast. But the Syrian Kurds lie at a dangerous crossroads between Turkey, Russia, Iraqi Kurds, Turkish Kurds, the United States, the Islamic State, and other armed groups.

The Islamic State locates its capital in Syria but did not settle there until after the onset of the Syrian war and the departure of U.S. military forces from Iraq. The group's connections to Syria are nevertheless of long standing. The Islamic State's predecessor organization, AQI, maintained networks in Syria throughout the U.S.-led coalition war in Iraq that began in 2003. Al-Qa'ida in Iraq used Syria's airports, road networks, and Syrian facilitators to help launder money and move foreign fighters to and from Iraq.[17] AQI, then the Islamic State, have consistently benefitted from cross-border tribal connections between

---

[14] The abbreviations PKK and PYD both derive from transliterations. Another is People's Protection Units (YPG), the military wing of the PYD.

[15] Andrew J. Tabler, Soner Cagaptay, David Pollock, and James F. Jeffrey, "The Syrian Kurds: Whose Ally?" Washington, D.C.: Washington Institute for Near East Policy, March 29, 2016.

[16] Antagonistic relations between Russia and Turkey have reinforced Russian relations with the Syrian Kurds.

[17] Bahney et al., 2010; Joseph Felter and Brian Fishman, *Al-Qa'ida's Foreign Fighters in Iraq: A First Look at the Sinjar Records*, West Point, N.Y.: Combatting Terrorism Center, 2007; JIC, "Iraq Security: External Support for Insurgents," October 7, 2004b (a declassified intelligence report presented as part of the Government of the UK Iraq Inquiry).

Iraq and Syria, particularly along the historic Euphrates River smuggling routes between al-Qa'im, Iraq, and Deir az-Zour, Syria.[18]

Abu Bakr al-Baghdadi, the Islamic State leader, established a strong presence in Syria in 2011, first as an offshoot of AQI. As noted in Chapter Two, al-Baghdadi attempted to incorporate Jabhat al-Nusrah—which he viewed as one of his subordinate elements—into the renamed the Islamic State. But Jabhat al-Nusrah rejected this unification effort, and the ensuing internecine squabble resulted in a split between the two groups and al-Baghdadi's withdrawal from al-Qa'ida.[19] This break placed the Islamic State in opposition to both Jabhat al-Nusrah and al-Qa'ida and to the larger array of groups seeking to overthrow Bashar al-Assad. These other groups receive support from the United States, Turkey, and the Gulf States. By mid-2013, al-Baghdadi began a concerted campaign to acquire territory in Syria, seeking to eject or absorb all Syrian opposition groups in the process. By early 2014, the Islamic State had established control of Raqqa and begun its expansion into Iraq, absorbing many of the original members of Jabhat al-Nusrah.[20] By 2015, the Islamic State controlled large portions of Syria's oil resources, eastern road networks, vital dams, and population centers.

External intervention—from the United States in the north and, to a lesser degree, from Russia, Iran, and Lebanese Hezbollah in the west—blunted and began to reverse some of the Islamic State's earlier gains. In 2016, Kurdish YPG dominated militia including some Syrian

---

[18] "U.S. Cross-Border Raid Highlights Syria's Role in Islamist Militancy," *CTC Sentinel*, November 15, 2008; Joseph Holliday, "Syria Update 13-01: Iraq-Syria Overland Supply Routes," Washington, D.C.: Institute for the Study of War, May 8, 2013.

[19] Reports detailing the Islamic State's relationship with Jabhat Fatah al-Sham—what was Jabhat al-Nusrah (JaN) through mid-2016—claim either that al-Baghdadi established JaN and then was rejected by JaN leadership when he attempted to unify them under the Islamic State of Iraq umbrella (renamed the Islamic State), or that the Islamic State and JaN were separate groups. For example, see Stern and Berger, 2015; and Charles C. Caris and Samuel Reynolds, *the Islamic State Governance in Syria*, Institute for the Study of War, July 2014.

[20] A good summary timeline of the Islamic State' rise in Syria can be found in Stern and Berger, 2015, pp. XVIX–XXVI. They provide detailed analysis of the timeline throughout the remainder of the book. Many alternative timelines exist, all with varying degrees of detail and agreement. None appears to be empirically definitive.

Sunni Arabs pushed back the Islamic State north of Raqqa. The Turkish border became less hospitable to the Islamic State's human and materiel smuggling efforts. Syrian government forces squeezed opposition territory from the west, temporarily recapturing the historic town of Palmyra. As with Iraq, the United States considers Syria to be area of active hostility, which has allowed U.S. forces to conduct an aggressive campaign against the Islamic State and other groups operating in the country.

Figure 5.1 shows the decline of Islamic State territorial control in Syria. The group held an estimated 3.3 million people (14 percent of the population) in fall 2014 and covered an area of roughly 47,497 km² (25 percent of the territory). By winter 2016-2017, a combination of Syrian, Turkish, Kurdish, and allied military operations had pushed the Islamic State out of territory in the northern and eastern Syrian provinces of Hasakah, Raqqa, and Aleppo. Islamic State control declined

Figure 5.1
Islamic State Control of Territory in Syria

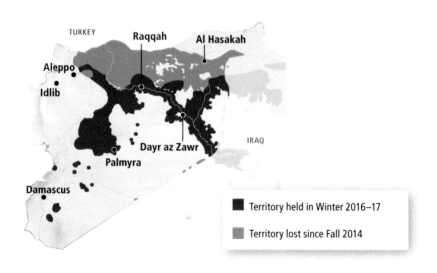

SOURCES: Fall 2014 estimates are based on U.S. Department of Defense, 2016a. Winter 2016–2017 estimates are based on authors' estimates of changes in control.
RAND RR1912-5.1

to 1.5 million people (or 6 percent of the population) and 29,695 km^2 (or 16 percent of the country).

Desired End State

It might be ideally desirable to end the civil war in Syria, then help the Syrian government regain control of Raqqa and the remaining Islamic State territory. But that war is not going to end any time soon. The alternative, therefore, is to support friendly local forces in liberating remaining Islamic State controlled territory and then to turn to the even more difficult task of ending the larger conflict.

The local organization most capable of taking Raqqa in the short term the Syrian Defence Forces (SDF), a mixture of Arabs and Kurds dominated by the YPG, a Kurdish militia. Raqqa and the surrounding areas are Arab, not Kurdish, however. Both the local population and most regional states would oppose this part of Syria falling under Kurdish control. Turkey, above all, will oppose any such extension of Kurdish authority. The United States has sought to bolster Arab elements within the SDF with the intent of using them to hold Raqqa and the surrounding region once the Islamic State has been driven out. It is not clear, however, that such an Arab force would be adequate to hold Raqqa against renewed Islamic State attacks, those of other Sunni militant groups affiliated with al-Qa'ida, and/or the Syrian regime.

Unless Turkey receives some assurances regarding the future of this territory, it will likely oppose any operation to liberate Raqqa, perhaps by moving into Kurdish-held territory, compelling SDF forces to be redeployed away from Raqqa to deal with the threat.

Even assuming Turkey's objections can be overcome and the Islamic State driven out of its capital, Washington will face further difficult choices. Should the United States continue to extend an air umbrella over the newly liberated province, fending off both regime and Turkish threats to an enlarged Kurdish zone of control? Alternatively, should the United States invite Russia and the Damascus regime to assume control of Raqqa and collaborate with Assad and his Russian (and Iranian) backers in mopping up remaining Islamic State strong points? Or should the United States declare victory and withdraw its forces from Syria, leaving the Kurds, the regime, and the Turks to sort out their differences?

None of these alternatives is very attractive. Kurdish control of the dominantly Arab province of Raqqa may not be sustainable, given both local and Turkish opposition. Collaborating with Assad would antagonize most American allies in the region and would be quite controversial both domestically and internationally, particularly after Assad's use of chemical weapons against civilians and rebels in Syria's Idlib province in April 2017. Asserting "mission accomplished" and withdrawing would likely replicate the Iraq experiences of George W. Bush in 2003 and Barack Obama in 2011, when such assertions proved hollow.

Even before it launches the operation to liberate Raqqa, therefore, the United States should propose interim arrangements for securing and administering the city and its surroundings that Turkey, Russia, and the local population will accept. We suggest that Washington should offer to place Raqqa, once liberated, under some form of international administration. This would require UN Security Council approval and, thus, Russian support. Moscow might be attracted to an arrangement that gave it a role in administering this region. The Turks and America's other regional allies would certainly prefer this arrangement to Kurdish or regime control.

Such an initiative would have both symbolic and practical effects. Raqqa and Mosul are the two cities most associated with the Islamic State's caliphate. So, investing in Raqqa's future and protecting it from conflict reoccurrence are crucial to the symbolism of the counter–Islamic State campaign. Practical considerations are also at play. Turkey will almost certainly block any flow of stabilization assistance to the city as long as it remains under Kurdish control.

Over the longer term, the United States must work to end the larger civil war. As long as the conflict continues, the Islamic State and other violent extremist groups, most notably the local branch of al-Qa'ida, will find fertile ground for growth.

U.S. and Allied Steps

The new U.S. administration should move briskly to complete the seizure of Raqqa, support its stabilization, and join in regional and broader international efforts to end the larger civil war.

Political and Governance

Employing Kurdish led forces to liberate Raqqa requires the United States to convincingly assure Turkey that Kurds will not occupy this region once it has been cleared of the Islamic State. This will in turn require some clear understanding between Washington and the Syrian Kurdish authorities. It also requires the availability of some alternative hold force. Once Raqqa and the surrounding region have been cleared, the United States will need to help that hold force resist attacks from residual Islamic State fighters, other violent extremist groups, and the regime. The latter threat might be deflected via some agreement with Russia and the other external parties to the conflict regarding the post–Islamic State administration of Raqqa. As noted earlier, one possibility is for the United States to propose placing Raqqa city and province under an interim international administration. Extending American military involvement further west, to encompass the several opposition held areas currently besieged by regime forces, could help protect a far larger number of Syrian civilians. But such a step would risk direct confrontation between American and Russian air forces. It would also provide a respite not just to the civilian population but also to the various militias, including the most extreme. The last group would likely take advantage of any such safe havens to renew attacks on regime-held areas. It is possible that such an American intervention could help advance a peace settlement, but the result might simply be an intensification of the fighting and a risk of escalation to U.S.-Russian conflict.

Rather than confronting the Damascus regime in the west of the country, Washington might usefully explore collaboration with Moscow in clearing what will be the last significant Islamic State stronghold in the east, the oil rich area around Dier ez Zur. Because this region contains all Syria's oil production, it is likely to be of much greater interest to the regime in Damascus than Raqqa is. Russia might be quite interested in securing American support in effecting its military operations.

Security

The SDF should be employed to isolate and then clear Raqqa and the surrounding region of Islamic State fighters. Turkish-supported Arab forces might also become involved in this assault. SDF forces should receive American support and be accompanied by American advisors. The United States has provided arms and ammunition to Arab units attached to the SDF. But out of deference to Turkish concerns, the United States has not equipped Syrian Kurdish forces. Turkey has argued that any support for the SDF will end up in the hands of the PKK, a terrorist group that has conducted attacks against Turkey for decades. Yet the United States should consider providing arms and training to the SDF to take back Raqqa and to overcome the Islamic State's use of snipers, suicide bombers, IEDs, and guerilla tactics. To help ameliorate Turkish concerns, the United States should insist that the SDF not provide resources to groups targeting Turkey and should cede predominantly Arab-populated territory liberated from the Islamic State to local forces. The United States might also support Turkish consolidation of a buffer zone in northwestern Syria and support Turkey's fight against the PKK.[21]

In addition to equipping SDF forces for the assault, the United States will likely need to introduce a limited number of additional American troops to provide, among other things, heavy fire support.

Holding and rebuilding Raqqa may prove much more demanding than taking the city. In Iraq these tasks have largely been left to Iraqi government forces and to international organizations, through which the United States and other donors funnel aid. Neither of these possibilities is available in Syria, where the regime is hostile and where international organizations, such as the UN and the World Bank, cannot operate freely in opposition-held areas. Further, Turkey will likely close

---

[21] See, for example, Antony J. Blinken, "To Defeat ISIS, Arm the Syrian Kurds," *New York Times*, January 31, 2017.

its borders to reconstruction assistance if Raqqa is held by Kurdish forces.

Although the United States may seek to mobilize and assist moderate Arab militia to hold Raqqa, these elements may prove inadequate to the task of defending the city against Islamic State remnants; other, more-extremist Arab militias; and regime forces. Yet it will be difficult for the United States, having successfully orchestrated a campaign to capture the Islamic State's capital, to abandon the city to any of these contenting factions.

Economic and Humanitarian

Among the most urgent task in post–Islamic State Raqqa will be dealing with unexploded ordinance and defusing booby traps. Reopening markets, encouraging local agricultural production, and restoring basic public services, including electricity, water, and hospitals, will also require external assistance. That assistance will have to come mostly from the United States at first because international assistance agencies cannot operate in opposition-held areas of Syria. It will be difficult to provide humanitarian and reconstruction assistance to areas liberated from the Islamic State unless the Turkish and Iraqi borders remain open. Some assistance might be flown in, but this would be very expensive, and the quantities would be limited

If and when the broader civil war can be ended, a much larger program of reconstruction and economic development should be launched. This should be shaped and led by international institutions, such as the UN and the World Bank, as is already being done in Iraq. But substantial American participation will be necessary if momentum is to be sustained and the processes structured in a manner that fosters an enduring peace.

Regional Dimension

The Syrian civil war has been perpetuated by outside actors. Historically, such conflicts end when one side wins or when both find themselves in a hurting stalemate, leading to a negotiated settlement. But outside actors can sustain this conflict indefinitely at relatively little cost to themselves and may therefore never feel compelled to accept such an outcome. As long as external players are ready to fight to the last Syrian, the war can continue.

Peace depends on putting forth some project for a reimagined Syria that both the Syrian parties and the outside powers can accept. This almost certainly involves a Syria that is sovereign within its present borders but much more decentralized than previously. Halting the fighting along the current battle lines in the west while continuing to clear eastern Syria of Islamic State fighters would be a step in this direction, The United States and Russia have twice attempted to do this, only to see the agreed ceasefires collapse. In late December 2016, Turkey and Russia made a third, and so far more successful attempt at such a cessation of hostilities. Whether or not this succeeds, continuing efforts of this sort are necessary first steps toward ending the war and beginning to rebuild the Syrian state, most likely based on a more-decentralized model.

CHAPTER SIX

Libya

Hopes that Libya would follow neighboring Tunisia's post–Arab Spring path toward democratic consolidation after the death of Muammar Qaddafi in 2011 were dashed when security deteriorated and the North African nation collapsed into civil war in summer 2014. Libya became a failed state with dueling governments, beset by conflict and facing a looming economic and humanitarian crisis. America and its European allies, led by the UN, worked to form a government of national unity out of the country's feuding parties, but progress was slow and halting. The Islamic State established footholds in the country, although its control of territory declined in 2016 with the successful ouster of Islamic State forces from Sirte. Still, the Islamic State remains a threat in Libya —as witnessed by the U.S. airstrike on an Islamic State camp on January 18, 2017—and there is a pressing need to take a series of political, security, economicand other steps to permanently deny it a sanctuary and establish a government with international and domestic legitimacy.

The Rise of the Islamic State in Libya

The Islamic State's expansion into Libya began around April 2014 in the eastern town of Derna, which was a hotbed of jihadi radicalism long before the Arab Spring.[1] At the height of the attacks against U.S. forces in Iraq, Derna had sent hundreds of fighters to join the ranks of

---

[1]   See Fred Wehrey, *The Struggle for Security in Eastern Libya* Washington, D.C.: Carnegie Endowment for International Peace, 2012.

AQI.[2] More recently, Derna's jihadist networks (and those of Benghazi) provided a steady stream of fighters to the Islamic State in Syria.[3]

In April 2014, a group of these fighters returned from Syria to Derna, formed the radical Islamic Youth Shura Council, and gradually took over control of the town, eventually pledging allegiance to Baghdadi.[4] The Islamic State seized the opportunity the Islamic Shura Youth Council offered by dispatching at least three of its managers to Libya and providing other forms of support.[5]

The Islamic State then sought to establish a second major front in its war for the caliphate in Libya. Although the Islamic State was forced to cede territory in Derna in 2015, it made significant inroads in and around the central Libyan town of Sirte. Because it was Qaddafi's former hometown, Sirte had been neglected and excluded in post-Qaddafi Libyan politics. By 2015, economic conditions there were poor, and insecurity was rife, making it ripe for inroads from Salafi-jihadists ready to offer some semblance of governance to the local population.[6]

Initially, Ansar al-Sharia in Libya, one of the groups responsible for the 2012 attack on the U.S. diplomatic compound in Benghazi, had provided rudimentary governmental service in Sirte.[7] In early 2015, however, the Islamic State effectively staged a coup and took over Sirte from Ansar al Sharia. In part due to the successes it had enjoyed in Iraq and Syria over the course of 2014, the Islamic State had increasingly attracted adherents from within the older group. In February

---

[2]   Felter and Fishman, 2007; David D. Kirkpatrick, "Libya Democracy Clashes with Fervor for Jihad," *New York Times*, June 23, 2012.

[3]   "Young Libyans Head to Join the Islamic State in Syria and Iraq," *Libya Herald*, September 8, 2014.

[4]   Meir Amit Intelligence and Terrorism Information Center, "ISIS in Libya: A Major Regional and International Threat," January 2016, pp. 27–28; Nathaniel Barr and David Greenberg, "Libya's Political Turmoil Allows Islamic State to Thrive," *Terrorism Monitor*, Vol. 14, No. 7, April 1, 2016.

[5]   Missy Ryan, "U.S. Officials: Chief of the Islamic State in Libya Thought to be Killed in Airstrike" *Washington Post*, November 14, 2015.

[6]   Usamah al-Jarid, "ISIL: The Road to Sirte Emirate" *Al-Wasat*, December 14, 2015.

[7]   "ISIS Militants Seize University in Libya's Sirte," Al Arabiya, February 19, 2016.

2015, the Islamic State beheaded 21 Egyptian Coptic Christians in Sirte and, over the course of the next few months, the Islamic State successfully pushed those who remained loyal to Ansar al-Sharia out and established full control over the city and several of its surrounding towns.[8] In the process, it also repulsed militia brigades that were aligned with Misrata and with which Ansar al Sharia had formerly coexisted. The Islamic State thus came into full control of a Libyan city of some 80,000 inhabitants, along with the neighboring towns of Bin Jawad and Nawfaliyah.

The Islamic State established itself as the local government, set up headquarters in the convention center, took over local television and radio stations, deployed religious compliance police, and began to administer sharia law. The group continued its practices of beheadings, crucifixions, and forced repentances. It financed these operations with a run of bank seizures, extortion of the local population, some profits from acting as a middleman for the burgeoning Mediterranean migrant traffic, and likely some direct financial support from the Islamic State in Iraq and Syria.[9] Its local leaders were from the Gulf, Levant, other North African countries, and Libya itself.[10] The Islamic State also expanded its presence into Benghazi, Ajdabiyah, Tripoli, Misrata, Derna, Sabratha, and possibly elsewhere. This presence in towns other than Sirte is best characterized as cellular or consisting of sympathizers within other Salafi-jihadist groups, although these cells can reportedly involve smaller-scale training camps and munition factories.[11]

Beginning in late 2015, Islamic State leaders in Iraq and Syria began to encourage foreign fighters to move from the Levant to Libya through official publications, such as *Dabiq*. Foreign fighters could enter Libya with relative ease overland from Tunisia, Chad, Egypt, and Sudan and by ship via the country's long coastline. The Islamic State's

[8] Aron Y. Zelin, "The Islamic State's Burgeoning Capital in Sirte, Libya" Washington, D.C.: Washington Institute for Near East Policy, Policywatch 2462, February 19, 2015.

[9] al-Jarid, 2015.

[10] Francesca Marmocchi, "Come Funziona il Califfato di Sirte" *L'Espresso*, December 4, 2015.

[11] Interviews, Tunis, October 2014.

membership in Libya included not only Libyans but also Tunisians, Algerians, Egyptians, Iraqis, Yemeni, Saudis, Nigerians, and other nationalities. There were an estimated 1,000 Tunisian foreign fighters in Libya.[12] Boko Haram developed increasingly close links to the Islamic State, and there were reports that Libyans led Boko Haram forces in Nigeria.[13] There were also some indications that the Islamic State in Libya established links with its partner affiliate in Egypt, the Wilayat Sinai (or Sinai Province).[14]

During its time in Sirte, the Islamic State had ample opportunity to reinforce its defenses, train, and build up its munitions stocks. It acquired most, if not all, of the many small and light arms types available to other armed groups in the country.[15] The Islamic State sought to expand its territory beyond Sirte, attacking the oil facilities at Al Sidr and Ras Lanuf. It was repulsed by the Libyan Petroleum Facilities Guard, a force controlled by federalist Ibrahim Jadran, and other local forces. The attacks raised the prospect that the Islamic State might seek to use Libya's oil as a source of revenue or, at a minimum, as a bargaining chip.

As it reinforced its position in Sirte, the Islamic State also conducted smaller-scale attacks elsewhere. In January 2015, it attacked the Corinthia Hotel in Tripoli. In May 2015, it attacked the western gates of Misrata. In January 2016, it bombed the Libyan police training academy in Zliten. Islamic State–aligned fighters were also active in Benghazi against the Libyan National Army of Khalifa Hiftar, the military commander of Libya's eastern government, as well as other groups.[16]

---

[12] UN, "Preliminary Findings by the United Nations Working Group on the Use of Mercenaries on Its Official Visit to Tunisia," July 2015.

[13] Jacob Zenn, "Wilayat West Africa Reboots for the Caliphate" *CTC Sentinel*, August 21, 2015b; Fulannasrullah, "Fulan's SITREP," blog, August 5, 2015.

[14] Meir Amit Intelligence and Terrorism Information Center, 2016, pp. 96–97.

[15] Small Arms Survey, "The Online Trade of Light Weapons in Libya," Security Assessment, No. 6, April 2016.

[16] See, for example, "ISIS Claims Deadly Car Bomb in Libya's Benghazi," Al Arabiya, February 27, 2016.

Its main focus during 2015, however, was on attacking neighboring Tunisia. The Islamic State attempted to put pressure on Tunisia's delicate political system, no doubt in hope of destabilizing it and opening the door to attacks on Algeria, which remains the prize of most jihadists in the region. The Islamic State cell in Sabratha, against which the United States conducted an airstrike in February 2016, was responsible for the attacks in Tunisia in 2015—at the Sousse Beach resort, at the Bardo Museum, and against a presidential guard bus in Tunis.[17] In March 2016, drawing on multiple sleeper cells in a strategy that had worked in Mosul, Iraq, the Islamic State also managed a larger-scale, cross-border assault on the Tunisian border town of Ben Guerdane. At least three squads began attacks on government buildings, and a conventional battle ensued. In this case, however, the Islamic State was repelled.[18]

The Islamic State exists amid a complex jihadist milieu. Many of Libya's other major jihadist groups are linked to al-Qa'ida in the Islamic Maghreb.[19] The Islamic State attempted to set itself apart from these other extremists. For the Islamic State in Libya, any organization that fails to pledge allegiance to its leader, Abu Bakr al-Baghadi, is an enemy.[20] Similarly, Islamic State operatives reject any of the groups in Libya that participated in Libya's post-Qaddafi democratic experiment.

Over the summer and fall of 2016, the United States provided air support to a campaign by Misratan militias that successfully pushed the majority of Islamic State fighters out of Sirte. Figure 6.1 shows the decline in Islamic State control between spring 2015 and winter 2016-2017. U.S. and United Kingdom (UK) special operations forces provided limited advice to support the successful Misratan advance. Misratan troops took heavy losses in the fight, as did the Islamic State.

---

[17] Declan Walsh, Ben Hubbard, and Eric Schmidt, "U.S. Bombing in Libya Reveals Limits of Strategy Against ISIS," *New York Times,* February 20, 2016.

[18] Multiple press reports.

[19] Thomas Joscelyn, "Al-Qa'ida in the Islamic Maghreb Backs Jihadists Fighting Islamic State in Derna, Libya" *Long War Journal*, July 9, 2015a.

[20] Thomas Joscelyn, "In Dabiq Magazine, Islamic State Complains About Jihadist Rivals in Libya," *Long War Journal*, September 13, 2015b.

Figure 6.1
Islamic State Control of Territory in Libya

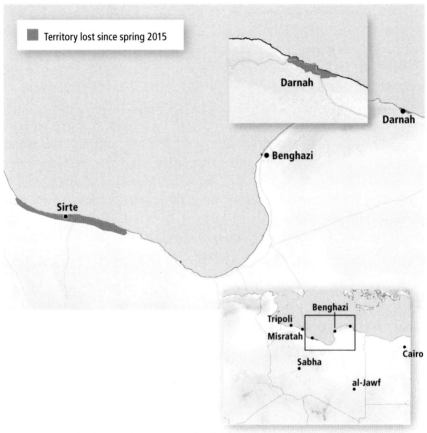

SOURCE: Issandr El Amrani, "How Much of Libya Does the Islamic State Control?" *Foreign Policy*, February 18, 2016; Eric Schmitt and Helene Cooper, "U.S. and Allies Weigh Military Action Against ISIS in Libya," *New York Times*, January 22, 2016; Meir Amit Intelligence and Terrorism Information Center, 2016; Thomas Joscelyn, "Islamic State's Safe Haven in Sirte, Libya Shrinks to a 'Single Neighborhood,'" *Long War Journal*, September 22, 2016; authors' estimates.
RAND *RR1912-6.1*

Many Islamic State fighters fled for other parts of the country, such as the southern Fezzan region, which borders Chad and Algeria. By winter 2016–2017, the Islamic State controlled virtually no territory in the country, although it did have cells in numerous areas.

Desired End State

Dealing with a dispersed Islamic State threat in Libya will be more difficult than denying it a fixed safe haven. As long as the country remains embroiled in civil war, advances against the Islamic State are likely to be transitory. The goal of U.S. policy should be to restore a legitimate national government, recognized as such internationally and internally, that has some capacity, however limited, to secure its territory and population.

While working toward that goal, the United States and its allies should continue to provide support to local Libyan militias as they go after the Islamic State in other areas.[21] Many of these militias, however, are linked to Salafi-jihadist networks themselves. Selecting one or more of them will require vetting for such links, in addition to assessing the militia's operational effectiveness. Additionally, showing preference for any of Libya's militias will be viewed negatively by other militias, whose cooperation is likely necessary to reestablish peace in the country over the long run. Salafi-jihadist groups will not be conclusively defeated in Libya until a minimally effective national government is established throughout the country.

U.S. and Allied Steps

A rollback strategy that permanently denies the Islamic State a foothold in Libya will require the emergence of a single government with international and domestic legitimacy and gradually expanding control over Libyan security forces. This will also require overcoming divisions among the currently competing regimes, securing the government against violent pressures from local militant groups, beginning to build regular security forces, and helping the government secure the loyalty and cooperation of nonjihadi militia forces throughout the country.

---

[21] See, for example, Nathalie Guibert, ""La France Mène des Opérations Secrètes en Libie," *Le Monde*, February 24, 2016.

Political and Governance

UN efforts to negotiate an end to the war made halting progress beginning in late 2015. Unfortunately, the UN backed government was challenged by the Tobruk-based powers, particularly because of the opposition of General Khalifa Hiftar, the powerful eastern commander. Hiftar's support in the east had been growing because of his successful, although highly destructive, efforts against extremists in Benghazi. Many in Libya and outside, however, still view Hiftar as an Egyptian proxy with presidential—or even dictatorial—aspirations. In 2016, the UN Special Envoy attempted to push beyond the stalemate with Tobruk by referencing a letter that a majority of the Tobruk parliament had signed as sufficient for the inauguration of the Government of National Accord, and most international powers subsequently recognized it as Libya's official government. If the Government of National Accord is to truly represent the Tobruk factions, however, agreement about Hiftar is likely still needed.

For the Government of National Accord to truly establish itself, it will need to further extend its control over the Tripoli militias while marginalizing the remaining hardline factions of the General National Congress. It is likely that the government will require international military and gendarmerie forces—heavily equipped police with militarylike training—to help protect its operations for an initial period, lest it meet the same fate as its post-Qaddafi predecessors. So far, however, the Government of National Accord has resisted such a deployment. Meanwhile, its effectiveness and legitimacy are declining due to its ongoing difficulties providing public services and governance for the divided country.

Characterizing the foreign force as a training mission would help overcome at least some of these obstacles. Building anything resembling a truly national army will still be a long and arduous process. Libya is still home to several hundred militias, and these are only loosely federated with larger formations. Even the forces of the "Libyan National Army" that are commanded by Hiftar represent a collection of militias rather than a unified fighting force. International actors will need to proceed gradually, using a carrot and stick approach that offers training and equipment to forces that demonstrate allegiance to the

Government of National Accord and that sanctions leaders of forces that do not cooperate. Any such agreement requires not only the support of Libya's local actors but also the cooperation of at least three key groups of external actors.

The first group consists of Egypt, Russia, the United Arab Emirates, and Saudi Arabia, which have been staunch supporters of the Tobruk-based House of Representatives and provided weapons and airpower to General Hiftar's efforts to drive other groups out of Benghazi and eastern Libya. In August 2014, for example, Emirati pilots flying from Egypt intervened directly, striking Islamist militants in Tripoli.[22] The United Arab Emirates have also provided arms directly to Hiftar.[23] Diplomatically, the support of this group would be needed not only for the initial agreement to form a confederal government but also in the event of a power-sharing arrangement in Benghazi or Sirte. In the latter case, the countries might be expected to offer stabilization forces.

The second group consists of countries that have supported the Tripoli government: Turkey, Qatar, and Sudan. The Tobruk government has frequently accused Turkey of ties to more-radical Islamist forces, including Ansar al-Sharia. Several shipments of weapons from Turkey have also been intercepted in the Mediterranean or on route from Sudan, in contravention of the UN arms embargo.[24] While there is no credible evidence that any of these countries is directly supporting the Islamic State, the cooperation of all of them will be necessary to bring the broader Libyan political crisis in which the Islamic State thrives to an end. These external parties will need to actively embrace the objective of eliminating not only the Islamic State, but also Ansar al-Sharia and other jihadist groups. This may be difficult because of the connections between the Islamist forces that these countries support and many of the jihadist groups.

---

[22] David D. Kirkpatrick, "Leaked Emirati Emails Could Threaten Peace Negotiations in Libya" *New York Times*, November 13, 2015.

[23] Girgio Cafiero and Daniel Wagner, "The UAE and Qatar Wage a Proxy War in Libya" *Huffington Post*, December 14, 2015.

[24] Jonathan Schanzer, "Turkey's Secret Proxy War in Libya?" *The National Interest*, March 17, 2015; Fahim Tastekin, "Turkey's War in Libya" *Al-Monitor*, December 4, 2014.

A third group includes Libya's immediate neighbors, especially Tunisia and Algeria. Both Tunisia and Algeria are reluctant to openly countenance any Western intervention in Libya. They will need to be brought into the discussions regarding Libya's future and the composition of any international stabilization force. In addition, they will need to reinforce their own efforts to counter radicalization, fight the groups on their soil, and strengthen border controls.

Security

Although not on the scale of the challenge in Iraq, the military requirements for a successful strategy to roll back the Islamic State in Libya may be significant. If other Islamic State safe havens emerge in the wake of its ouster from Sirte, the United States and other allied countries will likely need to conduct airstrikes against fixed the Islamic State command-and-control points, munitions depots, and training facilities. In the event that Libya's own militias provide the bulk of the force for such operations, the United States and its allies may need to deploy special operations forces to support the Libyans, as well as intelligence, targeting, and direct support. Unlike with Iraq, Syria, and Afghanistan, the United States has generally not considered Libya an area of active hostilities for lethal action, as outlined in the White House's PPG.[25] For much of 2016, however, the White House did include the area around Sirte as a combat zone, so U.S. government agencies could conduct targeted strikes without going following the PPG.[26] This allowed U.S. military forces to conduct a more efficient campaign against an adaptive network of extremist groups, including the Islamic State. Since Libya has an active insurgency and will likely remain a sanctuary for Salafi-jihadist networks in the foreseeable future, the United States should consider including Libya in its list of countries where there are active hostilities.

Demining, counter–IED, and other counterordinance capabilities will also likely be necessary. These capabilities will almost certainly

---

[25] White House, 2013.

[26] Charlie Savage, "U.S. Removes Libya from List of Zones with Looser Rules for Drone Strikes," *New York Times*, January 20, 2017.

need to come from Libya's foreign partners. Ideally, France, Italy, and potentially the UK could provide a significant part of the naval, air, and policing forces required for the operation. This is probably within the reach of these nations, although the United States will have to provide certain specialized requirements. German reconstruction funds and police forces would be equally desirable in a European Union (EU), North Atlantic Treaty Organization (NATO), or other framework.

Meanwhile, protection will be needed against Islamic State attacks elsewhere in Libya—especially Tripoli and Misrata. The Islamic State will likely attempt to conduct attacks elsewhere in the country to distract its attackers, spread out their resources, and sow turmoil within their ranks. Local security forces may require international support in areas that have been liberated from the Islamic State.

At the same time, government facilities across the country will need to be hardened against follow-on attacks from the Islamic State and the other Libyan Salafi-jihadist groups that will likely attempt to take the mantle of Libyan jihad from the Islamic State. Figure 6.2 shows the number of Islamic State attacks in Libya between 2014 and 2017, which peaked at 23 attacks per month in fall 2016. Protecting government facilities from future attacks will require forces and intelligence collection and analysis capabilities to protect the infrastructure. In some areas, Libyan militias may provide these defenses, but effective intelligence collection and analysis will require capabilities beyond those of a typical Libyan militia.

In addition, financial, cyber, covert, and overt military measures will need to be taken to destroy the Islamic State facilitation networks that exist in Derna, Benghazi, Misrata, and elsewhere in Libya. Success in destroying these networks may require financial inducements to tribes currently facilitating the Islamic State, such as the Warshafana and Qaddafa. Libya's border will also need to be reinforced to stem the influx of foreign fighters. This will require development of effective border guards, the establishment of technical systems in Libya's major ports of entry, and improved relations between the central government and the southern tribes that historically have controlled Libya's southern trade routes.

Figure 6.2
Islamic State Attacks in Libya

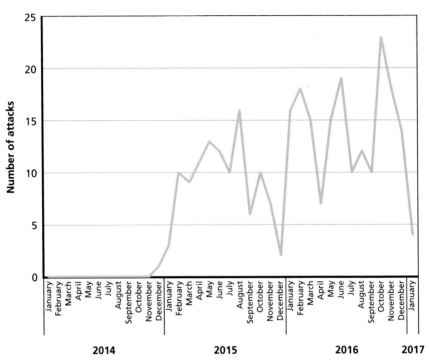

SOURCE: IHS Janes, 2017.
RAND RR1912-6.2

Measures to strengthen Egypt and, especially, Tunisia's ability to prevent foreign fighters from entering or exiting the country will be needed, as well as maritime operations to further check inflows of foreign fighters from Iraq and Syria. Such border control will need to be provided by the neighboring states until the Libyan government is in a position to do its share. The employment of U.S. reconnaissance and intelligence assets could significantly improve border and maritime control and aid local partners' efforts.

Economic and Humanitarian

Beyond these military and diplomatic steps, external powers should prepare for humanitarian relief, along with the logistics and other measures necessary to support that relief. Since military operations may lead to further displacement of the population, preparations for increased refugee flows into Tunisia and Egypt may be needed. Over the medium term, Libya also faces an economic cliff if it is unable to rectify is deteriorating balance-of-payments situation. Libya imports much of its food from abroad. The decline in oil prices and the reduced production due to the war have forced the country to draw down its once sizeable national reserves to cover a gaping current account deficit.

Improvement in overall economic conditions will be a necessary (but not sufficient) means of reducing the appeal of the Islamic State and other groups in Libya. Outside Benghazi and Sirte, the destruction of Libya's civil war to date has been fairly limited, so economic reconstruction to Libya's former level of development may not be onerous. However, economic growth in Libya will remain largely centered on the country's extractive industries, given the lack of other obvious sources of national revenue. Increasing the output of oil with renewed investment should be possible once the civil war has ended. The United States should also encourage implementation of some type of equitable revenue sharing.

Regional Dimension

Stabilizing Libya will require convincing Egypt and the Gulf States to work together, rather than supporting various sides competing for power. Some form of international peacekeeping presence may become necessary, and in that case, European states should be pressed to provide contingents. Unifying Libya under a single government will advance efforts to counter the Islamic State and other extremist groups, contribute to regional efforts in this regard, particularly in Tunisia, and significantly relieve migrant pressures on Western Europe.

The Islamic State in Libya has managed to threaten Tunisia, help strengthen its position in the Sinai, and build connections to sub-Saharan Africa—notably to Boko Haram. A rollback strategy that defeats the Islamic State in Libya should be a blow to the Islamic State across North Africa. But Niger; Sudan; Mali; and, to a lesser degree,

Chad are nevertheless susceptible to spillover effects if the Islamic State is chased out of Libya.

Algeria may also suffer the aftereffects of any successful operation in Libya. Groups operating along the Tunisian border and in the southern reaches of the country could provide new opportunities for Islamic State expansion. Support for Algeria's Islamic State affiliate, Jund al-Khilafah, could grow. There could also be renewed support for al-Qa'ida in the Islamic Maghreb, which is still based in Algeria's Kabylie mountains and continues to operate throughout southern Algeria. In either case, intensified cooperation with Algeria should be pursued to the extent that Algeria is willing.

In Tunisia, the Islamic State could attempt to build on the remnants of Ansar-al Sharia Tunisia just as it had in Libya. Doing so would be more difficult; the environment is less permissive because of Tunisia's somewhat more-capable security services. To prevent potential spillover effects in Tunisia, the United States and its allies will need to redouble their efforts to strengthen that country's nascent democratic institutions, reform the ministry of interior, strengthen the borders, design and implement effective strategies to counter violent extremism, and energize the flagging economy. Tunisia is the world's leading per capita exporter of foreign fighters, with more than 1,000 estimated in Libya alone. Tunisia's domestic political environment is fragile.

CHAPTER SEVEN
Nigeria

Boko Haram is an indigenous Nigerian extremist group operating in the Lake Chad Basin of West Africa. The group chose to affiliate itself with the Islamic State in 2015. It has become the deadliest of the Islamic State's affiliates. At its peak, it controlled the most territory of any of the Islamic State provinces outside Syria and Iraq. As with the Islamic State elsewhere, Boko Haram has suffered significant setbacks in the past two years while its extreme nihilism has taken a toll on its support base and even strained relationships with Islamic State leadership. It is not clear how deep Boko Haram's commitment to the Islamic State brand is, or how long that connection might survive the collapse of the actual caliphate in Iraq and Syria.

With the assistance of the international community, the countries of the Lake Chad Basin have made significant progress in combatting this group to the extent that Boko Haram can no longer claim to control significant population centers. The Buhari administration of Nigeria demonstrated greater will and capacity than its predecessor. Regional partners and the international community likewise made important contributions in addressing the cross-border aspect of the Boko Haram threat. Still, continued improvement in security-sector reform, interagency coordination, and regional cooperation are critical to sustaining this trajectory.

The Rise of Boko Haram in the Lake Chad Basin

Boko Haram seeks to purify Islam from what it considers to be heretical innovation [*bid'a*]. Its name, which roughly means the "Prohibition of Western Education" in Hausa, was given to the group by its detractors in reference to Boko Haram's antipathy toward secular education, which it manifests in the targeting of students and teachers.[1] Members of Boko Haram do not apply this label to themselves. Instead, adherents refer to themselves as either members of a precursor organization called the Sunni Group for Preaching and Jihad [Jama'at Ahl al-Sunna lil Da'wa wa al-Jihad] or as members of the Islamic State West Africa Province, based on the organization's 2015 pledge of loyalty to Islamic State leader Abu Bakr al-Baghdadi.

The group has passed through several phases.[2] The first can be dated to 2002, when the Sunni Group for Preaching and Jihad was established by Muhammad Yusuf in Muslim-majority northern Nigeria. During this period, Boko Haram pursued political change by backing religious conservatives in local elections, growing its base through microcredit programs and other outreach efforts. It also established what it considered to be a model community on the principle of *hijra* [emigration], in which Muslims withdraw from corrupt society to recreate an ideal alternative based on the example of the Prophet Mohammad's pious companions.[3]

The most important locales for Boko Haram at this time were its camp outside Kannama village (Yobe State, Nigeria), where it sought to recreate an "authentic" Muslim community, and Maiduguri (Borno

---

[1]   Lauren Ploch Blanchard, "Nigeria's Boko Haram: Frequently Asked Questions," Washington, D.C., Congressional Research Service, R43558, March 29, 2016.

[2]   Both outside analysts and the group's leadership have used *phases* to describe the evolution of Boko Haram. See Simon Gray and Ibikunle Adeakin, "The Evolution of Boko Haram: From Missionary Activism to Transnational Jihad and the Failure of the Nigerian Security Intelligence Agencies," *African Security*, Vol. 8, No. 3, September 2015, and "Wālī Gharb Ifrīqīya: Al-Shaykh Abu Musa'b al-Barnawi," *An Naba'*, No. 41, August 2016. *An Naba'* is the Islamic State's biweekly Arabic-language publication.

[3]   Zacharias Pieri and Jacob Zenn, "The Boko Haram Paradox: Ethnicity, Religion, and Historical Memory in Pursuit of a Caliphate," *African Security*, Vol. 9, No. 1, March 2016.

State, Nigeria), where it sought to promote the adoption of *sharia* by Nigeria's northern neighbors. Looking back, a current Boko Haram leader describes this period as preparatory phase for future jihad: "[Muhammad Yusuf] called the people to [jihad], but at that point he did not begin his direct jihadist action even though he announced that the primary objective of the organization was jihad."[4]

In the mid-2000s, the group moved to a second phase in its evolution, embarking on violent confrontation with the state. What began with small-scale attacks in Yobe State of Nigeria—where Boko Haram attempted to carve out its own model community—quickly escalated, reaching a crescendo in 2009. Nigerian security forces killed many of the group's members in clashes in Maiduguri, including its leader Muhammad Yusuf, who died while under detention. This event led to the selection of an even more violent successor, Aboubakar Shekau, and further radicalization of the group's rank and file.[5] Shekau increased the tempo of Boko Haram's guerilla attacks and focused on the armed wing of its organization to the exclusion of its other elements. Although Boko Haram became increasingly militant, it remained a local phenomenon. The United States had not yet designated Boko Haram a foreign terrorist organization and Boko Haram had yet to establish strong relationships with regional or international terrorist networks.

The suicide bombing of a UN facility in Nigeria's capital in September 2011 signaled that Boko Haram had larger aspirations. This represented the group's first major attack on foreign interests. The attack occurred soon after Boko Haram members began receiving training at al-Qa'ida in the Islamic Maghreb camps in the Sahel. This shift in capabilities and targeting represents the third phase in Boko Haram's development. As Boko Haram evolved, so did the international community's approach. The United States declared Boko Haram a foreign terrorist organization in 2013 and increased the use of existing collab-

---

[4] "Wālī Gharb Ifrīqīya . . . ," 2016.

[5] Virginia Comolli, "The Regional Problem of Boko Haram," *Survival*, Vol. 57, No. 4, August–September 2015.

orative arrangements, such as the Trans-Sahara Counterterrorism Partnership, to support Nigeria and its neighbors in countering the group.[6]

Boko Haram embarked on its fourth phase in 2014 when it transitioned from guerilla tactics to taking and holding territory, declaring an Islamic state under its control. It was at this time that Boko Haram drew international condemnation for kidnapping nearly 300 Nigerian schoolgirls in Chibok. The attack was initially seen as a symbol to rally efforts against the group, only to become a symbol of government ineptitude after the Jonathan administration failed to track and free the captives.[7] During this period, Boko Haram became more indiscriminate in its use of force, killing an estimated 5,000 civilians in 2014 and up to 2,000 in a single incident in early 2015.[8] In addition to its increased lethality, Boko Haram expanded the geographic scope of its operations to the neighboring countries of Cameroon, Chad, and Niger.

After joining with the Islamic State in March 2015, Boko Haram began to lose territorial control but expanded its offensive operations outside Nigeria. It was responsible for just over 400 attacks from March 2015—the month of its pledge—until the end of that year. Of those attacks, roughly three-quarters took place in Nigeria. Cameroon, Chad, and Niger were the targets of the remaining attacks.[9] Most of the attacks outside Nigeria took place in border areas. However, Boko Haram also penetrated a neighboring capital, N'Djamena, Chad, when it carried out bombings that killed 37 people in June 2015. Boko Haram's territorial control was further reduced in 2016 following Nigerian and allied military operations, and Boko Haram forces retreated to the Mandara Mountains along the Nigeria-Cameroon border.

---

[6] Blanchard, 2016.

[7] Goodluck Jonathan was President of Nigeria from 2010 to 2015. Jonathan is a Christian from the south of Nigeria who succeeded a Muslim from the north of the country, Umaru Yar'Adua, when the latter died while in office.

[8] U.S. Department of State, *Country Reports on Terrorism 2015*, Washington, D.C.: Bureau of Counterterrorism and Countering Violent Extremism, June 2016.

[9] These figures are derived from the data from Global Terrorism Database at the University of Maryland, undated. From March 1, 2015 through the end of that calendar year, Boko Haram carried out 406 attacks in the four countries of interest. Of these, 299 were in Nigeria, 28 in Niger, 26 in Chad, and 53 in Cameroon.

   As Figure 7.1 illustrates, Boko Haram lost considerable ground in Nigeria between 2014 and 2017. Boko Haram controlled 1,330,115 people (0.7 percent of the population) and 18,019 km^2 (2 percent of the territory) in fall 2014. By winter 2016–2017, Boko Haram control had declined to 332,841 people (a 75-percent drop) and 6,041 km^2 (a 67-percent decrease) from 2014 levels.

   As the preceding overview demonstrates, Boko Haram passed through at least four distinct phases. Notwithstanding those changes, several important constants help explain the group's staying power. One is the historical legacy the group can draw on to recruit members. Nigeria may seem odd territory for the caliphate, but Boko Haram portrays the goal of establishing an Islamic state as an extension of

Figure 7.1
Islamic State Control of Territory in Nigeria

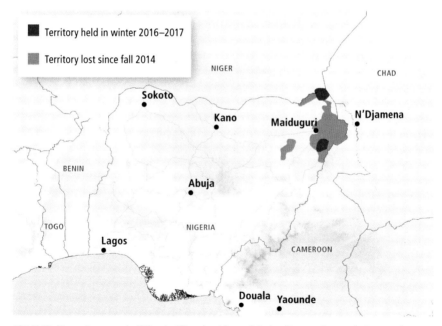

SOURCE: Evan Centanni, "War in Nigeria: Map of Boko Haram Control, September 2014)," *Political Geography Now*, September 29, 2014; Njadvara Musa, "No Progress Until Sambisa Forest Is Cleared of Boko Haram," *Guardian* (Nigeria), November 21, 2016; Blanchard, 2016; "Boko Haram Attacks Jere, . . . ," 2016; authors' estimates.
RAND *RR1912-7.1*

Nigeria's precolonial history. For the group's adherents, this marks a return to a more authentic system of governance that was interrupted first by British rule and then by the Westernized Nigerian elite that led the country after independence.

To make this argument, Boko Haram plays up the two most successful Islamic empires that stretched over Northern Nigeria: the Sokotu caliphate of Usman dan Fodio, which spanned northwest Nigeria, and the Kanem-Borno empire, which covered much of Boko Haram's current area of operations in northeast Nigeria and the broader Lake Chad Basin. Boko Haram sees itself as the new standard-bearer for this historical movement.

Another enduring feature of Boko Haram is the inroads it has made into the Kanuri ethnic group. Boko Haram's top leadership is Kanuri; the group operates in Kanuri territory; many of Boko Haram's rank and file are Kanuri; and its leadership often adopts the moniker *al-Barnawi* (or from Borno State, where the Kanuri predominate). This should not be interpreted to mean that Boko Haram is a front for Kanuri nationalism; Boko Haram privileges religious identity over ethnic identity and is pursuing a religiously inspired project.[10] Rather, the significance of its Kanuri ties is that Boko Haram uses this connection to recruit within the community, playing on Kanuri perceptions that they are disadvantaged relative to other Nigerians, including southern Christians and Hausa- and Fulani-speaking Muslims. Boko Haram has fought the tradition of large dowries that operate as an obstacle to marriage among lower classes, an appealing initiative among poorer Kanuri.[11] In the same vein, Boko Haram is reported to pay its fighters a competitive monthly salary and to convey status by providing motorbikes and the promise of marriage.[12]

---

[10] Alex Thurston, "'The Disease Is Unbelief': Boko Haram's Religious and Political Worldview," Washington, D.C.: Brookings Institution, Analysis Paper No. 22, January 2016.

[11] Olabanji Akinola, "Boko Haram Insurgency in Nigeria: Between Islamic Fundamentalism, Politics, and Poverty," *African Security*, Vol. 8, No. 1, March 2015.

[12] Pieri and Zenn, 2016.

This recruitment strategy fits with Boko Haram's master narrative, which includes a combination of victimhood and exclusivism.[13] Boko Haram presents itself as the champion of a community deprived of its culture by locals imitating Western values. According to this narrative, Boko Haram is a particularly committed defender because it has suffered government repression. The theme is evident in the group's description of the death of its first leader, Muhammad Yusuf, while in the custody of security forces.[14] In 2009, clashes between the group and the state are estimated to have killed as many as one thousand Boko Haram members, reinforcing the victimization narrative. As for Boko Haram's exclusivism, much of its rhetoric focuses on the dilution of authentic Islamic practices by corrupt leaders. To counter this heretical innovation, Boko Haram is quick to evoke *takfir* (the excommunication of a Muslim, punishable by death), which the group uses to justify violence against their coreligionists.

Over the years, intrajihadi disputes have splintered the movement, and tensions are still evident today. The most visible split in the movement is between Boko Haram and two rival factions, Ansaru and the Movement for Oneness and Jihad in West Africa. These splinter groups reveal three main types of division within the Lake Chad branch of the jihadi movement. The first is simple leadership disputes. This factor is most visible in the tension between Ansaru and Boko Haram. Each is led by one of Mohamed Yusuf's deputies, with Ansaru emerging after its leader lost out to Shekau in the effort to succeed Yusuf.[15] The second sort of division revolves around territory and bases of support. The strongest followings for Ansaru and the Movement for Oneness and Jihad in West Africa are in northwestern Nigeria and the Middle Belt region of the country; Boko Haram is strongest in the Kanuri

---

[13] Thurston, 2016.

[14] See Abu Musa'b al-Barnawi's description of the event: "The government apostate attacked the Center for Preaching [markaz al-da'wa] in Maiduguri called the Ibn Taymiya Center. It was the Amir of the group, Abu Yusuf may god have mercy on him, who was the most prominent martyr in that aggression" ("Wālī Gharb Ifrīqīya . . . ," 2016).

[15] Jacob Zenn, "A Biography of Boko Haram and the Bay`a to al-Baghdadi," *CTC Sentinel*, Vol. 8, No. 3, March 2015a.

northeast.[16] The third division revolves around ideology and, in particular, disagreements within Salafi-jihadist circles over Boko Haram's expansive use of *takfir*. Ansaru is much closer to al-Qa'ida's vision, which seeks to confront the "near enemy" without slipping into indiscriminate violence against fellow Muslims.[17] In contrast, Boko Haram shows little concern for Muslim casualties.

This third division involved a dispute between Boko Haram's putative leader, Aboubakar Shekau, and a challenger, Abu Mus'ab al-Barnawi.[18] The particulars of the dispute were rooted in whether it was acceptable to excommunicate—and thus kill—Muslims who live within a corrupt Muslim society but are not actively involved in opposition to it. Both Islamic State leadership and Boko Haram agreed that it was permissible to excommunicate the corrupt rulers, but Boko Haram went a step farther and argued that it was justified to excommunicate and kill Muslims who passively accepted that rule.[19] In that sense, Boko Haram achieved the dubious distinction of being even more violent than Islamic State's core leadership.

Desired End State

Along the spectrum of nihilism, Boko Haram is at the far end of the continuum even relative to other Islamic State provinces. Since Boko Haram is neither unified nor seen as a provider of security, it is one of the more vulnerable Islamic State affiliates.[20]

---

[16] Zenn, 2015a.

[17] Zenn, 2015a.

[18] The dispute is reminiscent of then Al-Qai'da deputy Ayman al-Zawahiri's dispute with Abu Musa'b al-Zarqawi, the former leader of AQI, over Zarqawi's particularly virulent strain of sectarianism.

[19] For Boko Haram, those who refuse to accept this principle are guilty of *irjā'*, postponing judgment on a fellow Muslim's faith. See "Message from the Soldiers," video message from Boko Haram fighters loyal to Aboubakar Shekau, August 7, 2016.

[20] The Center for Civilians in Conflict conducted 250 interviews with citizens, finding that they overwhelmingly blame Boko Haram for the insecurity they face, despite reservations about the capability and professionalism of the security forces (Kyle Dietrich, "'When the

In addition to Boko Haram's inherent weaknesses, the effort to combat the group has received a boost from new leadership in Abuja; the introduction of the Multinational Joint Task Force (MNJTF) to serve as a mechanism for addressing the group's cross-border reach; and increased involvement from the United States and other Western powers that provide unique capabilities, most notably in the area of intelligence, surveillance, and reconnaissance for tracking and targeting Boko Haram militants. Nigeria has a poor track record in prosecuting effective counterinsurgency, and Boko Haram expanded to a force of several thousand that, at its peak, controlled 18,019 km² of territory. But, on balance, the group is vulnerable to significant rollback.

Given these relatively favorable conditions, Nigeria and its international partners should adopt an end state that aims to leave Boko Haram broken, with its remaining cadre contained to the Sambisi Forest in northeast Nigeria, without recourse to safe haven in a neighboring country. While this end state is ambitious and contingent on steps that are described in subsequent sections, it is achievable and should be prioritized and resourced given the tremendous human toll wrought by Boko Haram. Figure 7.2 depicts attacks by Boko Haram in Nigeria, which peaked at nearly 40 attacks per month in summer 2015 and then declined in 2016 as the group lost territory. The data includes attacks before and after Boko Haram pledged *bay'ah* to the Islamic State in March 2015.

U.S. and Allied Steps

Achieving this end state will require a steadfast commitment from the United States and its partners in support of Nigeria and its neighbors.

Political and Governance

Washington's frustrations with Abuja boiled over during the Jonathan administration, largely over the issues of corruption, human rights

---

Enemy Can't See the Enemy, Civilians Become the Enemy': Living through Nigeria's Six-Year Insurgency," Washington, D.C.: Center for Civilians in Conflict, 2015).

Figure 7.2
Islamic State Attacks in Nigeria

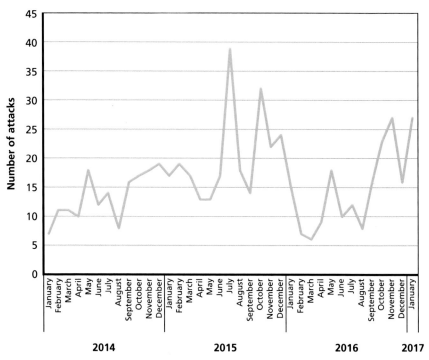

SOURCE: IHS Janes, 2017.
RAND RR1912-7.2

abuses, and general ineptitude. The low point in relations came in
2014, after the U.S. intervened to scuttle an Israeli arms sale of attack
helicopters to Nigeria, and Abuja responded by cancelling a U.S. training mission to assist a Nigerian battalion preparing to combat Boko
Haram.[21] U.S.-Nigerian cooperation under President Muhammadu
Buhari has improved. The new president possesses some natural advantages as a northerner who knows the terrain and spent the bulk of his
professional life in the Nigerian military.

---

[21] Eric Schmitt and Dionne Searcey, "U.S. Plans to Put Advisers on Front Lines of Nigeria's
War on Boko Haram," *New York Times*, February 25, 2016.

Under the Jonathan administration, assistance appeared to be a governed by a *quid pro quo* logic rather than Abuja taking a genuine interest in enhancing the nation's capabilities to confront a shared understanding of the threat. The new president has taken the counterinsurgency mission more seriously, creating the possibility for a more productive partnership with Nigeria's neighbors and the United States.

Security

Nigeria, its neighbors, and international partners have also taken significant steps to improve the effectiveness of the campaign against Boko Haram. Specifically, the joint task force established in 2011 introduced a mechanism for better interagency coordination among Nigeria's armed forces, internal security, intelligence agencies, and border guards to combat Boko Haram.[22] Two years later, regional coordination was strengthened via the creation of an MNJTF, a regional military force authorized by the African Union and led by a Nigerian with deputies drawn from the other Lake Chad Basin countries. Neither of these initiatives completely solved the bureaucratic challenges and sovereignty sensitivities that had undermined previous efforts, but they were important steps in the right direction.

The United States and other key Western partners, particularly France, supported this regional force by providing intelligence, surveillance, and reconnaissance and training and advising missions. Roughly 250 U.S. military personnel support these activities, all deployed throughout the region in noncombat roles.[23] While U.S. support cannot be easily reduced to a dollar figure, the United States has provided more than $400 million in counterterrorism aid specific to the Boko Haram threat.[24] Much of this takes the form of low-visibility activities, although Boko Haram is well aware of Western support. In an August 2016 interview, Abu Musaʻb al-Barnawi noted:

---

[22] Gray and Adeakin, 2015.

[23] Blanchard, 2016.

[24] Blanchard, 2016.

> They [i.e., Chad, Cameroon, Nigeria, and Niger with Western support] direct their ruthless war via a joint operations room in Niger. If they want to mount an attack on us, the American and French Special Forces in Niger send drones to surveil the areas, then the Joint Forces attack under thick air cover.[25]

In addition, the United States does not consider Nigeria to be an area of active hostilities as outlined in the PPG—such as Iraq, Syria, and Afghanistan.[26] Nigeria and its coalition partners have been able to effectively deal with Boko Haram thus far, suggesting that it is probably not necessary for the United States to conduct significant direct action in the country.

The most significant changes President Buhari introduced included injecting new urgency into the campaign against Boko Haram, moving the MNJTF headquarters to Maiduguri, dismissing ineffective senior leaders from the military, and stressing the need for security forces to respect human rights during their operations.[27] Further professionalizing the Nigerian security apparatus is a long-term project crucial to sustaining progress against Boko Haram.[28] Notwithstanding initial steps at reform, President Buhari inherited security forces that the U.S. judged as having "perpetrated extrajudicial killings, and engaged in torture, rape, arbitrary detention, mistreatment of detainees, and destruction of property."[29]

There are several steps partners can take to further support Nigeria and neighboring countries in the Lake Chad Basin as they combat Boko Haram. The first is to fill out and diversify the MNJTF. The African Union has authorized MNJTF to field 8,700 soldiers drawn from the armed forces of Nigeria, Niger, Chad, Cameroon, and Benin.

---

[25] "Wālī Gharb Ifrīqīya . . . ," 2016.

[26] White House, 2013.

[27] Dietrich, 2015.

[28] International Crisis Group, "Nigeria: The Challenge of Military Reform," June 6, 2016.

[29] U.S. Department of State, "Nigeria 2015 Human Rights Report," *Country Reports on Human Rights Practices for 2015*, Washington, D.C.: Bureau of Democracy, Human Rights, Labor, 2015a.

However, the force is largely comprised of personnel from two countries—Nigeria and Chad—who operate within their own national constructs rather than as a truly joint force. Since Boko Haram has a cross-border area of operations and recruits heavily from the Kanuri population, which also spreads across borders, it is critical that the MNJTF develop into a genuinely integrated effort.

Another area in which the international community can support regional partners is in designing risk mitigation strategies for dealing with the irregular local defense forces—called civilian joint task forces (CJTFs)—that local communities have established to protect themselves against Boko Haram incursions. As other counterinsurgency campaigns have demonstrated, local defense forces can be critical to meeting the requirements for collecting intelligence and holding territory seized from insurgents. By some accounts, CJTFs have played an important role in efforts against Boko Haram. Nigerian authorities have also taken some initial steps to integrate these forces into a more formal chain of command, thus mitigating the risk that of CJTFs becoming predatory forces that eventually pose a security challenge to their individual communities or to the state.[30]

Given that the United States and Western partners have recent experience—both positive and negative—with local defense forces in prosecuting counterinsurgency campaigns, Western countries are well placed to advise the Nigerians on approaches that maximize the benefit from CJTFs while avoiding the pitfalls that can accompany reliance on nonstate security actors. U.S. experience includes the Citizen Armed Force Geographical Unit in the Philippines; the 2006 Sunni Awakening in Iraq's Anbar Province; the Afghan local police; various local forces in Iraq and Syria, including the YPG, Peshmerga, Sunni Arab "National Mobilization"; and Misratan militias in Libya.[31]

Western countries also need to consider how best to use intelligence, surveillance, and reconnaissance to incentivize regional part-

---

[30] Dietrich, 2015.

[31] For a good review of this issue, see Austin Long, Stephanie Pezard, Bryce Loidolt, and Todd C. Helmus, *Locals Rule: Historical Lessons for Creating Local Defense Forces for Afghanistan and Beyond*, Santa Monica, Calif.: RAND Corporation, MG-1232-CFSOCC-A, 2012.

ners to adopt best practices in their counterinsurgency operations. That leverage is somewhat diminished by the fact that Nigeria fields its own Chinese-manufactured unmanned aerial vehicles—the CH-3 variant—for surveillance and strike. This poses a difficult policy question regarding whether Western partners want to assist Nigeria in providing intelligence that can be used to inform Nigeria's own strikes. Such strikes would presumably decrease the risk of civilian casualties, given the quality of the intelligence, surveillance, and reconnaissance, but could also enable a partner with a troubling record of human rights violations to take on such missions. The stakes are high, as demonstrated by Nigeria's mistaken airstrike on an IDP camp in January 2017 that killed dozens, including local Red Cross staff.[32]

The United States and its Western partners can make several further contributions to the fight against Boko Haram. The first would be to continue pressing for reform of the Nigerian security services that will make recent gains sustainable over the long term. In particular, this means reigning in the corruption that erodes the capability of Nigerian security forces by depriving them of resources. It also means greater accountability for human rights violations that alienate security forces from the communities they are mandated to protect and whose support they need to carry out their mission. A second contribution is to work with the Nigerian government on a plan that allows the state to leverage the contributions of local defense forces but without creating the conditions for these forces to evolve into a menace to security themselves. This will require a thoughtful design and execution of demobilization, disarmament, and reintegration of these forces once they are no longer required. The poor state of Nigeria's formal security apparatus suggests that the conventional approach of integrating the forces into existing institutions may not be the right one. Whether that means CJTFs remains as a separate institution or demobilize entirely is a Nigerian decision but one Western partners are well placed to advise on, given their own experience working through nonstate security actors.

---

[32] Dionne Searcey, "Nigerian Jet Mistakenly Bombs Refugee Camp, Killing Scores," *New York Times*, January 17, 2017.

Economic and Humanitarian

Continued humanitarian and development assistance will be needed for this region. Fighting in the Lake Chad Basin has created a significant humanitarian crisis. In Niger's Diffa region on the northeastern border of Nigeria, for example, more than 280,000 people were displaced in 2016 because of the fighting. Most of the displaced do not live in refugee camps but in ramshackle settlements next to a national highway. The closing of markets and suspension of trade contributed to an economic downturn.[33] The region was already in dire shape. Of the 20 million people living in the Lake Chad Basin, 9.2 million were in need of lifesaving assistance in 2016; 5.2 million people were severely food insecure; and 2.7 million were forced from their homes.[34]

Regional Dimension

Since Boko Haram continues to operate throughout the region—including in the neighboring countries of Chad, Cameron, Benin, and Niger—multinational cooperation will remain critical over the long run. There has already been some cooperation through the MNJTF, with financial assistance from outside donors. The EU provided $54 million to support the construction and maintenance of MNJTF headquarters in N'Djamena and sector headquarters in Cameroon and Niger. The EU also provided transport and communication assets to help improve coordination and command of military operations.[35] The United States should continue providing equipment, logistics support, and training to MNJTF countries. Still, the MNJTF has been plagued by a series of political, logistical, technical, and financial challenges

---

[33] Lucas Destrijcker, "Boko Haram Refugees in Niger Find Safety, But Lack Aid," Al Jazeera, September 27, 2016.

[34] UN High Commissioner for Refugees, "Lake Chad Basin Emergency Response," Geneva, July 2016b.

[35] Federica Mogherini, EU High Representative/Vice-President of the Commission; Neven Mimica, EU Commissioner for International Cooperation and Development; and Smail Chergui, AU Commissioner for Peace and Security, "Joint Communiqué," August, 1, 2016.

that have undermined its effectiveness.[36] One key area of future cooperation is improving border security to help identify and interdict Boko Haram's movement across borders.

Washington may also want to consider a more robust posture in the region. While the United States has military bases in East Africa, particularly in Djibouti, it has nothing comparable in West Africa, despite significant activity from the Islamic State and other Salafi-jihadist groups. The United States is apparently investing at least $50 million in a new drone base in central Niger, although there may be restrictions in what the U.S. military can do and how many U.S. forces or aircraft can be stationed there. Even with a base in Niger, the United States might consider negotiating access arrangements with one or more other countries in the region to station U.S. military forces and fly combat and surveillance aircraft. U.S. access in Africa has been notoriously difficult because of political sensitivities, making it important to ensure some redundancy.

Overall, major progress has been made in the fight against Boko Haram. The group's extreme ideology—and operationalization of that ideology through atrocities against civilians—has further antagonized the communities in which it seeks to operate. In addition to Boko Haram's own missteps, the Nigerian government has demonstrated better leadership under the current Buhari administration and has improved regional coordination with neighbors to address the shared threat. Western partners should continue to assist in these efforts to consolidate current gains and work toward an end state in which Boko Haram lacks the capability to threaten regional security.

---

[36] William Assanvo, Jeannine Ella A. Abatan, and Wendyam Aristide Sawadogo, "Assessing the Multinational Joint Task Force Against Boko Haram," Pretoria, South Africa: Institute for Security Studies, West Africa Report No. 19, September 2016.

CHAPTER EIGHT

Egypt

Egypt's tumultuous transition has created fertile conditions for the growth of the Islamic State in that country. Following the 2011 demonstrations in Tahrir Square, Egypt has been buffeted by political upheaval, the flow of weapons from the Libyan uprising, and the release of hardened jihadists from Egypt's prisons. At the same time, Egypt's military has been stretched by balancing its security role with a more direct hand in governing. Terrorist organizations have taken advantage of the circumstances, most notably in the Sinai, where an Islamic State affiliate is waging an insurgency against the state. Egypt's approach to combatting the Islamic State, which has mixed counterterrorism objectives with the threat to delegitimize political opposition, has contributed to the challenge.

Egypt, with the support of the international community, has the capability to degrade the Islamic State and improve security in Egypt and the region. By exploiting that group's inherent weaknesses and adopting best practices in counterterrorism and counterinsurgency, Egypt can keep the Islamic State from controlling population centers in the Sinai; weaken its network in Upper Egypt, Cairo, and the Delta; and limit its ability to use Libya and Egypt's Western desert region as sanctuary.

The Rise of the Islamic State in Egypt

The Islamic State–Sinai Peninsula seeks to overthrow the Egyptian government, which it claims to be an intermediate step to "liberating"

Jerusalem.[1] Until it reaches that stage in the struggle, the Islamic State–Sinai Peninsula is devoted to establishing an Islamic emirate in the Sinai that is ruled by its interpretation of sharia law. Since November 2014, the group has recognized Abu Bakr al-Baghdadi as the overall caliph of the state they seek to build and has encouraged other jihadist groups to accept his leadership, so as not to divide efforts. Perhaps the most prominent theme in the Islamic State–Sinai Peninsula's discourse is revenge [al-tha'r], with the group often describing its operations as revenge for wrongs perpetrated against Muslims. This reasoning applies not only to its attacks on Egyptian security forces but also to its attacks on foreign interests, such as the Russian airliner it downed, which it described as retribution for Russian involvement in Syria.[2]

As with other Islamic State provinces, the so-called Sinai State was established by a preexisting jihadi group which "rehatted" after pledging an oath of allegiance to the Islamic State in 2014. The predecessor group, Ansar Bayt al-Maqdis, emerged during the chaotic period following Egypt's 2011 uprising.[3] Today the Islamic State's main area of operations is the Sinai Peninsula, although its roots are transnational in that it has ties to Palestinian militant groups and carries out attacks on the Israeli border in addition to its more-frequent operations inside Egypt. A vacuum of authority in neighboring Libya has also enabled the group to take refuge on the border and open a second front against the Egyptian state in its sparsely populated Western desert region.

The focus of this section is on the Islamic State–Sinai Peninsula; however, breakaway factions that remain loyal to al-Qa'ida operate well beyond the Sinai Peninsula. The peninsula, and more specifically a

---

[1]   Media Office of Sinai State, "Min Wilayat Sayna' ila Bayt al-Maqdis [From Sinai State to Jerusalem]," November 2015.

[2]   Media Office of Ninawa Province, "Isqāt al-Tā'ira al-Rūsīya Thā'ran li Ahalina fī Bilād al-Shām [Downing of the Russian Plane Is Revenge for Our People in the Levant]," November 2015.

[3]   Going back further, Islamic State's lineage in the Sinai can be traced to at-Tawhid wa al-Jihad and the Mujahideen Shura Council, both of which preceded Ansar Bayt al-Maqdis. See Mustafa Zahran, "al-Tanzhīmāt al-Musallaha fī Saynā' wa Imkānīyāt at-Tamadud Dākhilian [Armed Groups in the Sinai and their Potential to Spread Internally]," Istanbul: Egyptian Institute for Political and Strategic Studies, December 20, 2015.

triangle within in that connects the medium-sized towns of Rafah, Al-Arish, and Sheikh Zuwaid, is where the Islamic State–Sinai Peninsula operates most freely.[4] The Islamic State–Sinai Peninsula enjoys sufficient freedom of movement in this area to mount assaults against checkpoints, security outposts, and administrative buildings. More than hit and runs, these attacks can leave the Islamic State–Sinai Peninsula in control of a neighborhood for hours before security forces can expel the attackers. As for the more populous Nile River valley, terrorist networks that grew out of Ansar Bayt al-Maqdis but subsequently split with the Islamic State–Sinai Peninsula over the latter's oath to the Islamic State share the territory with the Sinai State. The best known of these networks are those loyal to Hisham 'Ashmawi, who is believed to be behind many operations in the Nile Valley and Western Egypt.[5]

Although Egypt is the Arab world's most populous country, the Islamic State–Sinai Peninsula is not as large as some other Islamic State affiliates. Whereas Boko Haram and the Islamic State's Libyan province can claim upwards of 5,000 fighters, estimates put the Islamic State–Sinai Peninsula's strength at several hundred to perhaps 1,000 fighters.[6] But this group's smaller numbers have not prevented it from maintaining a high tempo of operations in northeast Sinai or carrying out periodic spectacular attacks, most notably the assassination of Egypt's Prosecutor General in 2014 and the downing of a Russian civilian airliner that killed more than 200 people after its takeoff from

---

[4]   The largest of the three towns and the capital of North Sinai governorate is al-Arish, with an estimated population of 176,294 (about 40 percent of the governorate's total population). See the official North Sinai Governorate website.

[5]   Hisham 'Ashmawi is 35-year-old jihadist leader who previously served in Egypt's special forces. After being expelled from the military for his extremist views, he established a terrorist cell with other former security personnel. He is believed to have travelled to Syria in 2013 to receive additional training and experience. Egyptian authorities believe he is behind the failed assassination attempt on then–Interior Minister Mohammed Ibrahim, the successful assassination of Prosecutor General Hisham Barakat, and the Farfara Oasis attack in Western Egypt that killed 22 soldiers. See Salwa El-Zoghby, "15 Ma'lūma 'an Hisham 'Ashmawi, al-'Aql al-Mudabbir li Ightiyāl al-Nā'ib al-'Amm [15 Facts About Hisham 'Ashmawi, the Mastermind of the Assassination of the Prosecutor General]," *al-Watan*, July 2, 2015.

[6]   U.S. State Department's Counterterrorism Bureau, "Country Reports on Terrorism 2015," June 2016; Tahrir Institute for Middle East Policy, "Wilayat Sinai," undated.

Sharm El Sheikh in 2015. The group controls little territory or population but does enjoy freedom of movement in parts of the Sinai (see Figure 8.1) and in the desert that spans Western Egypt and Eastern Libya. But it has not established an overt base of operations that serves as its capital. The Islamic State's control of territory did not change much between 2015 and 2017. It remained relatively steady in an area that covered 910 km², with a population of approximately 100,000

Figure 8.1
Islamic State Control of Territory in Egypt

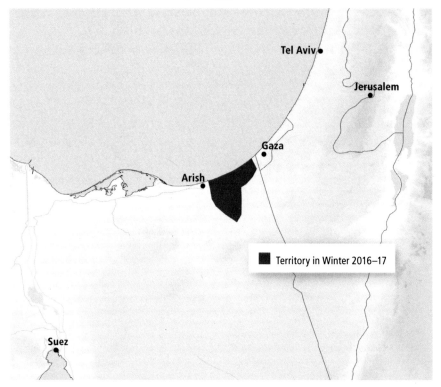

SOURCE: Jantzen W. Garnett, "An Islamic State in the Sinai," *Journal of International Security Affairs*, No. 28, Spring/Summer 2015; "Sinai Province: Egypt's Most Dangerous Group," British Broadcasting Corporation, May 12, 2016; Yasmin Faruki, Jenna Gowell, and Laura Hoffman, "ISIS's Wilayat Sinai Launches Largest Offensive in Sheikh Zuweid," Washington, D.C.: Institute for the Study of War, July 2, 2015; authors' estimates.
RAND RR1912-8.1

residents, particularly around such villages as Sheikh Zuweid. This represents roughly 0.1 percent of Egypt's total size and population.

The Islamic State–Sinai Peninsula's limitations in manpower are somewhat offset by its access to relatively advanced weapons. Specifically, it has acquired a rocket arsenal that it has used to launch occasional attacks on Eilat Israel. The group has also used antitank weapons, demonstrated first in a cross-border attack on Israel and again in an attack off the coast of Rafah in which onshore assailants are suspected to have fired an antitank missile to strike an Egyptian coast guard vessel.[7] And the Islamic State–Sinai Peninsula has also shown some limited antiair capability, most notably when it shot down an Egyptian helicopter in the Sinai using a man-portable air-defense system.[8] In addition to its access to relatively advanced weapons, the Islamic State–Sinai Peninsula has penetrated the operational security of Egyptian security forces. Its car bombings of security installations; hijacking of an Egyptian naval vessel; and assassination of key security officials, such as Mohammed Mabrouk, all indicate insider knowledge of the forces it targets.[9]

Early in its existence, Ansar Bayt al-Maqdis was best known for bomb attacks on Egypt's natural gas infrastructure that highlighted a contentious political issue: Cairo's sale of energy to Tel Aviv at what many Egyptians perceived to be below-market rates. But the group remained obscure until 2012, when it launched an ambush of Egyptian security forces in the Sinai border town of Rafah, killing 16 soldiers as they were breaking their Ramadan fast. That attack led then-President Mohamed Morsi to sack his defense chief, replacing him with a general from military intelligence he believed to be more pliant, 'Abdel Fattah El-Sisi, who would depose him a year later.

---

[7]   Bill Roggio, "Islamic State Strikes Egyptian Naval Vessel off Sinai Coast," *Long War Journal*, July 16, 2015.

[8]   Mohamed Bassiuni 'Abd al-Halim, "al-Hurūb al-Hajīna: Dalālāt Imtilāk al-Irhābīyīn lil Sawārīkh Mahmūla fī al-Sharq al-Awsat [Hybrid Wars: Evidence of Terrorist Acquisition of Portable Missiles in the Middle East]," Cairo: Regional Center for Strategic Studies, April 26, 2016.

[9]   Mokhtar Awad and Samuel Tadros, "Bay'a Remorse? Wilayat Sinai and the Nile Valley," *CTC Sentinel*, Vol. 8, No. 8, August 2015.

The Islamic State–Sinai Peninsula has targeted Egyptian secu-rity forces, killing hundreds in the process.[10] It has also expanded its operational footprint, carrying out attacks in Cairo, the Nile Delta region, and western Egypt, although its center of gravity remains in the al-Arish, Rafah, and Sheikh Zuwaid area of northeast Sinai. The group's most common tactics are car bomb attacks on security installa-tions; IED attacks on convoys; small-arms attacks on desert outposts; and assassinations of officials from the Egyptian Ministry of Defense, Ministry of Interior, and judiciary. The group goes so far as to ask sym-pathizers among the Egyptian public to report on local security forces, providing intelligence that can be operationalized in its assassinations.[11]

In addition to its campaign against Egyptian security forces, the group targets Egyptian Copts, such as bombing St. Mark's Cathedral in 2016, and foreign interests, such as downing of the Russian civilian airliner in 2015. The group is also notorious for attacks against com-munities in the Sinai that it accuses of being informants, with reprisals taking the form of beheadings used to deter future cooperation with Egyptian security.[12] Figure 8.2 summarizes attacks in Egypt between 2014 and 2016, which peaked at more than 30 per month in summer 2016. The data include attacks both before and after Ansar Bayt al Maqdis formally pledged *bay'ah* to the Islamic State in November 2014.

The Egyptian security services have waged an intense but at times counterproductive campaign against the Islamic State–Sinai Penin-sula. The government has stressed the military dimension of its cam-paign and defaulted to the use of conventional military tactics, such as helicopter gunship attacks on suspected terrorist hideouts.[13] To counter

---

[10] Omar Ashour, "Sinai's Stubborn Insurgency," *Foreign Affairs*, November 8, 2015

[11] Ali Abdelaty and Ahmed Aboulenein, "Islamic State Extending Attacks Beyond Sinai to Egyptian Heartland" Reuters, January 25, 2017.

[12] See, for example, Islamic State-Sinai Peninsula's warning that, "For anyone who provides assistance in any form to the apostate army or police . . .we will carry out the legitimate pun-ishment. There will be no distinction between the apostate and whoever helps him" (Sinai State, "Tahdhīr wa wa'īd li min a'ān junūd ar-ridda wa at-tandīd [Warning and Threat to Anyone Who Helps the Condemned Soldiers of Apostasy]," communiqué, March 26, 2015).

[13] Zack Gold, "Salafi Jihadist Violence in Egypt's North Sinai: From Local Insurgency to Islamic State Province," The Hague: International Centre for Counter-Terrorism, April 2016.

**Figure 8.2
Islamic State Attacks in Egypt**

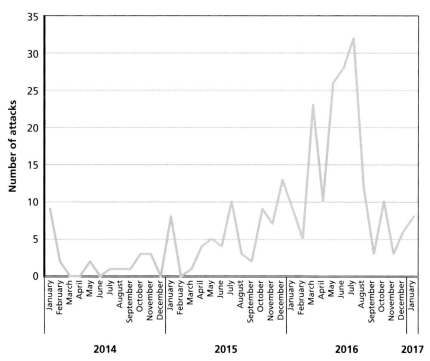

SOURCE: IHS Janes, 2017.
RAND *RR1912-8.2*

smuggling and coordination between Egyptian and Palestinian militants, the regime razed a 1-km buffer zone along its border with Gaza, bulldozing residential areas in the process. And Cairo has declared emergency law in the Sinai, which enabled curfews and afforded security forces wide discretion in detaining suspects. Not surprisingly, the Islamic State–Sinai Peninsula seized on these tactics to allege government repression and mobilize public support against the regime.[14] The

[14] The Islamic State–Sinai Peninsula has issued four videos under the heading "Crimes of the Alliance of Jews and Apostate Army against our people in the Sinai." All allege to show excessive use of force, the destruction of property including homes and farms, and the Egyptian government's recruitment of local informants. The Jihadology website has posted a series of four videos, the fourth of these (the page has links to the other three) is Islamic State,

group's efforts are aided by a legacy of distrust of the central government stemming from the area's relative underdevelopment; the military's seizure of coastal land, particularly in South Sinai, for its own
economic interests; Sinai's isolation during the period of Israeli occupation (1967–1982); and the tribal nature of local communities that
distinguish the Sinai from the urban areas of mainland Egypt.[15]

The Islamic State–Sinai Peninsula is the most lethal terrorist
organization in Egypt, but not the only one. The U.S. government has
also designated Ajnad Misr, a group known for small bomb attacks in
Cairo, as a foreign terrorist organization. Legacy designations remain
in place for radical groups, such as al-Gama'a al-Islamiya, that operated
in Upper Egypt in the 1990s. In addition, terrorist cells, such as those
directed by Hisham 'Ashmawi, are often lumped together with the
Islamic State–Sinai Peninsula, given that they also grew out of Ansar
Bayt al-Maqdis, although 'Ashmawi's group remains loyal to al-Qa'ida
and split with the Islamic State–Sinai Peninsula over the issue.[16]

The Egyptian regime's definition of which groups qualify as terrorist organizations is more expansive than Washington's. For example,
Cairo labeled the Muslim Brotherhood a terrorist entity in 2013 under
a far-reaching law in which posing a "threat to national unity" is sufficient grounds for designation.[17] The U.S. government has not followed
suit, although some members of the Muslim Brotherhood advocated
for violence, and some disaffected members of the Muslim Brotherhood joined the ranks of Ajnad Misr and even the Islamic State–Sinai
Peninsula.[18]

"Documenting the Crimes of the Alliance of the Jews and Army of Apostasy Against Our
People in the Sinai #4—Wilāyat Sīnā' (Sinai)," February 9, 2015 (with links to earlier videos
in the series).

[15] Mohannad Sabry, *Sinai: Egypt's Linchpin, Gaza's Lifeline, Israel's Nightmare*, Cairo:
American University in Cairo Press, October 2015.

[16] Awad and Tadros, 2015.

[17] John Kerry, "Certification Pursuant to Section 7041(a)(6)(c) of the Department of State,
Foreign Operations, and Related Programs Appropriation Act, 2015" May 12, 2015.

[18] Eric Trager and Marina Shalabi, "Egypt's Muslim Brotherhood Gets a Facelift: The
Movement's Young Leaders Turn Revolutionary to Stay Relevant," *Foreign Affairs*, May 20,
2015.

Desired End State

Given the depth of grievances in northern Sinai, the Egyptian regime's often counterproductive approach to counterterrorism, and the specter of Egyptian fighters returning home from Syria and Iraq, a realistic end state will inevitably fall short of the ideal in which the Islamic State–Sinai Peninsula and like-minded groups are eliminated altogether.[19] An achievable end state that would serve the goals of Egypt and the international community includes denying the Islamic State–Sinai Peninsula the ability to hold population centers, denying the group sanctuary and a supply line from the desert that spans eastern Libya and western Egypt and connects with the Sinai, and limiting the group's ability to sustain its weak network in the Nile Delta or expand its network to Upper Egypt.

Although a more democratic Egypt would be laudable, a political transformation in Cairo, which is unlikely in either the near or medium term, is not a requirement for degrading the Islamic State–Sinai Peninsula. The end state outlined above can be realized through changes in the counterterrorism and counterinsurgency strategies the Egyptian regime employs.

U.S. and Allied Steps

A more effective rollback strategy would deny the Islamic State–Sinai Peninsula freedom of movement by eliciting cooperation from credible local leaders—particularly from the Tarabin and Sawarka tribes—to facilitate a local check on Islamic State expansion. A second step is improving civilian security in the most vulnerable areas—currently, the northeast portion of the Sinai Peninsula, in which al-Arish, Rafah, and Shaikh Zuwaid are the largest population centers. Improving security

19 Zack Gold and Elissa Miller, "Egypt's Theory of Terrorism," *Foreign Affairs*, June 16, 2016. In addition, between 600 and 1,000 Egyptians have travelled to Syria and Iraq to fight for the Islamic State. See Hardin Lang and Muath Al Wari, "The Flow of Foreign Fighters to the Islamic State Assessing the Challenge and the Response," Washington, D.C.: Center for American Progress, March 2016.

in these communities is not just desirable but also a means of enhancing the government's ability to cultivate the intelligence required to penetrate the Islamic State–Sinai Peninsula's network. A third component of a successful rollback strategy would be to strengthen the same communities against the group's recruitment. Improved security will help in this regard but needs to be supplemented by targeted economic development that creates opportunities for the region's population.

Political and Governance

One component of a more effective rollback strategy should be engagement with tribes in the Sinai Peninsula that can become allies of the state in pushing back the Islamic State's encroachment on their traditional influence. At present, the Islamic State–Sinai Peninsula has shown some ability to recruit individual fighters from Sinai's tribes, but it would be a misstatement to suggest that there is anything akin to a pro-Islamic State tribe on the peninsula. Just the opposite; the Tarabin, one of the major tribes in the areas of North Sinai in which the Islamic State–Sinai Peninsula is most active, announced the intention to fight the group after it had carried out several assassinations of leading sheikhs from their federation.[20] Closer coordination between tribal elements and the 2nd Land Army, which has responsibility for Egyptian military operations in North Sinai, could help limit the Islamic State–Sinai Peninsula's freedom of movement. At present, cooperation is constrained by the inability of Egyptian forces to protect communities that are vulnerable to Islamic State reprisals and a continued resentment of the Egyptian state that can lead some residents to tolerate or sympathize with the Islamic State–Sinai Peninsula, despite its brutality.

Based on its experience supporting local communities to resist the Islamic State in Syria and Iraq—and before that, AQI—the United States should advise Egypt on how to better employ local actors in counterterrorism and counterinsurgency operations. In general, Cairo has pursued a quid pro quo approach to relations with Sinai tribes,

---

[20] "Qabā'il Sīnā' Tatlub Mawāfaqat al-Jaysh 'ala Qitāl Ibnā'iha li Dā'sh [Sinai Tribes Ask for the Army's Agreement That Their Sons Fight ISIL]," Al Arabiya, April 28, 2015.

offering sweeteners, such as the release of Sinai residents jailed for smuggling and other offenses, in return for specific forms of cooperation. This conditional one-off engagement needs to evolve into sustained cooperation that builds from trust. Investment in the Sinai that benefits local residents is one way for the Egyptian government to signal its intentions. However, economic assistance should be supplemented by a commitment to civilian security that communicates shared sacrifice. The United States and its Arab partners, such as Jordan, that were critical to the Anbar Awakening in Iraq can assist Cairo by distilling the lessons from that experience including the shortcomings that led to its reversal.

Security

The main vehicle for channeling U.S. assistance to Egypt is the annual foreign military financing allotment, which by precedent—not by treaty—is funded at $1.3 billion. In spring 2015, the U.S. administration adopted a policy change linking the security assistance provided through foreign military financing to four missions: counterterrorism, border security, Sinai security, and maritime security.[21] The policy was designed to start a process of shifting Egypt's acquisitions away from those suited for conventional military operations to counterterrorism. Although an admirable goal, the near-term effect on Egypt's ability to combat the Islamic State–Sinai Peninsula will be limited because the policy change is not scheduled to take effect until fiscal year 2018.[22]

---

[21] Jeremy Sharp, "Egypt: Background and U.S. Relations," Washington, D.C.: Congressional Research Service, RL33003, February 25, 2016.

[22] Whether Egypt is open to a shift in its acquisition priorities to better align with the terrorism threat it faces remains unclear. There are reasons to be dubious given the Egyptian Armed Forces' long-standing investments in M1A1 tanks and F-16 fighter aircraft; the political economy of acquisition decisions, in which the military's economic interests figure heavily; and the need to at least appear to be building a military to deter Israel, given public sentiment on that issue. American leverage is also undermined by the fact that the policy change did not take effect until the new U.S. administration took office—which could then choose to embark on a different course—and that the policy carves out funds for sustainment of weapons systems already in Egypt's arsenal. Through recent purchases of Raphael fighters and Mistral ships from France and continued security cooperation with Russia,

Should this policy succeed, it could require decades to transform the orientation and force structure of a military as large as the one in Egypt.

What the United States can do in the near term is to advise and train Egyptian security forces in counterterrorism and counterinsurgency best practices. Egypt's current approach to security provision in the Sinai is reactive and prioritizes the security of the mainland over the peninsula. This approach is reflected in Egypt's garrisoning of security forces in outposts that are there to respond to security incidents, as well as in Egypt's establishment of checkpoints on major roads to prevent the Islamic State–Sinai Peninsula from moving men and materiel to the mainland. The deployment of military forces to the Sinai and the continuation of checkpoints on the major roads crossing the Suez Canal are necessary but should be supplemented by the introduction of a population-centric strategy in which internal security forces establish a presence in the Sinai Peninsula's population centers. The goal would be to create conditions under which local residents have the confidence to report on Islamic State–Sinai Peninsula activities, providing the government with intelligence necessary to penetrate and ultimately to break the terrorist network.

Economic and Humanitarian

The United States can also help Egypt advance its objectives via targeted economic development projects in the Sinai that are designed to demonstrate the government's commitment to improving the welfare of this area.[23] At present, all the government's top officials in North Sinai are former generals from its armed services, reinforcing a perception that the government's view is that the territory is a security problem rather than a constituency to be served and integrated into the

---

Egypt has demonstrated that American conditions can be countered by diversifying security relationships.

[23] To be clear, the rationale for such investment is based on an assumption that economic development and an improvement in service delivery in this region will make local populations more receptive to cooperating with government counterterrorism efforts. There is insufficient information on the profile of Islamic State–Sinai Peninsula fighters to know if they themselves are from lower socioeconomic status groups or are engaging in a misguided attempt to champion the cause of neglected populations.

country.[24] Perhaps the Egyptian military can be encouraged to move a few of the factories that it owns to this region. The United States should also encourage the development of better land transportation in and to the region, tax incentives for investment, and the placement of some government offices there.

Egypt's official statistics suggest a highly variable employment picture in North Sinai. In 2013, Egypt's Central Agency for Public Mobilization and Statistics (CAPMAS) ranked North Sinai as having the seventh worst unemployment rate (15.7 percent) of the country's 27 governorates. A year later, CAPMAS reported a much improved picture (11.3 percent unemployment), which, if accurate, would rank North Sinai better off than the national average.[25] This large swing may be due to data-quality issues or may reflect the ups and downs of the security situation, smuggling, and tourism on the region's livelihood. Whatever the true magnitude of unemployment and other development challenges in North Sinai, the perception of underdevelopment and central government neglect is a common theme in the Islamic State–Sinai Peninsula's messaging that should be addressed.[26] And given that the population of North Sinai encompasses just over 450,000 residents, roughly 5 percent of Egypt's total population, doing so is attainable.[27]

---

[24] At the time of this writing, the Governor of North Sinai is General Abd al-Fattah Harhour; the Secretary General is General Sameh Abdullah; and the Deputy Secretary General is General Mohammed Ibrahim al-Saadni.

[25] In 2013, North Sinai's unemployment rate was estimated at 15.7 percent, 2.5 percent higher than the national average of 13.2 percent. In 2014, North Sinai's unemployment rate was estimated at 11.3 percent, 1.7 percent less than the national average of 13.2 percent. See CAPMAS, "Statistical Yearbook—Labor," 2015.

[26] Mohamed Shoman, "Kayfa Nantasir 'ala al-Irhāb fī Sīnā'? [How Can We Be Victorious over Terrorism in Sinai?]," *Al-Hayat*, November 5, 2014.

[27] On its website, CAPMAS recorded North Sinai's population at 458,983 as of March 8, 2017.

Regional Dimension

Within the region, the partners best positioned to support Egypt in advancing Sinai's development are Saudi Arabia and the United Arab Emirates, which have become the major benefactors of the Sisi regime since the July 2013 removal of then-President Morsi. Fortunately, the Gulf Cooperation Council (GCC) states do appear attentive to the challenge and have launched several initiatives to improve the welfare of Sinai communities. Specifically, the GCC states and the Arab Fund for Economic and Social Development have pledged more than $2 billion to Sinai development projects.[28] Several important steps lie ahead, including the disbursement of funds and execution of the projects, to say nothing of testing the assumption that the investment will lead to improved perceptions of government legitimacy and decrease the pool of Islamic State–Sinai Peninsula recruits. Despite these "ifs," GCC efforts are a step in the right direction and should be encouraged for balancing what to date has been Egypt's military-centric approach to combatting terrorism.

Israel is another important partner for Egypt in its campaign against the Islamic State–Sinai Peninsula. By many accounts, cooperation between Cairo and Tel Aviv is at a historic high.[29] Public sensitivities constrain the two countries from discussing the scope of cooperation, but it includes coordination of security force deployments and some intelligence sharing. One practical example of cooperation against the Islamic State–Sinai Peninsula is Israel's waiver of the force thresholds established in the Sinai by the military annex of the Camp David Accords.[30] It can also be assumed that Cairo and Tel Aviv have closely coordinated on combatting smuggling via tunnels under the

---

[28] "Misr: Lajna Barlamānīya Tuqirr Barnāmaj Khādim al-Haramayn li Tanmīya Sīnā' [Egypt: A Parliamentary Committee Approves the Program of the Custodian of the Two Holy Shrines for the Development of the Sinai]," *Al-Hayat*, June 13, 2016.

[29] David Schenker, "How the Israeli Drone Strike in the Sinai Might Backfire," *Atlantic*, August 13, 2013.

[30] David Schenker, "Security Challenges in Egypt Two Years After Morsi," testimony before the House Foreign Affairs Subcommittee on the Middle East and North Africa, December 16, 2015.

Gaza border. When threatened directly, Israel has carried out cross-border operations, such as launching a drone strike against Ansar Bayt al-Maqdis militants preparing to launch rockets from the Sinai into Israel in 2013. Sustaining these efforts will be crucial to Egypt's progress against the Islamic State–Sinai Peninsula.Given the current level of cooperation between Israel and Egypt, there is no present need for the United States to play a greater role as a facilitator of cooperation between the two countries. However, changes in the leadership of the governments in either capital could create conditions under which the United States may need to become more engaged.

The Islamic State–Sinai Peninsula is a serious threat to Egypt's security that, if left unattended, could further undermine stability in the country's mainland. In addition to the risks the Islamic State–Sinai Peninsula poses to Egypt, the Islamic State's presence on the Libyan border exacerbates that conflict and could tempt Egypt into cross border operations that would further strain its military forces.

A successful rollback strategy to weaken and ultimately defeat the Islamic State–Sinai Peninsula would reorient the current campaign— which is heavy on conventional military operations—toward a comprehensive approach based on sustained tribal engagement, the prioritization of civilian security in northeast Sinai, and development projects. The United States has some channels for influencing the Egyptian government. But the success of the campaign will ultimately depend on the Egyptian government's willingness to forgo its scorched-earth approach for a more enlightened strategy. Egypt is unlikely to morph into an ideal partner, but degrading the Islamic State–Sinai Peninsula need not wait on an unlikely democratic transition. Adoption of best practices in counterterrorism and counterinsurgency should be sufficient to make progress against the Islamic State–Sinai Peninsula and would advance both Egypt's interests and those of the international community.

CHAPTER NINE

Afghanistan

The Islamic State has struggled to maintain a presence in Afghanistan. Since 2014, it has attempted to expand a beachhead in South Asia by leveraging existing militant networks. Islamic State leaders have called this land "Wilayat Khorasan," a reference to the historical region that encompassed parts of Iran, Central Asia, Afghanistan, and Pakistan.[1] Yet the Islamic State–Khorasan Province, as Islamic State leaders refer to this branch, controls virtually no territory except for tiny areas in such districts as Deh Bala, Achin, and Naziyan in Nangarhar Province of eastern Afghanistan. In addition, the Islamic State–Khorasan Province has conducted only a handful of attacks, failed to secure the support of most locals, struggled with poor leadership, and faced determined opposition from other local insurgent groups, most notably the Taliban.

The United States should continue to work with the Afghan and Pakistan governments to target the Islamic State's leadership, undermine its limited support base, counter its extremist ideology, and improve governance at the national and local levels.

The Rise of the Islamic State in Afghanistan

For Islamic State leaders, Khorasan has significant historical, religious, and strategic implications with the prophecy of a Muslim army storm-

---

[1] *Khorasan* comes from the Persian language and means "where the sun arrives from."

ing across the Middle East and into Jerusalem.² This comes from a hadith—a record of the traditions and sayings of the Prophet Mohammad—that says: "When you see the black flags coming from the direction of Khorasan, you will join their army."³ In 2014, Islamic State leaders communicated with militant groups in South Asia to gauge the possibility of helping expand the Islamic State's influence in the region. The Islamic State began conducting an information campaign through word of mouth, printed material, and other forums. Islamic State sympathizers, for example, distributed a 12-page printed booklet titled "Fateh" (or *victory* in Pashto) in Pashtun areas of Afghanistan and Pakistan.⁴ As TTP spokesman Shahid Shahidullah remarked in late 2014:

> Oh our brothers, we are proud of you in your victories. We are with you in your happiness and your sorrow . . . . All Muslims in the world have great expectations of you. We are with you, we will provide you with mujahedeen and with every possible support.⁵

South and Central Asia seemed a promising market for the Islamic State. The region had a long history of supporting jihadist groups, dating back to the anti-Soviet wars in the 1980s. It has relatively weak governments, which have provided an opportunity to secure safe havens in areas with little or no official interference; ongoing wars backed by foreign countries, which could be used in an attempt to delegitimize the governments in Kabul and Islamabad as foreign puppets; and a religious and historical importance as part of Khorasan. Islamic State leaders also determined that there were serious problems with the ide-

² See, for example, Ali H. Soufan, *The Black Banners: The Inside Story of 9/11 and the War Against al-Qaeda*, New York: W.W. Norton, 2011, p. xvii.

³ Abu 'Abd Allah Muhammad (quoted in John Thorne, "What's in the Internet Videos Posted by Tamerlan Tsarnaev," *Christian Science Monitor*, April 28, 2013).

⁴ The Islamic State conducted a recruitment campaign in Pashtun-dominated areas of Pakistan in 2014. See, for example, Zahir Shah Sherazi, "Islamic State Footprints Surface in Parts of Bannu," *Dawn* (Pakistan), November 14, 2014.

⁵ The TTP statement was reprinted in "Pakistan Taliban Vow Support for ISIS Fighters," *Al Arabiya*, October 5, 2014. Also see Zahir Shah Sherazi, "Six Top TTP Commanders Announce Allegiance to Islamic State's Baghdadi," *Dawn* (Pakistan), October 14, 2014.

ology and strategic vision of several local groups, including al-Qa'ida and the Afghan Taliban. In 2015, the Islamic State launched a blistering public attack against al-Qa'ida and the Afghan Taliban, accusing them of having gross shortcomings regarding the teaching of *tawhid* [the oneness of God] to their members. The Islamic State accused both of a litany of offenses: focusing on tribal law over sharia; establishing a close alliance with Pakistan's intelligence agency; failing to effectively conquer and control territory; neglecting to target Shi'a (or "Rafidi"); adopting "un-Islamic" practices, such as wearing amulets; establishing a hierarchical structure that excluded many rank-and-file fighters; and erroneously recognizing international borders (instead of supporting a pan-Islamic caliphate).[6]

The Islamic State also brazenly criticized the Afghan Taliban leader, Mullah Muhammad Omar, for practicing a bankrupt, distorted version of Islam. One of the few groups that escaped the Islamic State's excoriation was TTP, which was formed in December 2007 as an umbrella organization among various Pakistani militant groups hostile to that regime. "They were upon great good," concluded one article in *Dabiq*, referring to the TTP. "They carry the Salafi creed and hope and strive to establish the laws of Islam in their region."[7]

In fall 2014, the Islamic State sent representatives to Pakistan to meet with several local militants, including some TTTP leaders. Around the same time, Pakistan officials began receiving reports of pro–Islamic State leaflets in FATA.[8] Hafiz Saeed Khan, former chief of TTP's Orakzai branch in Pakistan's tribal areas, agreed to become the leader of the Islamic State's South Asia branch. His deputy was Abdul Rauf Khadim, an Alizai tribesman from Helmand Province who had defected from the Afghan Taliban.[9] A key component of the Islamic State's campaign was utilizing Saeed and Khadim's established net-

---

[6]   Abu Jarir ash-Shamali, "Al-Qa'idah of Waziristan," *Dabiq*, No. 6, December 2014 (1436 Rabi' Al-Awwal).

[7]   ash-Shamali, 2014, p. 46.

[8]   Author interviews with U.S., Afghanistan, and Pakistan officials, 2016.

[9]   On the background of early Islamic State leaders in Afghanistan and Pakistan, see, for example, "'IS Khorasan' Chief Dies in Afghan Drone Strike," *Dawn* (Pakistan), July 12,

works to recruit fighters in eastern and southern Afghanistan. Saeed was particularly helpful in developing the Islamic State's footprint in Pakistan's tribal areas and such nearby Afghan border provinces as Konar and Nangarhar, where some TTP operatives fled following Pakistani military operations in 2014. Khadim was helpful in developing the Islamic State's network in Baluchistan Province of Pakistan and such southern and western Afghan provinces as Helmand, Farah, and Zabol.[10] In January 2015, the Islamic State formally announced the establishment of Khorasan Province:

> Indeed, the mujahidin from amongst the soldiers of the Khilafah have fulfilled the conditions and met the requirements for the declaration of Wilayat Khorasan. They have announced their bay'ah to Amirul Mu'minin (may Allah preserve him) Khalifah Ibrahim, and he has accepted it and appointed the noble Hafiz Saeed Khan (may Allah preserve him) as the wali of Wilayat Khorasan, and appointed as his deputy the noble Abdul Rauf Khadim Abu Talhah (may Allah preserve him).[11]

Around this time, U.S., NATO, Pakistan, and Afghanistan officials became alarmed at the Islamic State's growing presence in the region. On February 9, 2015, a U.S. aircraft locked onto Khadim in southern Afghanistan and fired a missile, killing him and destroying the vehicle he was traveling in. Afghanistan's intelligence agency, the National Directorate of Security, quickly announced that Khadim "was killed along with his five companions in Sadat village of Kajaki district of Helmand province."[12] He was soon replaced by his deputy, Mullah

---

2015, and Farhan Zahid, "Islamic State in Afghanistan Ready to Capitalize on Mullah Omar's Death," *Terrorism Monitor*, Vol. 13, No. 18, September 3, 2015.

[10] Borhan Osman, "The Shadows of 'Islamic State' in Afghanistan: What Threat Does it Hold?" Afghanistan Analysts Network website, February 12, 2015; Borhan Osman, "The Islamic State in 'Khorasan': How It Began and Where it Stands Now in Nangarhar," Afghanistan Analysts Network website, July 27, 2016a.

[11] Mujāhid Shaykh Abū Muhammad al-'Adnānī ash-Shāmī, "Say, 'Die in Your Rage!" video message, January 2015.

[12] National Directorate of Security, written statement, Afghanistan, February 9, 2015. The statement said: "Today at 1:28 p.m. [3.58 a.m. ET] in a successful operation, Abdul Rauf

Abdul Razzaq Mehdi. The Taliban also became among the most virulent opponents of the Islamic State. As then–Taliban leader Akhtar Mohammad Mansour pointedly noted in a message to Islamic State fighters, it was important that the fighting in Afghanistan come "under one banner" and one leadership—that of the Taliban.[13] Taliban leaders strongly objected to the Islamic State's desire to establish a separate chain of command in Afghanistan with a separate leader, Abu Bakr al-Baghdadi. In response, Islamic State spokesman Abu Muhammad al-Adnani referred to the Taliban as allies of Pakistani intelligence, creating a spiral of accusations that led to a series of Taliban offensives against the Islamic State.[14] The Taliban routed Islamic State fighters in the southern Afghan provinces of Helmand and Farah in fall 2015.[15]

As previously noted, the Islamic State in Afghanistan and Pakistan focused on co-opting local militants to expand its networks. This strategy included several components. First, the Islamic State attempted to exploit local grievances. Following the death of several TTP leaders, including Hakimullah Mehsud in 2013, Hafiz Saeed Khan and several of his colleagues in Pakistan became increasingly disenchanted with TTP. Saeed had apparently been one of the main contenders for TTP's top spot but was passed over. In southern Afghanistan, Abdul Rauf Khadim was a long-standing Taliban military leader who had risen to prominence after the United States released him from the detention camp at Guantanamo Bay, Cuba, in 2007. Yet he became increasingly disgruntled with the Afghan Taliban. One issue was the ascendancy of Akhtar Mohammad Mansour, an Ishaqzai tribesman, in the Tali-

---

also known as 'Khadim' was killed along with his five companions in Sadat village of Kajaki district of Helmand province. He was the commander of [the Islamic State] in southern Afghanistan."

[13] Letter from Haj Mullah Akhtar Mohammad Mansour to Abu Bakr al-Baghdadi, June 2015. For a translation, see S. J. Prince, "Read: Taliban Writes Letter to ISIS Leader Baghdadi," Heavy website, June 16, 2015.

[14] Osman, 2016a.

[15] On Islamic State efforts to establish a foothold in southern Afghanistan, see Osman, 2015, and Osman, 2016a.

ban's inner shura. Khadim was an Alizai Pashtun.[16] Consequently, the Islamic State recruited some disgruntled former TTP and Afghan Taliban members, as well as some operatives from the Islamic Movement of Uzbekistan. In Pakistan, Islamic State leaders also developed ties to the Lal Masjid [Red Mosque] in Islamabad, which served as a nexus for extremists.[17]

Second, the Islamic State headquarters in Syria and Iraq doled out some money to attract supporters. The group had accrued substantial financial resources in Iraq and Syria from such activities as selling oil and stolen goods, kidnapping, extortion, seizing bank accounts, and smuggling antiquities.[18] The Islamic State was willing to provide some finances—perhaps as much as several hundred thousand dollars—to build networks in South Asia. In addition, the group's seizure of territory in Iraq and Syria attracted some extremists in the region who wanted to ally with what they viewed as a successful violent jihadist group.

Third, the Islamic State took advantage of weak local governance to establish a foothold. Nangarhar Province in Afghanistan is perhaps the clearest example. Both the Afghan government and the Taliban had failed to control in parts of Nangarhar. The Afghan government and its security forces had virtually no presence in most districts along the Spin Ghar mountain range south and east of Jalalabad.[19] The Taliban had little control, in part because the area included different insur-

---

[16] Osman, 2016a.

[17] "Pakistani Taliban Splinter Group Again Pledges Allegiance to Islamic State," *Long War Journal*, January 13, 2015.

[18] For the history of how the Islamic State and its predecessor organizations have been financed, see Patrick B. Johnston, Jacob N. Shapiro, Howard J. Shatz, Benjamin Bahney, Danielle F. Jung, Patrick K. Ryan, and Jonathan Wallace, *Foundations of the Islamic State: Management, Money, and Terror in Iraq, 2005–2010*, Santa Monica, Calif.: RAND Corporation, RR-1192-DARPA, 2016.

[19] David Mansfield, "The Devil Is in the Details: Nangarhar's Continued Decline Into Insurgency, Violence and Widespread Drug Production," brief, Kabul: Afghan Research and Evaluation Unit, February 2016.

gent groups and fractured tribal dynamics.[20] In such districts as Achin, Deh Bala, and Nazian, the Shinwari tribal structure has almost completely broken down.

Using this strategy, the Islamic State–Khorasan Province established an organizational structure led by an emir, with a deputy emir and a central shura with such committees as intelligence, finance, propaganda, and education. After the death of Hafiz Saeed Khan in 2016 in a U.S. strike, the Islamic State appointed Abdul Hasib, a former Afghan Taliban member, as emir of the Islamic State–Khorasan Province. Islamic State leaders reached out to other militant groups in the region. By late 2016, the Islamic State–Khorasan Province included roughly 1,000 to 2,000 fighters, a slight decrease from 2015.[21] The group attempted to expand its presence in Afghanistan into such Afghan provinces as Konar and Nuristan. The group also conducted a small number of attacks in the region, such as ones against a police convoy in Quetta in August 2016, Pakistan attorneys at a hospital in Quetta in August 2016, Hazara protesters in Kabul in July 2016, and the Pakistan consulate in Jalalabad in January 2016.[22] Despite this activity, the Islamic State controlled little territory, except a few areas in Nangarhar Province; conducted only a handful of attacks; failed to secure the support of most locals; and struggled with poor leadership.

---

[20] Multiple insurgent groups have operated in Nangarhar, such as the Taliban, Hezb-e Islami, various Salafi groups, al-Qa'ida, TTP, Lashkar-e Islam, Jama'at-e Islam, Jama'at ul-Ahrar, Junud-e Khorasan, and Ansar ul-Islam. See Borhan Osman, "Descent into Chaos: Why Did Nangarhar Turn into an IS Hub?" Afghanistan Analysts Network website, September 27, 2016b.

[21] Author interviews with U.S., Pakistan, and Afghanistan officials in 2015 and 2016. Several reports have almost certainly vastly overstated the size of the Islamic State—Khorasan Province, putting it between 9,000 and 11,000. See, for example, Antonio Giustozzi, "The Islamic State in 'Khorasan': A Nuanced View," London: Royal United Services Institute, February 5, 2016.

[22] Shafqat Ali, "70 Dead as Taliban Bomb Protest over Lawyer's Killing in Quetta," *Nation* (Pakistan), August 8, 2016; Kunwar Khuldune Shahid, "What Quetta Bombing Reveals About Islamic State and Pakistani Taliban," *Diplomat*, August 9, 2016; Syed Ali Shah, "14 Injured as Roadside Bomb Targets Judge's Police Escort in Quetta," *Dawn* (Pakistan), August 11, 2016; "Afghanistan Mourns Protest Blast Victims," Al Jazeera, July 23, 2016; Khalid Alokozay and Mujib Mashal, "ISIS Claims Assault that Killed 7 Near Pakistani Consulate in Afghanistan," *New York Times*, January 13, 2016.

Figure 9.1
Islamic State Control of Territory in Afghanistan

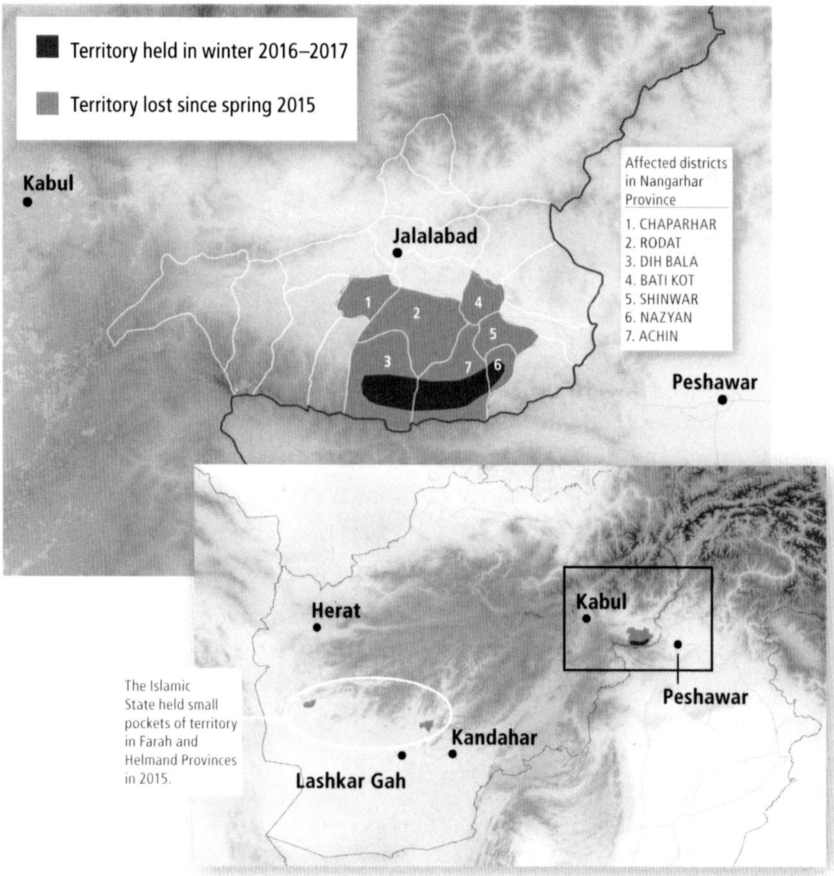

SOURCE: "IS Fighters Run Training Centre, Find Foothold in Farah," *Pajhwok Afghan News*, January 14, 2015; Harleen Gambhir, "ISIS in Afghanistan," Washington, D.C.: Institute for the Study of War, December 3, 2015; Kate Clark and Borhan Osman, "First Wave of IS attacks? Claim and Denial over the Jalalabad Bombs," Afghanistan Analysts Network website, April 22, 2015; Hamid Shalizi, "Exclusive: In Turf War with Afghan Taliban, Islamic State Loyalists Gain Ground," Reuters, June 29, 2015; Joseph Goldstein, "In ISIS, the Taliban Face an Insurgent Threat of Their Own," *New York Times*, June 4, 2015; "Afghan Official: IS Group Present in at Least 3 Provinces," Associated Press, June 28, 2015; Jessica Donati and Habib Khan Totakhil, "Afghan Spy Agency Enlists Villagers to Hold Off Islamic State," *Wall Street Journal*, April 5, 2016; Franz J. Marty, "On the Trail of the Islamic State in Afghanistan," *Foreign Policy*, April 5, 2016; Sune Engel Rasmussen, "ISIS in Afghanistan: 'Their Peak Is Over, But They Are Not Finished,'" *Guardian*, November 18, 2016; Osman, 2016a; authors' estimates.

RAND RR1912-9.1

As Figure 9.1 shows, the Islamic State's territorial reach peaked in spring 2015 when it controlled an estimated 511,777 people (1.9 percent of the population) and roughly 2,919 km^2 (less than 1 percent of the territory). Most of this territory was in the southwestern province of Farah and eastern province of Nangarhar, with small pockets in other provinces, such as Helmand. By winter 2016-2017, the Islamic State's control decreased to only 64,406 people (an 87-percent drop) and 372 km^2 (also an 87-percent drop) from 2015 levels.

Desired End State

Given substantial government weaknesses and that Afghanistan has been in a state of war almost continuously since the 1970s, it is important for the United States to set realistic goals in developing a roll-back strategy for the region. The intended end state in Afghanistan and Pakistan should be to eliminate the Islamic State's safe havens and prevent it from planning or otherwise facilitating attacks against the U.S. homeland and U.S. interests overseas. In addition, the United States should support national and local actors so that they are willing and able to prevent the Islamic State from reestablishing safe havens in the future. In the longer term, the U.S. goal should be peaceful, more prosperous, and better governed countries that contribute to regional security and stability.

For countering the Islamic State, Afghanistan is a particular priority because of the government's fragility and because the Islamic State could use the territory as a base for wider attacks. The United States and other foreign actors, such as NATO allies, India, China, the EU, and UN, should work to

- help sustain and strengthen the Afghan state
- prevent the establishment of safe havens for the Islamic State on Afghan soil
- maintain, in cooperation with Afghan partners, the U.S. forces and facilities essential to confront these threats

- contain and weaken the Taliban and other violent armed actors who refuse to negotiate a peaceful settlement
- change the behavior of regional players, particularly Pakistan, to encourage support for Afghan stability; this could involve sharpening the incentives, both positive and negative, that Washington and other outside actors offer Islamabad.

Were the Islamic State America's sole concern in Afghanistan, one might argue for leaving the country to the Taliban, which could probably be counted on to combat this competitor without the need for American involvement. But left to the Taliban, Afghanistan would continue to be a crossroads for various violent extremist groups and again become a sanctuary for al-Qa'ida. Combating the Islamic State in Afghanistan must therefore be part of a broader campaign to support an Afghan government willing to cooperate in the suppression of all such groups. A sound and well-supported anti-Taliban strategy can also be extended to deal with a local Islamic State presence.

U.S. and Allied Steps

Accomplishing these objectives will require a steadfast commitment from the United States and its partners; a long-term commitment from Afghanistan; a change in Pakistan's strategic calculus; coordinated international efforts that integrate political, security, and economic instruments; and engagement with regional neighbors, such as China, India, Iran, and Russia.

Political and Governance

Improving governance is important for countering the Islamic State–Khorasan Province. The Islamic State faces substantial hurdles in the region because of a crowded market of violent jihadist groups and the absence of an ideology with strong local roots. Populist militant groups in Afghanistan and Pakistan have generally latched onto local ideologies, such as Deobandism, which began around 1867 at the Dar ul-Ulum madrassa in Deoband, India.[23] The Islamic State's brand of Islam is not native to the region. The stigma of a foreign ideology has been a substantial barrier for al-Qa'ida, whose firebrand version of Salafi-jihadism has also not been popular among most locals.

Still, the Islamic State–Khorasan Province may be able to take advantage of weak governance to retain or expand its limited foothold. Afghanistan ranks among the lowest countries in the world in every category of governance—accountability, political stability, government effectiveness, regulatory quality, rule of law, and control of corruption—according to World Bank estimates.[24] Pakistan was not far behind, ranking among the bottom 30 percent of countries worldwide in each of these categories.[25]

Better governance is particularly important in Afghanistan, where the country faces a burgeoning insurgency that has allowed such groups as the Islamic State–Khorasan Province to gain a foothold.[26] Significant problems continue to plague Afghanistan's National Unity Government, such as widespread corruption, deteriorating economic conditions, disagreements over reconciliation with the Taliban, and competition for power among political elites. President Ashraf Ghani has clashed with the Afghan Parliament, and several major political issues remain unresolved. The political agreement that created the National Unity Government, which the United States helped broker, required the Afghan government to hold parliamentary and district council elections. Yet the elections are long overdue. The agreement also stipulated that Afghanistan convene a grand assembly of elders,

---

[23] Olivier Roy, *Islam and Resistance in Afghanistan*, 2nd ed., New York: Cambridge University Press, 1990, p. 57; Gilles Kepel, *Jihad: The Trail of Political Islam*, Cambridge, Mass.: Harvard University Press, 2002, p. 58.

[24] World Bank, 2017.

[25] The Worldwide Governance Indicators data for Pakistan are from 2015. Pakistan is ranked in the bottom 27 percent for voice and accountability, the bottom 1 percent for political stability, the bottom 27 percent for government effectiveness, the bottom 29 percent for regulatory quality, the bottom 24 percent for rule of law, and the bottom 24 percent for control of corruption.

[26] Scott Smith and Colin Cookman, eds., *State Strengthening in Afghanistan: Lessons Learned, 2001–2014*, Washington, D.C.: U.S. Institute of Peace, May 2016.

a *loya jirga*, from across the country to amend the Afghan Constitution and formally establish the position of prime minister. But Afghan political elites disagree about the timing of the elections and electoral reform. Some elites argue that the current election commission lacks legitimacy because of its flawed handling of the 2014 elections. They contend that elections cannot be held until the election process and the Independent Election Commission are reformed.[27]

Washington's most important political priority in Afghanistan should be to focus U.S. efforts on working with the Afghan government and political elites to improve governance and reach a consensus on contentious issues, such as electoral reform. U.S. diplomats and White House officials were instrumental in negotiating the agreement that led to the National Unity Government and should make a similar effort to overcome the differences on electoral reform to permit legislative elections to go forward. Afghanistan should not hold a loya jirga until there is a broader consensus on its ultimate purpose. Poorly organized parliamentary and district council elections marred by corruption and a contentious loya jirga would be more destabilizing than helpful.

Without expecting early results, Washington should also continue to encourage and promote regional support for an Afghan led process of reconciliation with the Taliban.

A more unified and competent Afghan government is critical to ensure that efforts against the Islamic State and other violent jihadist groups are sustained. A weak Afghan government would increase the possibility that militant groups, including the Islamic State, could take advantage of the vacuum. Efforts should also be made to counter Islamic State propaganda, which has included word-of-mouth efforts, written material, and the Islamic State–Khorasan Province's radio station, Khilafat Ghag [Voice of the Caliphate].[28]

---

[27] See, for example, Ali Yawar Adili and Martine van Bijlert, "Pushing the Parliament to Accept a Decree: Another Election Without Reform," Afghanistan Analysts Network website, June 10, 2016.

[28] "ISIS Launches Dari-Language Program on 'Voice of the Caliphate' in Nangarhar," *Nation* (Pakistan), January 28, 2016.

The Islamic State has used parts of Pakistan's FATA to recruit fighters, secure funding, and conduct operations. Under the Frontier Crimes Regulation, there are no regular police in FATA. Justice is draconian and lacks any appeal process. The Frontier Crimes Regulation is also a barrier to the free movement of people between FATA and the rest of Pakistan.[29] Pakistan should be encouraged to consider reform of FATA's legal structure.

A bigger challenge is ending Pakistan's support to militant groups, including the Afghan Taliban, which Islamabad uses as a foreign policy tool. While Pakistan security agencies have aggressively targeted Islamic State operatives, Islamabad's support to other militant groups undermines regional stability. The Islamic State–Khorasan Province has cooperated with a range of extremist groups operating in Pakistan, such as Lashkar-i-Jhangvi, Sipah-i-Sahaba Pakistan, Ahle-Sunnat-Wal-Jama'at, and TTP.[30] The Afghan Taliban has safe havens within parts of Pakistan and access there to funds and equipment. Washington's goal should be to change Pakistan's calculus over time, while recognizing that, whatever policies Washington adopts, Islamabad will likely not alter its Afghanistan policy quickly—even if civilian leaders in Pakistan favor such an outcome.

The new U.S. administration should review its options for dealing with Pakistan. For example, the United States could take further steps to pressure Taliban sanctuaries within Pakistan, with or without the support of Islamabad. The May 2016 killing of Mullah Mansour, the head of the Afghan Taliban, while he was traveling through southwestern Pakistan indicates the kind of direct action against the Taliban and the Haqqani Network that could make an important difference. The Obama administration and Congress have reduced military assistance to Pakistan in recent years and have curtailed Pakistan's access to foreign military financing. But even today's reduced amounts of U.S. assistance could be cut further. Targeted eco-

---

[29] See, for example, Robert Nichols, *The Frontier Crimes Regulation: A History in Documents*, New York: Oxford University Press, 2013.

[30] Tariq Parvez, "The Islamic State in Pakistan," Washington, D.C.: U.S. Institute of Peace, Peace Brief 213, September 2016.

nomic sanctions could be selectively applied against specific organizations and individuals; Washington could encourage other countries to consider similar steps. On the more positive side, Washington might also sketch out a vision of an improved relationship with Pakistan if Islamabad were to cut its ties with militant groups attacking both Afghanistan and India. This outcome would be highly desirable for broader American interests, given Pakistan's central role in the stability of the entire region—and its ability to upend that stability.

Security

The Islamic State–Khorasan Province has conducted a limited number of attacks in Afghanistan and Pakistan. Its operatives have also inspired attacks overseas, such as Riaz Khan Ahmadzai's axe attack in July 2016 on a German train.[31] The immediate security focus for the United States should be working with the Afghanistan and Pakistan governments to target Islamic State leaders and their support networks. In Afghanistan, the United States needs to continue partnering with such elite Afghan special operations units as the Ktah Khas, commandos, and Afghan national army special forces. U.S. and Afghan forces have already killed several Islamic State leaders, including Hafiz Saeed Khan, the Islamic State emir for Khorasan Province, in July 2016; an Islamic State operative named Sauban in January 2016; senior members Shahidullah Shahid and Gul Zaman in July 2015; and Mullah Abdul Rauf Khadim in February 2015.[32] In addition, several other senior Islamic State operatives defected from the organization, such as Muslim Dost in October 2015 and deputy emir Abdul Razzaq Mehdi in November 2015.[33] Afghan and U.S. forces have also killed larger numbers of Islamic State fighters in pitched battles, raids, and strikes.[34]

---

[31] Islamic State–Khorasan Province operatives had apparently been in touch with Riaz Khan Ahmadzai. Author interview with German officials, January 2017.

[32] Ismail Khan, "ISIS Leaders Reported Killed in Drone Strikes in Afghanistan," *New York Times*, July 9, 2015.

[33] Jibran Ahmad and Yeganeh Torbati, "U.S. Drone Kills Islamic State Leader for Afghanistan, Pakistan: Officials," Reuters, August 13, 2016.

[34] "Afghan Air Strike Against Islamic State Kills 40," *Dawn* (Pakistan), April 15, 2016.

Figure 9.2 highlights attacks from the Islamic State–Khorasan Province from 2015 to early 2017. The group conducted the fewest attacks of any Islamic State province that controlled territory. Islamic State–Khorasan Province attacks never exceeded nine attacks in a single month, compared to a high of more than 400 per month by the Islamic State in Syria.

Sustaining high-tempo direct-action operations to clear Islamic State areas will require continuing to develop an Afghan special operations capability. An aggressive campaign should involve continuing to designate Afghanistan as an area of active hostility under the PPG for the use of lethal force, giving the U.S. military flexibility to target the

Figure 9.2
Islamic State Attacks in Afghanistan

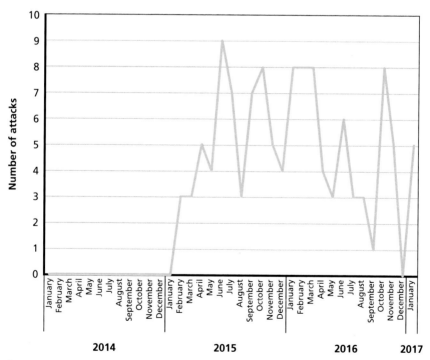

SOURCE: IHS Janes, 2017.

RAND *RR1912-9.2*

Islamic State.[35] In January 2016, the Obama administration gave the Pentagon legal authority to target the Islamic State after a request from Secretary of Defense Ashton Carter.[36] In addition to targeted strikes, U.S. and Afghan government forces need to work closely with tribes, subtribes, clans, and other local actors against the Islamic State. In southern parts of Nangarhar, for example, the population is mostly Ghilzai Pashtun from such tribes as the Shinwaris, although many tribes have fractured.[37] Support from these communities, along with such forces as the Afghan Local Police, is important to hold any areas that are cleared.

Afghanistan, with American support, should establish an enduring military and intelligence presence to counter the Islamic State and other militant groups in the areas in which they operate. The new U.S. administration should retain and perhaps modestly increase the current American force of 8,400 there now. It should also relax restrictions on certain activities, including air strikes and American advisors accompanying Afghan forces in the field. Afghanistan should be regarded as one of several "lily pads" in a global campaign against violent extremists. Unlike most other Islamic societies, Afghan leaders and most of the population want U.S. forces to stay. The United States should also work closely with countries participating in the NATO-led Resolute Support Mission to sustain their current numbers and roles. As part of a total non-U.S. NATO commitment of around 5,000, these countries include Italy in the west, with roughly 800 troops; Germany in the north, with approximately 800; and Turkey in the capital region, with 500. A sustained U.S.- and NATO-led security role is important, since a larger military role for Afghanistan's neighbors would be either infeasible (Afghans, for instance, continue to harbor animosity toward the Russians for their invasion in the 1980s and are even more hostile to Pakistan), increase regional security competition (a larger Indian

---

[35] White House, 2013.

[36] Gordon Lubold, "U.S. Clears Path to Target Islamic State in Afghanistan," *Wall Street Journal*, January 19, 2016.

[37] See, for example, Robert Kemp, "Counterinsurgency in Nangarhar Province, Eastern Afghanistan, 2004–2008," *Military Review*, November–December 2010.

security role would likely increase friction with Pakistan), or undermine American interests (an Iranian security role would be unwelcome in Washington).

The United States should also continue support for the Afghan security forces. Over the past several decades, no Afghan government has been able to sustain itself without support from outside powers. This has been particularly true when the country faced a serious security threat, as it does now. It is much cheaper for the United States and its allies to support Afghan security forces than it is to deploy large numbers of U.S. and other NATO soldiers. The United States should carry through on its commitment to providing roughly $4 billion per year through at least 2020 to help sustain the costs of the Ministries of Defense and Interior, improve retention of trained soldiers, and prevent a drop in salaries. The United States should also continue to build up the Afghan Air Force, which is plagued by low operational readiness, maintenance problems, and a lack of trained aircrew. In the long run, that air force can play a crucial role by conducting close air support missions and airlifts, relieving the United States of these tasks. The United States should provide additional training to the air force; supply additional light attack aircraft, such as the A-29 Super Tucano; and light attack helicopters, such as the MD-350.

In Pakistan, the army, police, and Directorate of Inter-Services Intelligence have all conducted operations against the Islamic State. The most significant challenge for Pakistan will likely remain the possibility that the Islamic State will gain inroads into Pakistan's broader extremist landscape. Aftab Sultan, director general of the Intelligence Bureau, acknowledged that the Islamic State had emerged as a threat because such local militant groups as Lashkar-i-Jhangvi, Sipah-i-Sahaba Pakistan, and TTP cooperated and provided assistance.[38] In 2015, Pakistan police and intelligence agencies arrested several Islamic State–Khorasan Province operatives in Karachi, revealing a network of educated, middle-class professionals who regularly donated to the

---

[38] Iftikhar A. Khan, "IS Emerging as a Threat, Warns IB Chief," *Dawn* (Pakistan), February 11, 2016. Also see, for example, "Islamic State a Serious Threat to Pakistan, Foreign Secretary Admits," *Dawn* (Pakistan), February 23, 2015.

group. Pakistan authorities uncovered a similar network in Lahore in December 2015.[39] Military operations in 2015 and 2016, such as Operation Zarb-i-Azb in Pakistan's tribal areas, cleared out Islamic State–Khorasan Province and other militant safe havens in the FATA, but a number of individuals shifted to Afghanistan or Balochistan. Pakistan must seek a joint effort with Afghanistan to combat this threat, focusing on border controls to stem the flow of militants between the two countries.[40]

Economic and Humanitarian

Economic and humanitarian challenges are more acute in Afghanistan than in Pakistan because of the government's fragility and the Taliban-led insurgency that has engulfed much of the country. The United States should continue working closely with the UN, the World Bank, International Monetary Fund, and major financial contributors to better address acute economic and governance challenges. Rather than focusing on a broad array of economic issues, U.S. diplomats might concentrate on forestalling developments that could increase public opposition to the government, such as a poor agricultural harvest, rising unemployment, and a prolonged energy shortage. An electricity blackout, such as the one that occurred in Kabul in January 2016 following the Taliban sabotage of Kabul's main power supply, could decrease morale and increase antigovernment sentiment, particularly if prolonged.

Next to Syria, Afghanistan has produced the second-largest number of refugees in the world, at 2.7 million.[41] This number could double or triple, as it did prior to 2002, if American and international support are not sustained.

---

[39] Tariq Parvez, "The Islamic State in Pakistan," Washington, D.C.: United States Institute of Peace, Peace Brief 213, September 2016.

[40] "Most IS Men in Afghanistan Are TTP Fighters," *Dawn* (Pakistan), August 1, 2016.

[41] Data are from UN High Commissioner for Refugees, "Facts and Figures About Refugees," Geneva, 2016a.

Regional Dimension

Every government in the region—including Afghanistan, Pakistan, Iran, India, Russia, and China—has expressed concern about the Islamic State and vowed to combat it. But there are several obstacles to regional cooperation. First, there is significant security competition among major powers in the region, most notably between Pakistan and India. Afghanistan has long been entangled in a "great game" among neighboring states and global powers.[42] Most of Afghanistan's neighbors prefer a stable central government in Kabul but want one that protects their own interests. New Delhi, for example, has enjoyed close relations with the Afghan government and sought to minimize Islamabad's influence and weaken anti-Indian terrorist groups. Pakistan, on the other hand, has attempted to minimize New Delhi's influence in Afghanistan and has supported pro-Pakistan proxy groups. An enduring U.S. commitment to Afghanistan may help alleviate some, although not all, of this security competition.

The rise of the Islamic State–Khorasan Province has raised concerns that some countries—such as Iran and Russia—might increase their cooperation with the Taliban to as a hedge against the Islamic State. The Taliban has been effective against the Islamic State in such Afghan provinces as Helmand and Farah. But Russian or Iranian cooperation with the Taliban would undermine long-term stability and ensure that the region continues to attract and give rise to violent extremist groups.

Cooperation on intelligence and border security among countries in the region is also important to counter the Islamic State. Intelligence cooperation varies considerably because of the security competition among these countries. Cooperation is relatively close between Beijing

---

[42] William Dalrymple, *Return of a King: The Battle for Afghanistan, 1839–42*, New York: Alfred A. Knopf, 2013; Diana Preston, *The Dark Defile: Britain's Catastrophic Invasion of Afghanistan 1838–1842*, New York: Walker & Company, 2012; Steve Coll, *Ghost Wars: The Secret History of the CIA, Afghanistan, and Bin Laden, from the Soviet Invasion to September 10, 2001*, New York: Penguin Press, 2004; Barnett R. Rubin, *The Fragmentation of Afghanistan: State Formation and Collapse in the International System*, New Haven, Conn.: Yale University Press, 1995.

and Islamabad, poor between Kabul and Islamabad, and almost non-existent between New Delhi and Islamabad. To effectively counter the Islamic State–Khorasan Province over the long run, the United States needs to help promote greater sharing of intelligence about Islamic State activities. Border security is also important, particularly with foreign fighters moving back and forth across the Afghanistan-Pakistan border and through Iran from—and to—Syria and Iraq. Kabul and Islamabad have coordinated some operations along their borders before, during, and after attacks on the Islamic State–Khorasan Province. This cooperation should be regularized. The United States may not be able to overcome the pervasive lack of trust among governments in the region, but it can help improve regional cooperation where there are pressing common interests, as in countering the Islamic State.

The Islamic State in Afghanistan and Pakistan might not survive as a distinct entity after the collapse of the actual caliphate in Iraq and Syria, but both countries will remain home to a wide variety of extremist groups, some of which, like al-Qa'ida, have aspirations that transcend the region. Thus, most of the efforts recommended above will need to be sustained even after the disappearance of the Islamic State–Khorasan.

PART III

The Global Campaign

CHAPTER TEN

The Ideological and Information Campaign

The Islamic State is a global operation. Central to this operation is the Islamic State's messaging. The group's ideology is often incoherent or shallow from a theological point of view, and its volunteers are often remarkably ignorant of their faith. But its brand—and its means of disseminating its ideas—is quite strong among many Muslim communities. This strength helps the group in many ways, enabling it to inspire attacks, attract recruits, and raise the morale of existing fighters. It also helps the Islamic State win over jihadists from rival organizations and can even shape the politics of the countries on its long enemies list.

As with other successful terrorist and insurgent groups, the Islamic State does not have one message, but many. In its propaganda, it stresses the group's successes, both militarily and in terms of governance; the heroic nature of its violence; and the need to defend Sunni Muslims from perceived oppressors. Strains of apocalypticism also are pronounced, and the group's "heroic" brand offers criminals, alienated Muslims, and even misguided idealists some sense of legitimacy and purpose. It also provides a powerful brand to local fighting groups that are unpopular or that otherwise seek to change their image.

These ideas are disseminated in part through a vast array of media operations. The Islamic State has proven particularly adept at using social media, spawning a massive propaganda machine to attract and inspire recruits. The Islamic State also used social media to provide recruits with practical information, such as how to go to Syria and Iraq, and how to stay in touch in general. Some of this propaganda is a top-down, directed operation, while other messaging is generated by low-level supporters contacting their immediate social circles. An array of preachers and other ideologues, often operating from friendly countries, promotes a message of sectarianism and legitimate violence in the name of Islam. To translate these messages into action, however, human contact is often vital. Social media and propaganda are commonly the first steps in moving individuals to join a terrorist or insurgent group, but facilitators' and recruiters' personal touches often are what make the difference between vague support and joining a group.

In part because of the Islamic State's messaging campaign, the core group in Iraq and Syria relies heavily on foreign fighters—more than 40,000 as of early 2017—for its operations in its Iraqi and Syrian heartland, as well as in its provinces, such as Libya, Nigeria, Afghanistan, and Egypt.[1] Such fighters come from around the world; one report found that more than 80 countries supplied fighters. Most alarmingly for the West, Europe sent more than 6,000 foreign fighters to Iraq and Syria, while more than 250 Americans have tried to travel to Syria, with at least a few succeeding.[2] Even as it pulls Muslim recruits to its heartland, the group also pushes violence and radical ideas outward from this base. The Islamic State has shown an ability to expand rapidly outside its core areas through a variety of strategies: sending and infiltrating its operatives around the world to conduct attacks, inspiring local Muslims to commit terrorism as part of local cells or as lone wolves and co-opting a range of existing jihadist groups.

This chapter seeks to answer the following questions: What are the components of the Islamic State's message outside its core areas? How is this message promoted to influence potential adherents? What options do the United States and its allies have to counter these efforts as part of a rollback strategy? The remainder of this chapter has six sections. The first section looks at the content of the Islamic State's messaging outside its core areas. The second examines the ways in which the Islamic State has spread this message. The third briefly examines the current and potential dangers of this spread. The fourth describes the desired end state, while the fifth presents an array of policy options

---

[1]   Author interview with U.S. officials, February 2017.

[2]   Hughes, 2016; Soufan Group, 2015.

for reducing and countering the spread. The chapter concludes by discussing some of the trade-offs and limits inherent in these ideas.

The Islamic State's Extraregional Objectives and Message

Most of the Islamic State's goals are local and regional, such as defending and expanding its caliphate in Iraq and Syria, opposing Muslims it considers deviant, and expanding its provinces in various Muslim countries. Nevertheless, the Islamic State has several objectives regarding Europe, the United States, and other areas outside its heartland. A long-term goal is to include the West in the caliphate, but even the Islamic State's more wide-eyed fanatics recognize this is not immediately achievable. Shorter-term goals primarily involve ideological validation, recruitment, morale-building, and revenge. Examples include the following:

- The Islamic State claims to be the leader of the world's Muslims. As such, Muslims around the world rallying to its banners validates its leadership and helps it attract even more recruits.
- Europe is an important source of foreign fighters for the Islamic State. More than 6,000 Europeans have gone to fight, as have thousands of Central Asians. Some of these fighters have assumed leadership positions in the Islamic State, but far more are cannon fodder, serving as suicide bombers or otherwise helping the Islamic State maintain a high pace of operations.[3]
- As the Islamic State has lost territory, it has used terrorist attacks outside the region to "prove" to its members in Iraq and Syria that it is taking the war to its enemies and inflicting more damage than it is receiving. There is good reason to assess that this message is not fully believed, as discussed later, but these attacks are an attempt to shore up morale.
- The Islamic State also seeks revenge. The United States, France, and other countries are bombing its forces, building up its local

---

[3]   Soufan Group, 2015.

enemies, and otherwise inflicting grave losses. The group and its leaders want to avenge these deaths.

The Islamic State's message mixes several components designed to attract recruits; shore up morale among existing supporters; and, to a lesser degree, intimidate its enemies. The components at times reinforce one another and appeal to a range of audiences: There is no single propaganda stream.[4] These elements include the following:

- *Success.* The Islamic State constantly brags about its successes. At its 2014 peak, the Islamic State controlled territory roughly the size of England. Its propaganda constantly showed dead enemies and Islamic State fighters on the march, complete with tanks and successful suicide attacks.[5] It confronted what it proclaimed to be Islam's enemies on many fronts and, judging by the rhetoric of its foes and its own propaganda, it was prevailing. Portraying itself as a winner enabled the Islamic State to distinguish itself from rivals, such as al-Qa'ida, which had suffered many setbacks and could boast fewer accomplishments, and allowed it to claim that it could reestablish an Islamic caliphate.
- *Ultraviolence.* The Islamic State regularly records and disseminates violent and shocking images, such as the execution of enemies, throwing homosexuals off buildings, burning a captured Jordanian pilot alive, and conducting seemingly endless beheadings. Such violence alienates many Muslims, and even fellow jihadists repeatedly criticize it.[6] However, this graphic violence appeals to a core demographic of young males and creates a violent image that the Islamic State cultivates. While this certainly is meant to

---

[4] William McCants and Charlie Winter, "Experts Weigh in (Part 4): Can the United States Counter ISIS Propaganda?" Washington, D.C.: Brookings Institution, July 1, 2015.

[5] Winter, 2015, p. 26.

[6] Willa Frej, "How 70,000 Muslim Clerics Are Standing Up to Terrorism," *World Post,* December 11, 2015; "Jihadi Preacher Latest to Condemn ISIS' Methods," Associated Press (via CBS News), February 6, 2015.

intimidate enemies, it also sends a message to existing members about the perils of betraying the group.[7]

- *Sectarianism.* The foreign fighter flow increased dramatically in 2013 and after until 2016, as the Syrian conflict shifted its image from a popular revolt against a dictatorial regime to a conflict between a Shi'a-'Alawi-Iranian-Hizballah axis against the Sunni world. The Islamic State, in contrast to al-Qa'ida, prioritizes sectarianism and has played up the "apostate" nature of Shi'a Muslims and their allies. Such rhetoric has proven enormously popular as the sectarian fault line has widened.[8]

- *Apocalypticism.* The Islamic State has also played up apocalyptic rhetoric, taking advantage of the prevalence of references to Syria in the sayings of the Prophet Mohammad and the belief among many Muslims that the messiah's return and end of times are near.[9] It argues that good Muslims are engaged in a cosmic battle against an array of enemies and that Syria is the battleground. Volunteers will be the vanguard who will bring about the victory of Islam in the final battles.

- *The good life in the Islamic State.* In contrast to its harsh violence and apocalyptic rhetoric, the Islamic State also offers a utopian vision. It plays up a range of images to highlight the joys of living under its rule, such as care for the elderly and medical treatment for children. Female volunteers even show images of baked goods in the shape of hand grenades and testify about being truly fulfilled. Men explain their sense of camaraderie. Numerous images depict a family-friendly land in which services are bountiful. The well-known use of sexual slavery is also a variant of this, a promise of rewards for those who fight in the name of Islam.

- *Islam under attack and the defender of the faith.* The Islamic State regularly shows coalition attacks on its forces, the deaths of

---

[7] Winter, 2015, p. 23.

[8] Charles R. Lister, *The Syrian Jihad: Al-Qaida, the Islamic State and the Evolution of an Insurgency*, New York: Oxford University Press, 2016a, p. 91.

[9] Pew Research Center, "Articles of Faith," in *The World's Muslims: Unity and Diversity*, Washington, D.C., August 9, 2012. For a broader discussion, see McCants, 2015.

Muslim civilians, and other images designed to provoke sympathy and outrage.[10] Such images allow the Islamic State to proclaim itself to be the defender of the true faith—in this case, a narrow and extreme interpretation of Salafi Islam—with all others being deviant or lax at best. Those who come to fight or stay home and act thus have both purpose and legitimacy. Their actions and violence are sanctified and have social support, if only among a minority of the community, while the group itself gains legitimacy as the shield of the Sunnis.[11]

Taken together, the propaganda offers recruits a vision of transformation. As Charlie Winter contends, the Islamic State "captures the imaginations of its potential recruits by offering both immediate change and the ability to transform their future in the long term."[12] The themes are also flexible. In 2016, for example, the Islamic State's viability and image of success came into question after steady coalition military progress that shrank the territory under the group's control. In response, the group played up the enmity of the West and the need to act there, downplaying the centrality of the physical state.[13]

Far less important to all this is the "Islamic" content of the Islamic State's propaganda. To be clear, the Islamic State plays up its interpretation of Islam, quoting Quranic verses and sayings of the Prophet Mohammad. Yet numerous studies have shown that its foreign recruits know little about Islam.[14] In contrast to al-Qa'ida, Islamic State ideologues do not focus on point-by-point rebuttals of clerical critics but rather try to shame their critics as lax or as puppets of Islam's enemies. In addition to inspiration, the Islamic State's messaging provides

---

[10] Winter, 2015, p. 25.

[11] Winter, 2015, p. 33.

[12] Winter, 2015, p. 6.

[13] Joby Warrick and Souad Mekhennet, "Inside ISIS: Quietly Preparing for the Loss of the 'Caliphate,'" *Washington Post*, July 12, 2016.

[14] For the latest study that affirms this general point, see Brian Dodwell, Daniel Milton, and Don Rassler, *The Caliphate's Global Workforce: An Inside Look at the Islamic State's Foreign Fighter Paper Trail*, West Point, N.Y.: Combating Terrorism Center, 2016.

considerable practical knowledge for supporters, giving them information on what to pack, how to travel to Syria and Iraq, whom to meet when they arrive, and which targets in the West to strike. Mohammed Hamzah Khan, for example, arranged online from his home in Chicago to meet contacts in Turkey who would facilitate his travel to Syria with his brother and sister.[15]

How the Islamic State Spreads Its Influence

The Islamic State spreads its messages and other forms of influence in a variety of ways. These include propaganda through a range of social media and other platforms, as well as the use of foreign fighters and other emissaries to increase support for the group and act as facilitators for those wishing to become active members. Some of the Islamic State's propaganda is top-down. It maintains active media services—such as al-Hayat Media Center and Amaq News Agency—that create and disseminate slick online magazines and that have developed innovative propaganda platforms, such as a mobile Android-based app for broadcasting its al-Bayan radio station. But much of its messaging is generated directly by low-level members. Various preachers from the Muslim world also play an important, if less direct, role, creating an environment conducive to the Islamic State's message.

All successful terrorist groups are masters of propaganda, but the Islamic State has proven particularly successful in leveraging social media, such as Twitter, Facebook, and Ask.fm, to spread its message. In 2015, the Islamic State had over 40,000 Twitter accounts, with about 2,000 of them in English. A RAND report found that the Islamic State drew on almost 80,000 accounts in total, including informal supporters and surrogates who were not directly tied to the group but passed on its propaganda.[16] Part of this is simply a reflection

---

[15] Peter Bergen, "Jihad 2.0: Social Media in the Next Evolution of Terrorist Recruitment," testimony before the U.S. Senate Committee on Homeland Security and Governmental Affairs, May 7, 2015, p. 5; Hughes, 2016.

[16] Bodine-Baron et al., 2016, p. 8.

of its demographics—the Islamic State's average foreign recruit in the United States is 25 years old—and younger people are frequent social media users.[17] However, it also reflects the centrality of social media to Islamic State recruiting and propaganda efforts. Bodine-Baron et al. found that many of the Islamic State accounts were exceptionally active—far more so than those of the group's opponents and critics.[18]

Social media offer cheap and effective propaganda capabilities, making it easy to disseminate information, including visually powerful video. Internet propaganda in general allows users to bypass established media outlets and create their own messages. Social media in particular almost automatically create networks that can complement face-to-face contacts and enables individuals to form relationships outside their neighborhoods, countries, or even regions. Social media also enable risky behaviors because a user's identity can be concealed.[19] As Lorenzo Vidino and Seamus Hughes argue, social media enables the Islamic State to trigger radicalization, help individuals leave for Syria, and incite them to attack in the United States and Europe.[20]

To identify potential recruits, Islamic State members monitor sites that are ostensibly peaceful but contain radical content. Potential supporters are identified and then separated and groomed using direct messaging or private and more potentially secure platforms, such as Telegram, Surespot, WhatsApp, Kik, and Skype, to provide more-focused attention.[21] As individuals engage more with social media, an echo-chamber effect occurs. Like-minded individuals reinforce the message, often at a rapid pace with extensive back and forth, with indi-

---

[17] Bergen, 2015, p. 3.

[18] Bodine-Baron et al., 2016, pp. 7–11.

[19] This draws on the ideas of Tim Stevens and Peter R. Neumann, *Countering Online Radicalisation: A Strategy for Action*, London: International Centre for the Study of Radicalisation and Political Violence, 2009, p. 11.

[20] Lorenzo Vidino and Seamus Hughes, *ISIS in America: From Retweets to Raqqa*, Washington, DC:. Center for Cyber and Homeland Security, George Washington University, December 2015.

[21] J. M. Berger, "Tailored Online Interventions: The Islamic State's Recruitment Strategy," *CTC Sentinel*, October 23, 2015, p. 19. See also Robert Graham, "How Terrorists Use Encryption," *CTC Sentinel*, June 16, 2016, and Hughes, 2016.

vidual tweets being reposted by hundreds of others. When such messaging is successful, individuals become isolated, exposed only to the ideas of the Islamic State—a process recruiters encourage by citing religious teachings that call for shunning non-Muslims and Muslims they consider to be insufficiently zealous.[22] Such efforts pay off. In his studies of American supporters of the Islamic State, analyst Peter Bergen found: "The only profile that ties American militants drawn to the Syrian conflict is that they are active in online jihadist circles."[23]

The virtual and personal intersect on social media. Individuals are able to meet former or current fighters or more experienced recruiters virtually.[24] In the past, individuals had to go to a radical mosque or community center for such exposure, but now they can hear war stories and gain practical advice on logistics without leaving their homes.[25] Even more important, the process is interactive, so they can receive encouragement and advice tailored to their individual circumstances.

Islamic State leaders invest considerable effort and resources in their social media presence. Much of their effort goes into creating material for propaganda—"evidence" of their successes and good intentions.[26] The Islamic State puts out propaganda in multiple languages. In addition to English and Arabic, it uses Russian, French, German, Turkish, Uyghur, and even Kurdish, among other languages. Islamic State leaders recognize that their importance and impact can grow in the media even as they lose territory and suffer other reverses, as they have since 2015.[27] Much of the propaganda effort, however, is bottom up, with low-level fighters, sympathizers outside Iraq and Syria, and other supporters tweeting and otherwise promoting the Islamic State's cause. Islamic State supporters produce videos, poems, essays,

---

[22] Vidino and Hughes, 2015; J. Berger, 2015.

[23] Bergen, 2015, p. 4.

[24] See Rukmini Callimachi, "ISIS and the Lonely Young American," *New York Times*, June 27, 2015.

[25] Winter, 2015, p. 7.

[26] Winter, 2015, p. 7.

[27] Charlie Winter, ISIS Is Using the Media Against Itself," *Atlantic*, March 23, 2016.

and spread official Islamic State pronouncements and images.[28] This enables the Islamic State to have a vast propaganda apparatus without maintaining a significant official infrastructure.[29]

The Islamic State also draws on a fertile environment created by preachers who trumpet sectarianism, hostility to Iran, the perfidy of the West, and other themes that match the Islamic State's propaganda.[30] In the past, such preachers proved vital in rallying support for different jihads, helping inspire young European Muslims to travel to foreign battlefields to fight.[31] For example, in Albania and Kosovo, both of which have a large per capita number of foreign fighters with the Islamic State, a small number of ultraconservative mosques funded by money from Persian Gulf states, such as Saudi Arabia, and staffed by preachers from that region have inspired strong anti-Western sentiment. Although these preachers claim not to support the Islamic State, they have created fertile ground for Islamic State recruitment by echoing its messages about Islam's enemies, the illegitimacy of European governments, the false nature of non-Salafi forms of Islam, and the need for young men to fight.[32] As one Kosovar counterterrorism official noted: "There is no evidence that any organization gave money directly to people to go to Syria. The issue is they supported thinkers who promote violence and jihad in the name of protecting Islam."[33]

---

[28] Winter, 2015, p. 18; Peter Neumann, "Countering the Virtual Caliphate," testimony before the Committee on Foreign Affairs, U.S. House of Representatives, 114th Cong., 2nd Sess., June 23, 2016.

[29] On Islamic State media operations, see Craig Whiteside, *Lighting the Path: The Evolution of the Islamic State Media Enterprise, 2003–2016*, Hague: International Centre for Counter-Terrorism, November 2016.

[30] For one review, see Geneive Abdo, *Salafists and Sectarianism: Twitter and Communal Conflict in the Middle East*, Washington, D.C.: Brookings Institution, 2015.

[31] Petter Nesser, *Islamist Terrorism in Europe: A History*, London: Hurst Publishers, 2014, pp. 37–40.

[32] Joby Warrick, "In Albania—NATO Member and U.S. Ally—Worries About the Emergence of ISIS," *Washington Post*, June 11, 2016b; Carlotta Gall, "How Kosovo Was Turned into Fertile Ground for ISIS," *New York Times*, May 21, 2016

[33] Gall, 2016.

The teachings of such preachers inspire individuals to join or otherwise support the Islamic State. In addition, they make the group's actions and teachings more palatable, creating broader support and allowing members to gain the support, or at least the toleration, of their communities. For similar reasons, a sympathetic community is less likely to work with police and intelligence services in their efforts to identify potential and actual Islamic State members.

In addition to the Islamic State's propaganda efforts, foreign fighters themselves play an important role as recruiters and facilitators, as well as combatants and terrorists. As noted earlier, the Islamic State has attracted more than 35,000 fighters from more than 80 countries. Most are from the Arab world, with Tunisia and Saudi Arabia being top nationalities. In Europe, France, the UK, Belgium, and Germany are major contributors and, for their size, so are Kosovo and Albania. Russian and Central Asia have also seen thousands of volunteers, although exact numbers are elusive.[34] Some return to their home countries, using their experience to promote the cause and attract impressionable young people. Others stay in touch from the war zone via social media, glorifying their own experiences to attract new recruits to the cause. They are often able to take individuals who are sympathetic to the group thanks to social media or other reasons and move them toward more active and violent participation. Not surprisingly, societies with many foreign fighters tend to have stronger relations with the Islamic State over the long term.[35]

Historically, cell creators and leaders have tended to be veterans of foreign jihads.[36] In addition, these veterans are trusted and can help with logistics, enabling volunteers to hook up with travel networks and then the groups themselves.[37] But propaganda is not enough. There is often an external human influencer who is pivotal during the radical-

---

[34] Soufan Group, 2015.

[35] Clint Watts, "When the Caliphate Crumbles: The Future of the Islamic State's Affiliates," War on the Rocks Website, June 13, 2016.

[36] Nesser, 2014, pp. 12–13.

[37] Clint Watts, "Foreign Fighters: How Are They Being Recruited? Two imperfect Recruitment Models," *Small Wars Journal*, June 22, 2008.

ization process.[38] One British religious leader explained that radicalization and recruitment are "all about who knows who. One guy knows a friend, and so on."[39] Returned foreign fighters are particularly important in countries where Internet penetration is low, such as Libya and Yemen.[40]

Foreign fighter flows appear to be declining dramatically, although it is difficult to tell if this is the start of a long-term reversal. According to U.S. Department of Defense estimates, numbers may have fallen by as much as 90 percent by the middle of 2016.[41] The large numbers of volunteers who have already gone to Syria, however, offer considerable reserves from which the Islamic State can draw. Still, returning foreign fighters also play a role in seeding new jihadist groups or in changing the orientation of existing insurgencies, making them more radical. In Algeria, Chechnya, Iraq, and elsewhere foreign fighters from previous conflicts often began by working with local groups but, over time, made the radical cause far more dominant. The Islamic State has used foreign volunteers as emissaries to groups in their home countries and has at times sent more fighters to bolster them.[42]

The Islamic State is increasingly trying to use foreign fighters to infiltrate Europe. The Islamic State's intelligence unit, often referred to as *Emni* or *Amn al-Dawla*, has branches focused on Europe, Asia, and the Arab world. Incoming recruits are processed, and some are vetted and selected for special training. Emni then sends foreign recruits back to their home countries to commit terrorist attacks there.[43] The foreign fighters' role becomes easier when they are under less pressure from

---

[38] Winter, 2015, p. 7. See also Stevens and Neumann, 2009, pp. 12–13 and Hughes, 2016

[39] As quoted in Stevens and Neumann, 2009, p. 13.

[40] Watts, 2008.

[41] Thomas Gibbons-Neff, "Number of Foreign Fighters Entering Iraq and Syria Drops by 90 Percent," *Washington Post*, April 26, 2016.

[42] For a discussion of this phenomenon, see Daniel Byman, "The Homecomings: What Happens when Arab Foreign Fighters in Iraq and Syria Return?" *Studies in Conflict and Terrorism*, Vol. 38, No. 8, 2015, and Byman, 2016b.

[43] Rukmini Callimachi, "How a Secretive Branch of ISIS Built a Global Network of Killers," *New York Times*, August 3, 2016.

local security services and when borders are porous. Until at least 2015, Turkey's border was relatively easy for European and Arab volunteers to cross into Syria.[44] Similarly, it is far easier for foreign fighters to return to serve as incubators when they go back to unsettled countries, such as Libya, than when they are going to countries with strong security services, such as Jordan.

The foreign fighter danger in the United States is less than that in Europe. The United States has far fewer foreign fighters per capita than most European countries. In addition, the United States does not have an established Salafi-jihadist infrastructure that facilitates travel and provides in-person reinforcement, in contrast to several European countries. In Kosovo and Albania, for example, the networks are extensive. Even in such countries as France, Spain, and the UK, the networks are weaker and more clandestine but still far more robust than in the United States. Islamic State security officials reportedly told their operatives that the United States was a far harder target than Europe.[45] As a result, the online component is more important for the United States.[46]

The Islamic State also has a limited presence in Asia. From 2014 to 2016, the group's recruitment efforts there have been minimal, and individuals who have declared loyalty to the group or acted in its name appear to have done so without direct contact with the group. The Islamic State claimed credit for a January 2016 attack in Jakarta that killed eight people and for several disrupted plots. In June 2016, it called for establishing a province in the Philippines. Indeed, some in Australia were prevented from going to Syria and decided to strike Australia itself. The Islamic State's propaganda calls for jihadists from the area who cannot travel to join the caliphate to instead "join the mujahideen in the Philippines." By 2016, roughly 1,000 Muslims from the region had traveled to fight in Syria. Most came from Indonesia, but there were also 110 Australians and around 100 Malaysians. Regional

---

[44] Steven A. Cook, "Is Turkey Really at the Table," *Politico*, November 42, 2015.

[45] Callimachi, 2016.

[46] Hughes, 2016.

security officials fear that, if these fighters return, they could set off a major terrorism wave.[47]

Resulting Dangers

Several dangers emerge from the Islamic State's efforts to reach out beyond its core areas to Europe, the United States, and other parts of the world. These include resources for the group, a greater ability to infiltrate operatives to conduct terrorist attacks and foster insurgencies, and a higher risk of lone strikes. Through its international efforts, the Islamic State is able to gain resources, in part financial but mainly human, in its struggle in the region. The group relies heavily on foreign fighters for suicide bombers and also for leadership positions. Foreign funding from donations or brought by foreign fighters is far less important to the group than taxation, but it remains one source of revenue and may grow in importance as the group's control over territory and taxable populations shrinks.[48]

The Islamic State can also infiltrate its operatives into the West and other countries. One impact of this infiltration is more-effective terrorist attacks, such as the November 2015 strikes in Paris. The Paris attackers were European citizens who had fought in Syria and returned. They were able to execute a coordinated and deadly attack—the worst Europe had seen in more than a decade. When a foreign fighter is part of a terrorist plot, it is both more likely to succeed and more lethal.[49]

---

[47] David Ignatius, "Southeast Asia Could Be a Haven for Displaced Islamic State Fighters," *Washington Post*, August 18, 2016; Conor Cronin and Phuong Nguyen, "Recalibrating the Islamic State Threat in Southeast Asia," commentary, Washington, D.C.: Center for Strategic and International Studies, July 7, 2016; Paul Ehrlich, "Islamic State's Asian Offensive," *Politico*, August 16, 2016.

[48] "Remarks by Assistant Secretary for Terrorist Financing Daniel Glaser at Chatham House;" Lina Khatib, "The Islamic State's Strategy: Lasting and Expanding," paper, Washington, D.C.: Carnegie Middle East Center, June 29, 2015.

[49] Thomas Hegghammer, "Resources," webpage, undated, provides data on jihadi plots in general and on foreign fighters in particular. See also Thomas Hegghammer, "Should I Stay or Should I Go? Explaining Variation in Western Jihadists' Choice Between Domestic and Foreign Fighting," American Political Science Review, Vol. 107, No. 1, February 2013.

Another effect of infiltration is that the Islamic State is better able to establish new provinces or co-opt existing groups, especially in parts of the developing world where governance is weak. Minor and often unknown local groups may take on the Islamic State brand to reinvigorate themselves. Some also assume the label to challenge al-Qa'ida. The impact is biggest in the Muslim world, particularly in states with weak security services or existing insurgencies. In such cases, Islamic State fighters find it easy to penetrate borders and are often welcomed by locals who seek their manpower and expertise.[50]

The Islamic State also encourages lone attackers, and this effort increased in 2016. Islamic State propaganda in 2014 stressed that recruits should try to go to Iraq and Syria to be part of the Islamic State's consolidation and expansion. Acting locally was generally encouraged when individuals could not travel to Iraq and Syria. Propaganda thus encouraged *hijra* [migration] to the Islamic State.[51] But it still left room for individuals to act on their own. By 2016, however, Islamic State English-language propaganda prioritized attacks in the West over action in the heartland. Before he was killed, the group's spokesman and external operations chief, Mohammad al-Adnani, told international followers: "The smallest action you do in the heart of their land is dearer to us than the largest action by us."[52] Even though the attacks themselves appeared to have involved no direct links to the United States and although the shooters had minimal knowledge of the Islamic State, the attacks in the United States in 2015 and 2016 in San Bernardino and Orlando, respectively, reflected this danger and were difficult to prevent.

In addition to such actions being hard to prevent, the Islamic State chooses some potential recruits to act as lone attackers because it doubts their loyalty and commitment. Rather than risk bringing in a potential spy, having them act as a lone attacker minimizes risk for

---

[50] Watts, 2016; Byman, 2016b.

[51] Vidino and Hughes, 2015.

[52] Tim Lister, "ISIS Rides Wave of Attacks as Its Core Territory Shrinks," CNN, June 14, 2016.

the organization.[53] In addition, some lone attackers have psychological issues or personal problems and are operationally inept, traits that make them undesirable as military recruits.[54] Social media are often particularly important for lone attackers because they lack a handler to direct their actions. Islamic State propaganda can suggest targets, while Islamic State recruiters often act as the "devil on the shoulder," in the words of FBI Director Comey, encouraging supporters to attack.[55]

Desired End State

Although the Islamic State's control of territory is declining in Syria, Iraq, and a few other places, its virtual reach and clandestine presence remain. The disappearance of the core caliphate may severely damage the Islamic State's capacity to recruit, inspire, and conduct far-ranging attacks, but this effect may become apparent only over time. With the loss of the core caliphate, the Islamic State will likely become *more* dependent on its virtual profile and international terrorism to sustain its brand. Realistically, the medium-term goal should be to discredit and diminish the Islamic State's message and to disrupt and hinder foreign fighters and other human carriers. This will not eliminate all its supporters, and some terrorist attacks are likely to occur. But it will reduce the number of overall terrorists, hinder their operations, and make detection more likely. It would also reduce the value of the global network to the Islamic State's core organization in Iraq and Syria.

---

[53] Vidino and Hughes, 2015.

[54] Ramón Spaaij, "The Enigma of Lone Wolf Terrorism: An Assessment," *Studies in Conflict & Terrorism*, Vol. 33, No. 9, 2010, pp. 866-867; Michael Becker, "Explaining Lone Wolf Target Selection in the United States," *Studies in Conflict and Terrorism*, Vol. 37, No. 11, November 2014.

[55] John Hudson, "FBI Director: For Would Be Terrorists, Twitter Is the 'Devil on Their Shoulder,'" *Foreign Policy*, July 8, 2015.

Countering the Islamic State's Expansion

To counter the Islamic State's ideology and global actions, the United States should adopt a rollback strategy that works with its allies and Internet companies to shape the information environment, improve border security and internal defense, adapt focused measures to counter violent extremism, disrupt the Islamic State in its core areas, and capitalize on the decline and destruction of the core caliphate.

Shaping the Information Environment

The Islamic State's heavy reliance on social media and other forms of communication to publicize its message and share information with recruits is both a vulnerability and a benefit for the group. U.S. intelligence and law enforcement agencies should continue to exploit social media to identify potential group members and to disrupt their activities. Such monitoring is particularly important when seeking to identify potential lone attackers or those with no direct international connection, as they may be encouraged by online operatives or may post their intentions online as a form of bragging and belonging. In 2016, the killer of a priest in France reportedly announced his intention to do so well in advance on social media.

To hinder Islamic State recruitment efforts, the United States should press social media companies, such as Google and Facebook, to tighten restrictions on accounts linked to the group. Given the decentralized nature or the Islamic State's social media presence, law enforcement approaches to Islamic State propagandists will require extensive international cooperation. Propagandists might be located anywhere globally and could take refuge in states with weak law-enforcement institutions that do not have even basic capabilities in digital forensics or criminal procedures involving high-tech crime. In addition to existing cooperation, the United States will need to expand its cybercrime capacity-building efforts to help countries develop the institutional capacity to effectively pursue Islamic State extremists.

Covertly, the United States can also plant disinformation in the Islamic State's network. The group is already highly suspicious of perceived infiltrators—some potential foreign fighters are rejected or even executed as potential spies—and playing on this paranoia is appropriate. Messages might highlight the presence of moles, discuss the likelihood of defections, and otherwise sow distrust within the group's ranks. Israel, for example, attributes information gleaned from signals intelligence to human spy networks, creating the impression that a group has been thoroughly penetrated and thus leading its leaders not to trust subordinates.[56] The United States should also carefully consider how offensive cyberattacks on extremist sites and networks could be potentially used. Although there is always the risk that cyberoperations might simply be a game of whack-a-mole that will merely push the Islamic State elsewhere online, cyberoperations can also impose real costs. Possible steps might include taking down sites, altering them to pass on false contact information, presenting distorted propaganda, or otherwise sowing confusion and mistrust. Given the global nature of the Internet—and the fact that Islamic State sites might be hosted anywhere, including in allied or adversarial territory—unilateral cyberattacks will raise policy and legal complications. So, the United States should collaborate with partners to build their capacities and willingness to participate in joint cyberoperations against the Islamic State's online presence. Although certain cyberoperations might be covert, some important offensive actions will produce visible effects, so the United States and partners should also be prepared to explain publicly why they took the actions they did.

Countermessaging is also important, albeit exceptionally difficult. In theory, delegitimizing the message of the Islamic State and tarnishing its image can diminish fundraising and recruitment. In practice, however, government efforts are often cumbersome and cautious. Further, in a climate of conspiracy and paranoia, government funding for private efforts can be counterproductive.[57] Governments are also not able to engage in online conversation rapidly. Social media statements must be vetted, in contrast with the Islamic State's model, in which low-level recruiters can fire off hundreds of messages in a short

---

[56] See Daniel Byman, *A High Price: The Triumphs & Failures of Israeli Counterterrorism*, New York: Oxford University Press, 2011, for a discussion of Israeli intelligence methods.

[57] Stevens and Neumann, 2009, p. 43.

period.[58] Consequently, U.S. government social media campaigns like these are likely to have at best a limited impact. The U.S. government has already absorbed lessons from some of its prior missteps and has created a new Global Engagement Center, housed at the State Department, to provide grants to credible third parties to produce and amplify the countermessages the third parties create.

The best voices are former recruits or others with firsthand experience in the group.[59] They can talk credibly about the dismal conditions in the Islamic State, the killing of other jihadists, and other problems that run counter to the image the group promulgates. Saudi Arabia discredited the jihadists that opposed the kingdom in the mid-2000s by portraying their members as deluded criminals who were ignorant of Islam. In a program called "Jihad Experiences, the Deceit," former members of the group went on television to explain their mistakes, claim they were brainwashed by unscrupulous jihadist leaders, and describe the wanton cruelty of group leaders while religious leaders condemned the group's message.[60] The Abu Dhabi based Sawab Center has launched an original "defector's campaign" that focuses on testimonials from Islamic State defectors describing the true and harsh reality of life under the Islamic State.

The focus should not be on convincing Muslims in general or on engaging in theological debates but rather on reaching the small group that is attracted to the Islamic State's propaganda of success. In addition, the countermessage—in counterpoint to the Islamic State's message—must be segmented, recognizing that different audiences respond to different counterarguments.[61] Discrediting and, ideally, flipping returned foreign fighters is vital because they often seed new cells or serve as centers of recruiting networks. Many of these recruits, how-

---

[58] J. M. Berger, "Making CVE Work: A Focused Approach Based on Process Disruption," The Hague: International Centre for Counter-Terrorism, May 2016, p. 9.

[59] See, for example, Anne Speckhard and Ahmet S. Yayla, *ISIS Defectors: Inside Stories of the Terrorist Caliphate*, McLean, Va.: Advances Press, 2016.

[60] Abdullah F. Ansary, "Combating Extremism: A Brief Overview of Saudi Arabia's Approach," *Middle East Policy*, Vol. 15., No. 2, Summer 2008.

[61] Neumann, 2016.

ever, still hold views that are anathema to U.S. policy and its values, and any support for their anti-Islamic State agenda must be balanced by broader U.S. policy concerns.

An even more difficult challenge is convincing allied states, such as Saudi Arabia, to increase restrictions and pressure on preachers in the kingdom and affiliated charity networks that promote extremism overseas and in the kingdom itself. Saudi textbooks, for example, contain "derogatory and intolerant references to Shia and non-Muslims," according to the U.S. Department of State, while Saudi television broadcasts "sectarian hatred and intolerance."[62] The kingdom and other partners have tolerated such preachers and networks because they seek to gain the goodwill of the clerical establishment and to promote hostility toward Iran. In the past, however, governments have proven able to exert both formal and informal pressure effectively, and the Islamic State's hostility to these regimes makes cooperation more likely. However, the ongoing rivalry with Iran and the weak legitimacy of many Arab regimes will limit the extent of allied efforts.

Helping Refugees and Targeting Propagandists

The United States and its partners must also step up efforts to integrate and care for refugees in the Middle East and in Europe. So far, the refugees in the United States have not been linked to any terrorism in the homeland. In Europe, the Islamic State has exploited the refugee pipeline to send in operatives and is seeking to recruit from among the many refugees and inspire them to commit lone attacks. The refugees are not going back anytime soon, and the risk of alienation and recruitment by extremist groups rises if they do not find jobs and if their children are not educated. Palestinian refugees formed the core of many terrorist groups in the 1970s and 1980s. Syrian refugees, most notably those that are not well integrated into host country societies, could well do the same.

In the United States, the limited number of Syrian refugees should be assisted in finding jobs and integrated into host communities— a relatively simple task, given the small numbers, but one made harder

---

[62] U.S. Department of State, *Country Reports on Terrorism 2015*, Washington, D.C.: Bureau of Counterterrorism and Countering Violent Extremism, June 2016.

by Islamophobia and antirefugee sentiment.[63] As Europe has taken in far more refugees, the demands of integration are more considerable. One estimate put the figure at roughly $30,000 per refugee.[64] The asylum that European states, such as Germany, give requires long-term funding for education of refugee children, jobs programs, and other forms of assistance to assimilate and integrate refugees. This will require billions of dollars over time. Actively targeting recruiters and propagandists, as well as those who directly use violence, is also vital. Often, a relatively small number of recruiters have a disproportionate effect and so cannot easily be replaced—a pattern that is now holding true for the Islamic State.[65] The group suffers tremendously when these individuals are jailed, forced into hiding, or killed.

Facilitation networks in Turkey have been particularly important to the Islamic State, given that country's long border with Iraq and Syria and the extensive travels back and forth that foreign fighters have enjoyed along the border. Ankara long allowed foreign fighters considerable freedom but has cracked down more recently on transit routes and the Islamic State's infrastructure in Turkey. Such efforts have led the Islamic State to strike back with repeated terrorist attacks in Turkey. Washington should continue to offer Turkey technical assistance and political support and help with refugees to encourage the country to continue and expand its crackdown. Technical support might include providing additional sensor and surveillance technology to help Turkey monitor its border and sharing more signals intelligence on potential terrorist activity within Turkey itself. For the refugees, financial support is vital so that Turkey has the resources to police camps and educate refugee children. Washington should also encourage Turkey to assimilate refugees because they are not likely to return to Syria soon.

---

[63] For polling on Islamophobia in the West, see Gallup, "Islamophobia: Understanding Anti-Muslim Sentiment in the West," webpage, undated.

[64] Rob Williams, "Syrian Refugees Will Cost Ten Times More to Care for in Europe than in Neighboring Countries," *Independent*, 2016.

[65] Timothy Holman, "'Gonna Get Myself Connected': The Role of Facilitation in Foreign Fighter Mobilizations," *Perspectives on Terrorism*, Vol. 10, No. 2, 2016. See also Dodwell, Milton, and Rassler, 2016.

Give Extremists Off-Ramps

Efforts to fight the root causes of terrorism are often attractive to policymakers seeking a nonmilitary way of fighting terrorism. However, the analytic community lacks a robust understanding of why individuals join terrorist groups, and, in any event, such measures must be tailored carefully to succeed. Targeting communities as a whole, rather than focusing on individuals already engaged at least to some extent with recruitment and propaganda, is likely to fail or even backfire.[66]

To encourage family members and friends to work with security officials, off-ramps are vital, both for those who might join the Islamic State and for returning foreign fighters. Programs in Saudi Arabia and Indonesia offer possible models; individuals are given a mix of religious education, counseling, family support, and employment to change their attitudes toward the state and turn them against the radical group.[67] Families and friends may not turn in a potential terrorist if they believe the only alternative is sending him or her to jail. Similarly, some foreign fighters want to leave Syria or Iraq after becoming disillusioned with the group but may not return, fearing a lifetime in jail.[68] Counseling; probation; and, perhaps, limited and light prison sentences in some cases might be a better mix, although of course those committed to violence must be jailed. Attention also needs to be paid to the danger of radicalization of those in prison. Europe has developed several promising pilot projects in this area, although the scale is small so far.[69] A desire to look strong in the face of terrorism and the risk of mistakes, however, make it politically easier to always pursue maximal penalties, even though such an approach may backfire. Gaining com-

---

[66] Berger, 2016, p. 3.

[67] For overviews of these programs, see Roel Meijer, ed., *Counterterrorism Strategies in Indonesia, Saudi Arabia, and Algeria*, The Hague, Netherlands: Clingendael, 2012. The authors in the volume are quite cautious, however, in their conclusions on these programs' effectiveness.

[68] For one example, see Adam Goldman, "'I Am Fed Up with This Evil': How an American Went from Ivy League Student to Disillusioned ISIS Fighter," *Washington Post*, June 30, 2016

[69] Bergen, 2015, p. 15; Eric Rosand, Taking the Off-Ramp: A Path to Preventing Terrorism," War on the Rocks website, July 1, 2016.

munity support is particularly important for countering lone attackers. Their activity may be observed by neighbors, or they may confide online or to close friends.

Promoting online education for youths is also valuable. Most youth online education in the West focuses on sexual predators. Broadening this education to focus on other risky behaviors, including joining Salafi-jihadist groups, such as the Islamic State, would provide more warning and erect another barrier to terrorist recruitment.[70] One area that might also be explored is suicide prevention, for which there is broad education about warning signs and 24/7 hotlines.

Defeating the Core Organization

Defeating or at least disrupting the Islamic State in its heartland in Iraq and Syria is also vital for reducing its international influence. Much of the group's propaganda is about its image as a winner and the benefits of living in an Islamic State. Taking that away would be a serious blow. The territorial and financial losses the group has suffered since 2014 led to a dramatic decrease in the number of volunteers by 2016.[71] Similarly, forcing the group's leaders and recruiters to hide makes it harder for them to have sustained contact with potential recruits or exercise command and control when they seek to seed or acquire new provinces.

Limits and Trade-Offs

Because the Islamic State relies on an image of success to attract recruits, setbacks in one arena may push it to do more operations in another. So advances against the core group in Iraq and Syria may, at least for a time, lead to more terrorism in the West. Thus, U.S. and allied successes against the group might be viewed as failures by citizens understandably more focused on the deaths of dozens in their own country than the deaths of thousands of Islamic State victims abroad. In the long term, shrinking and eventually ending the Islamic State's

---

[70] Stevens and Neumann, 2009, p. 39.

[71] Gibbons-Neff, 2016.

base will have a significant payoff. Until then, however, more terrorism may result.

Success against the Islamic State might lead some recruits to go to Jabhat Fateh al-Sham (previously known as Jabhat al-Nusrah) or other terrorist groups. Some experts argue that this al-Qa'ida affiliate is potentially more dangerous to the United States than the Islamic State, given the al-Qa'ida core's emphasis on attacking the West over targets in the Muslim world.[72] Perhaps the two most troubling returnees to the United States were tied to Jabhat Fateh al-Sham, not the Islamic State.[73]

Because terrorism is likely to continue, regardless of what happens to the Islamic state, efforts to promote domestic resilience are vital. Even before the Paris and Orlando attacks, polling found that more Americans felt more unsafe than they did in September 2002, in the aftermath of the 9/11 attacks. This was a surprising finding, given that terrorism on U.S. soil has since been relatively low by modern historical standards.[74] Similarly, terrorism concerns in Europe are high, increasing support for far-right political movements there.

Finally, when considering new arenas into which the Islamic State might expand, the United States should recognize the risks of creating new enemies and of overstretch. Some regions, such as Indonesia, might best be left with allies, such as Australia, in the lead; still others, such as parts of Central Asia, may not meet a threat level worthy of a high level of U.S. attention. Still, intelligence monitoring and cooperation with regional security services is worthwhile, as is contingency planning should the perceived threat change. Diminishing the Islamic State's global appeal is difficult, demands cooperation with allies and partners, and will require a range of instruments. If it succeeds, it is likely to do so incompletely and in fits and starts. But a comprehensive rollback strategy that targets both the hard and soft power of the

---

[72] Charles Lister, *Jihadi Rivalry, The Islamic State Challenges al-Qaida*, Washington, D.C.: Brookings Institution, January 27, 2016b.

[73] Bergen, 2015, p. 9.

[74] Mark Murray, "ISIS Threat: Fear of Terror Attack Soars to 9/11 High, NBC News/WSJ Poll Finds," NBC News, September 9, 2014.

Islamic State can tarnish the group's image, hinder its operations, and over time make it far less dangerous.

CHAPTER ELEVEN

Recommendations

U.S. success against the Islamic State and other Salafi-jihadist groups will depend to a great extent on the capacity and will of its local partners in Africa, Europe, the Middle East, and Asia. Previous chapters have outlined steps to counter the Islamic State in countries in which it has controlled territory—Iraq, Syria, Libya, Nigeria, Egypt, and Afghanistan—and beyond, where it continues to organize and inspire attacks. In this chapter, we seek to integrate these findings and make specific recommendations to weaken and ultimately defeat the Islamic State. The U.S. goal should be to reduce the Islamic State to a clandestine network that holds no physical territory, controls no meaningful population, and poses no major threat to the United States at home or abroad. We also cost out, at least in rough terms, the necessary American commitment of military manpower and economic resources.

Recent American efforts have helped undermine Islamic State territorial control in Iraq, Syria, Afghanistan, Libya, and Nigeria. But continuing along the same lines is unlikely to prevent a return of the Islamic State or another Salafi-jihadist organization without taking additional measures.

Intensify Military Efforts in Syria

The lack of an acceptable local government partner in Syria has complicated American efforts to roll back the Islamic State. Washington has found an effective partner in the SDF, which includes a mix of Kurdish and Sunni Arab forces. The SDF has isolated Raqqa and is poised for an assault on the city, but it lacks the heavy weaponry that may be necessary for success. Turkey is opposed to any further extension of Kurdish control within Syria and equally opposed to any American effort to arm Kurdish forces within the SDF. Washington must therefore choose whether to ignore Turkish objections and arm the SDF, seek direct Turkish Army participation in the assault, or add some American units to the assault force. Waiting for the Turkish Army and its Syrian allies to arrive will require postponing the operation some months, with an uncertain end result. Arming the Kurdish-dominated SDF and introducing additional American forces into Syria, beyond the special operations troops already there, may be the fastest and surest way of retaking the Islamic State capitol.

Even before it launches the operation to liberate Raqqa, the United States should propose interim arrangements for securing and administering the city and its surroundings that Turkey, Russia, and the local population will accept. We suggest Washington should offer to place Raqqa, once liberated, under some form of international administration.

Delegate Authority Downward

The United States should review the policy guidance for authorizing lethal force overseas and consider loosening constraints in two ways for counterterrorism operations. First, the White House should revamp the process used to approve strikes against the Islamic State and other terrorist groups. The PPG outlining the Obama administration's policy toward drone strikes in locations outside "areas of active hostilities" did not precisely define that term.[1] However, administration lawyers included such countries as Iraq, Syria, and Afghanistan.[2]

---

[1] White House, 2013.

[2] See, for example, Heather Brandon, "Will Obama's Targeted Killing Policy Say What 'Areas of Active Hostilities' Means?" *Lawfare*, May 5, 2016, and Christian Schaller, "Using Force Against Terrorists 'Outside Areas of Active Hostilities'—The Obama Approach and the Bin Laden Raid Revisited," Journal of Conflict Security Law, Vol. 20, No. 2, February 2, 2015.

Other countries in which the United States considered or conducted lethal action—except, briefly, Libya—were not considered areas of active hostility. For these countries, the PPG detailed prescriptions for the bureaucratic, legal, and operational process to conduct lethal force. U.S. agencies had to follow a process that involved developing operational plans for taking direct action, conducting an interagency review of operational plans, organizing principals and deputies to meet and review the operational plans, and presenting options to the president of the United States. The PPG also outlined which specific senior U.S. officials had to review proposals to capture or kill terrorists and what factors they had to consider.[3]

While the PPG offered many benefits, including an emphasis on minimizing civilian casualties, it also had problems. To begin with, its criteria for what constituted areas of active hostilities were unclear. It appeared to cover countries with protracted armed violence between government forces and organized insurgent groups in which the United States faced a national security threat. If that were the intention, such countries as Libya should also be considered areas of active hostilities.[4] So should a handful of countries, such as Somalia and Yemen, with insurgencies involving al-Qa'ida affiliates and other Salafi-jihadists. In addition, the PPG process was overly bureaucratic. U.S. agencies had to follow a cumbersome process that was sometimes inefficient and a poor use of time for senior policymakers, including individuals at the Deputies Committee level. Too often, they debated *tactics* rather than focusing on *strategic* issues, such as the overall campaign plan, cooperation with allied nations, and ways to deal with political and governance challenges. The authorization process also required extra and sometimes unnecessary work for military units to prepare for senior meetings.

---

[3] White House, 2013.

[4] The International Criminal Tribunal for the former Yugoslavia defined a *non-international armed conflict* as occurring "whenever there is . . . . Protracted armed violence between governmental authorities and organized armed groups or between such groups within a State." See, for example, International Committee of the Red Cross, "How Is the Term 'Armed Conflict' Defined in International Humanitarian Law," opinion paper, March 2008.

Finally, such groups as the Islamic State have become increasingly adaptive and decentralized, requiring the United States to be equally efficient and flexible.[5] The Islamic State has inspired and plotted attacks in Europe, North America, Africa, Middle East, and Asia. And it is becoming more proficient in utilizing commercially available encrypted communications technologies and new systems, such as unmanned aerial vehicles. When the PPG was written, the Islamic State did not exist in its current form. Indeed, the evolution of such groups makes it important for the United States to establish a streamlined approval process for lethal action in war zones.[6]

The White House should consider expanding the number of areas of active hostilities on a case-by-case basis to include more locations where the Islamic State has established a significant presence and where the United States is supporting local forces. When American ambassadors and commanders cannot agree, disputes should be referred to Washington. But otherwise, there should be more discretion for action at the local level in active military theaters, such as Libya, Somalia, and Yemen, on the basis of clearly established guidelines, as is already the case in Afghanistan, Iraq, and Syria. The United States should continue interagency deliberation at lower levels of the U.S. government, and the White House should still hold senior policymakers—including military officials—accountable when there are mistakes. The United States should also conduct direct action, such as raids by U.S. special operations forces, only when there is near certainty that the action can be taken without injuring or killing noncombatants.[7] In addition, the White House should make a concerted effort to be transparent about strikes overseas, both in discussing the results of operations and explaining the legal and policy framework for authorizing them.[8] With

---

[5] Christopher S. Chivvis and Andrew M. Liepman, *Authorities for Military Operations Against Terrorist Groups: The State of the Debate and Options for Congress*, Santa Monica, Calif.: RAND Corporation, RR-1145-1-OSD, 2016.

[6] See, for example, Luke Hartig, "U.S. at Crossroads on Drone Ops," CNN, August 21, 2016.

[7] White House, 2013, p. 1.

[8] Hartig, 2016; Chivvis and Liepman, 2016.

some types of operations, such as hostage rescue missions and special operations raids, authorizing the deployment of U.S. military boots on the ground should still involve senior-level deliberations because the U.S. foreign policy implications are particularly significant. The use of lethal force outside designated areas of active hostilities should as well.

Second, the United States should relax restrictions on U.S. military forces accompanying local forces into combat environments. U.S. soldiers, including special operations forces, have at times been prevented from moving past the "last cover-and-conceal" position during operations because of security concerns.[9] Because of this risk aversion, U.S. forces have had to rely on partner forces in such countries as Syria to conduct missions ranging from seizing terrorist personnel and materiel (what the military refers to as *sensitive site exploitation*) to conducting strikes. Partner forces are not always reliable and many have interests different from those of the United States. These authorizations are often held at the combatant command level, not at the White House. But they have been overly restrictive. Consequently, the U.S. military should loosen restrictions on forward-deployed U.S. forces and push down authority to local U.S. commanders.

Expand Basing Access in North and West Africa

The United States should expand its force posture in West and North Africa. The threat from the Islamic State and other Salafi-jihadist groups in these regions remains high; the current posture is inadequate; and the collapse of the Islamic State's caliphate in Iraq and Syria may trigger the return of a large number of North Africans to the region. The U.S. global defense posture consists of forces rotationally deployed and permanently garrisoned abroad, the facilities and supporting infrastructure that make up the U.S. military footprint, and the agreements that enable the United States to have an overseas military presence (such as mutual defense treaties, status of forces agreements, and access

---

[9] *Last cover-and-conceal position* refers to the final location that U.S. soldiers can hide before going to the target.

agreements). Today, thousands of U.S. troops are stationed in hundreds of military facilities overseas, conducting activities from training with partner nations to conducting combat operations with them.[10]

Figure 11.1 highlights the U.S. overseas basing posture in Europe, Africa, Asia, the Middle East, and Australia. It includes two categories of installations: main operating bases and forward operating sites. The figure excludes locations to which U.S. military personnel are temporarily deployed for train-and-assist programs, cooperative security locations used for contingency operations and regional training, and loca-

Figure 11.1
U.S. Force Posture in Europe, Africa, the Middle East, and Asia

RAND *RR1912-11.1*

---

[10] Michael J. Lostumbo, Michael J. McNerney, Eric Peltz, Derek Eaton, David R. Frelinger, Victoria A. Greenfield, John Halliday, Patrick Mills, Bruce R. Nardulli, Stacie L. Pettyjohn, Jerry M. Sollinger, and Stephen M. Worman, *Overseas Basing of U.S. Military Forces: An Assessment of Relative Costs and Strategic Benefits*, Santa Monica, Calif.: RAND Corporation, RR-201-OSD, 2013.

tions used for combat support and intelligence-collection operations in countries in which basing agreements with the host government do not exist.

Figure 11.1 suggests several issues. First, U.S. military posture is robust in Afghanistan and Iraq, as discussed earlier in the report, where counterterrorism and counterinsurgency operations have been ongoing—or nearly ongoing—since 2001 and 2003, respectively. In Afghanistan, for example, the United States has bases in Kabul, Bagram, Kandahar, and Jalalabad and more than 8,000 troops. In Iraq, U.S. military forces use a number of bases across the country, such as al Asad Air Base in Anbar Province, to conduct operations against the Islamic State. The United States also has a force presence of more than 5,000 soldiers in Iraq. These bases can be helpful to support the CIA and other intelligence units that play important counterterrorism and counterinsurgency roles.

Second, U.S. posture is limited in several regions in which the Islamic State and other Salafi-jihadist groups pose significant threats, particularly North and West Africa. The current posture has affected U.S. counterterrorism operations in several ways. In some cases, weather in southern Europe or the Mediterranean has hampered efforts to move aircraft quickly from southern Europe to Africa. Some European countries have also prohibited the United States from flying some types of missions from their bases, including operations to capture or kill terrorists. In addition, limited basing in Africa makes it challenging for U.S. quick-reaction forces to respond adequately to crises in West and North Africa and has forced the U.S. military to plan for emergencies from bases in such locations as Rota, Spain. Finally, inadequate basing in Africa, including too few forward arming and refueling points, limits the reach-and-response time of U.S. aircraft.

Consequently, the United States should increase its posture in West and North Africa. While the United States has bases in East Africa, particularly in Djibouti, it has no major bases in Libya, Nigeria, Algeria, Egypt, and Chad—despite significant activity from the Islamic State and other Salafi-jihadist groups. The United States is investing in a base in central Niger, although there may be restrictions on what the U.S. military can do and how many U.S. forces or aircraft can be stationed there. Even with a base in Niger, the United States should consider negotiating with other countries in the region to station U.S. military forces and fly combat and surveillance aircraft. U.S. basing access in Africa has been notoriously difficult because of political sensitivities, making it important to ensure some redundancy. The Pacific also presents a potential challenge if there is a resurgence of Islamic State–linked groups in the Philippines, Indonesia, or Thailand. Even in countries in which the U.S. military does have a presence, such as the Philippines, the local political climate has become much more tenuous for U.S. forces.[11]

Tighten Restrictions on Islamic State Internet Access

To counter the Islamic State's ideology and global actions, the United States should redouble efforts to shut down social media accounts linked to the Islamic State, establish closer collaboration with social media companies, conduct offensive cyberoperations, and give extremists off-ramps. While Chapter Ten provides a more detailed set of suggestions to counter the Islamic State's ideology, we focus on one issue here: tightening restrictions on Islamic State accounts.

To hinder Islamic State recruitment efforts, the United States should work with social media companies to increase restrictions on accounts linked to the group. In 2015 and 2016, several social media companies, such as Twitter, became more active in suspending Islamic State–linked accounts that violated terms of service. Such motivated efforts help diminish the Islamic State's social media presence but could also result in law enforcement and intelligence services losing important sources of information. To grapple with this tension, the United States should work with companies to develop trusted flagging mechanisms, algorithms, and perhaps "robust hashing" techniques developed by computer scientists, such as Dartmouth College professor Hany Farid, who can identify which accounts pose national

---

[11] See, for example, Jane Perlez, "Philippines' Deal with China Pokes a Hole in U.S. Strategy," *New York Times*, November, 2, 2016.

security threats.[12] Companies have been largely receptive to similar mechanisms in the UK and EU.[13] In creating such a nodal point for engagement with companies, the United States should be wary of the perception of government censorship and should closely consult with companies as transparently as possible.

There are other productive avenues for partnership between the government and Internet companies. Google, Facebook, and other major companies thrive by tracking their users for advertising and revenue purposes. The same computerized techniques that enable targeted advertising to everyday users can be repurposed for identifying Internet-use patterns associated with potential Islamic State recruits and, once identified, serving them pinpointed countermessages and information about off-ramp options. In addition, such organizations as the Gen Next Foundation have partnered with Silicon Valley companies, such as Google, to develop and implement the "redirect method," which uses a mixture of Google's search advertising algorithms and YouTube's video platform to discourage possible Islamic State recruits from joining the group.

The U.S. government should encourage broader use of these efforts and further assist companies by compiling useful, shareable analysis about the Islamic State to help them better understand the challenge and further motivate action. Silicon Valley and Washington have had strained relations at times, including between the Federal Bureau of Investigation and Apple over encryption. But through collaboration and trust-building, the United States can more effectively promote the notion that companies have an ethical and security responsibility to counter the Islamic State's use of their services.

Restricting extremist access to social media and redirecting possible recruits requires companies to devote staff time and engineering resources to detecting such content and closing it down. Voluntary compliance with government importuning may not be sufficient to

---

[12] Joseph Rago, "How Algorithms Can Help Beat the Islamic State," *Wall Street Journal*, March 11, 2017.

[13] See, for example, Alex Hern, "Facebook, YouTube, Twitter, and Microsoft Sign EU Hate Speech Code," *Guardian* (UK), May 31, 2016.

persuade these companies to spend as much money, time, and effort as the task optimally requires. The United States and other governments should set out clear requirements and consider what additional levels of regulation and assertions of liability might be applied to secure maximum compliance. In doing so, consideration will need to be given to sustaining a cooperative relationship with these companies and avoiding precedents that might lead governments to unnecessarily impinge on Internet freedom.

The Islamic State will likely adapt by creating new accounts and taking other steps, but this adaptation may fall short. Although the Islamic State had tens of thousands of accounts on Twitter, for example, it relied heavily on a small fraction of these for much of its social media presence.[14] One study found that the number of Islamic State Twitter accounts fell from 2014 to 2016, in part because of more-aggressive efforts to shut down their accounts: "Over time," the study concluded, "individual users who repeatedly created new accounts after being suspended suffered devastating reductions in their follower counts."[15] Because of such crackdowns, the Islamic State now uses more peer-to-peer and encrypted methods that are harder to detect but reach far fewer people and require more of its operatives' time. Account takedowns are also far more effective when accompanied by prosecutions or other means of stopping the propagandists more permanently.[16]

Strengthen Partner Capacity to Secure and Govern Territory

The United States should rebalance its counterterrorism campaign and focus on preventing a resurgence of Salafi-jihadist groups after the

---

[14] J. M. Berger and Jonathon Morgan, *The ISIS Twitter Census: Defining and Describing the Population of ISIS Supporters on Twitter*, Washington, D.C.: Brookings Institution, 2015, p. 3.

[15] J. M. Berger and Heather Perez, "The Islamic State's Diminishing Returns on Twitter: How Suspensions Are Limiting the Social Networks of English-Speaking ISIS Supports," Washington, D.C.: George Washington University Program on Extremism, February 2016, p. 4.

[16] Stevens and Neumann, 2009, p. 27.

Islamic State loses its control of territory and a decline in its brand. While military force is necessary to target the Islamic State and undermine its control of territory, it is not sufficient. Military operations that take territory away from the Islamic State will likely be transitory unless these areas are effectively secured and administered by local authorities and unless the underlying factors that gave rise to insurgency are more effectively addressed. Developments in Iraq highlight this challenge. In early 2017, several months after Iraqi forces liberated the western city of Fallujah from Islamic State control, residents were disenchanted because of a lack of reconstruction, services, and jobs. Much of the city had been destroyed during the fighting, and the anemic pace of reconstruction threatened to rekindle the same type of resentment toward the Iraqi government that had given rise to the Islamic State in the first place.[17]

Consequently, an important—perhaps the most important— component of rollback should be to help local regimes improve governance and deal more effectively with grievances leveraged by the Islamic State and other Salafi-jihadist groups. We examine these issues in the countries where the Islamic State has controlled territory: Iraq, Syria, Libya, Nigeria, Egypt, and Afghanistan. A key theme from these cases is that U.S. policymakers need to better understand the *specific* political and other factors that allowed the Islamic State to establish a foothold and to focus U.S. diplomatic and development efforts on better addressing them.

Iraq

Sunni Arab disenfranchisement has been among the most important causes of instability in Iraq and an important source of recruits for the Islamic State. Current military efforts to undermine Islamic State territorial control in such cities as Fallujah, Ramadi, and Mosul have so far done little to ameliorate local grievances. The Islamic State's loss of territory could heighten ethnic, sectarian, tribal, political, and other

---

[17] Guillaume Decamme and Salam Faraj, "Patience Wears Thin in Fallujah, 6 Months after IS Ouster," Agence France Presse, January 18, 2017; Rick Gladstone, "Iraqis Take Eastern Mosul from Islamic State," *New York Times*, January 19, 2017.

tensions as Sunni, Shi'a, Kurdish, and other actors struggle for control of the liberated areas; outside powers, such as Iran, attempt to expand their influence; and the Iraqi government attempts to reestablish its authority. An important component of rollback in Iraq should involve encouraging implementation of an Iraqi government reconciliation plan that directly addresses collective Sunni Arab grievances. U.S. diplomats and military personnel can and should aid in the implementation of this plan. The United States should seek to boost ongoing Iraqi government reform efforts. The objective should be to build toward an eventual constitutional convention, which will allow all parties—Sunni, Shi'a, Kurd, and other minorities—to have another opportunity to ensure that their roles and livelihoods are protected.

Syria

The political and governance challenges in Syria are immense. Alawi Arab Ba'athists have dominated the Syrian government at the expense of other groups, notably Sunni Arabs. Syrian Kurds have a longstanding history of opposition to the Assad regime. Some Kurdish political and military groups also have close ties with the radical anti-Turkish PKK, placing them in opposition to the government of Turkey. At a minimum, the United States should establish and help protect a zone of relative safety covering Raqqa province once the Islamic State has been driven out. This will require Washington to establish arrangements for securing and administering Raqqa, once liberated, that Turkey, Russia, and the local population will accept.

Libya

Ending Libya's civil war is essential for undermining the Islamic State over the long run. Of particular importance is improving governance in Libya. A political agreement in Libya will likely require both the support of Libya's local actors and the cooperation of at least three key outside groups. The first consists of Egypt, the United Arab Emirates, and Saudi Arabia, which have been staunch supporters of the Libyan House of Representatives and provided weapons and airpower to General Hiftar's efforts to drive other groups out of Benghazi and eastern Libya. A second group includes the actors that have supported the Tripoli government, including Turkey, Qatar, and Sudan. A third group involves Libya's immediate neighbors, especially Tunisia and Algeria. Both Tunisia and Algeria are reluctant to openly countenance any Western intervention in Libya. They will need to be brought into the discussions regarding Libya's future and the composition of any international stabilization force. In addition, they will need to reinforce their own efforts to counter radicalization, fight the groups on their soil, and strengthen their border controls. The United States should provide a range of security assistance to strengthen the defense and law enforcement institutions of Tunisia, a sole positive remnant of the Arab Spring, and to prevent the further spread of terrorism. The United States should also help Sudan better secure its northwestern border with Libya to prevent Islamic State fighters from traveling to and from Libya, as well as help Sudan interdict weapon smuggling and human trafficking.

Nigeria

The most significant political change in Nigeria has been the improved performance under President Buhari. Washington's frustrations with Abuja boiled over during the administration of his predecessor, Goodluck Jonathan, largely over the issues of corruption, human rights abuses, and general ineptitude. The United States should continue to foster a cooperative relationship with the Nigerian government and support regional cooperation through the MNJTF. The United States should also continue to encourage the Nigerian leadership to address the corruption that helped generate popular sympathy for the Boko Haram insurgency.

Egypt

The United States should encourage more Egyptian government engagement with tribes in the Sinai Peninsula to persuade them to push back the Islamic State–Sinai Peninsula's encroachment on their traditional lands. The Tarabin, one of the major tribes in North Sinai, where the Islamic State is most active, announced their intention to fight the Islamic State after the group carried out several assassinations of leading sheikhs from their federation. Closer coordination between tribal elements and the 2nd Land Army that has responsibility for Egyptian military operations in North Sinai could help limit the Islamic State's freedom of movement. Cooperation is currently constrained by the inability of Egyptian forces to protect communities that are vulnerable to Islamic State reprisals and a continued resentment of the state that can lead some residents to tolerate or sympathize with the Islamic State–Sinai Peninsula, despite its brutality. Cairo has pursued a quid pro quo approach to relations with Sinai tribes, offering sweeteners, such as the release of Sinai residents jailed for smuggling and other offenses, in return for specific forms of cooperation. This conditional engagement needs to evolve into sustained cooperation. Investment in the Sinai that benefits local residents is one way for the Egyptian government to signal its intentions.

Afghanistan

The Islamic State faces substantial hurdles in the region because of a crowded market of violent jihadist groups. Improving governance is important to counter the Islamic State–Khorasan Province and other groups. Washington's most important political priority in Afghanistan should be to focus U.S. efforts on working with the Afghan government and political elites to improve governance and reach a consensus on contentious issues, such as the status of Afghanistan's chief executive officer and elections. U.S. diplomats could play an important role in helping broker a compromise on electoral reform and providing financial aid and technical support so that elections can eventually occur. In Nangarhar Province, where there is a small Islamic State footprint, the United States and the Afghan government should continue to work with local communities, such as Shinwari tribal leaders, to undermine the Islamic State's support base.

The Islamic State has used some parts of Pakistan's FATA to recruit fighters, secure funding, and conduct operations. Pakistan is unlikely to turn the FATA into a governed territory any time soon. A bigger challenge is Pakistan's support to militant groups, which it utilizes as tools of foreign policy toward Afghanistan and India. Pakistan's support to militant groups calls for a fundamental review of available U.S. options. The Obama administration and Congress reduced military assistance to Pakistan in recent years and also curtailed the use of foreign military financing. But even today's reduced amounts of U.S. assistance could be cut further. Targeted economic sanctions could be selectively applied against specific organizations and individuals. Washington might also sketch out a vision of an improved relationship with Pakistan if Islamabad would show more forthright and consistent support for the goals of NATO in Afghanistan. This outcome would be highly desirable for broader American interests, given Pakistan's central role in the stability of the entire region.

Aid to State Building

The main focus for American economic assistance in all these countries should be improving the capacity of local authorities to secure and administer territory and populations liberated from the Islamic State. The United States should also leverage such assistance to promote steps to ameliorate the underlying grievances that facilitated the emergence of the Islamic State. This is obviously easier to do where a legitimate local authority exists, including one willing to work with the United States and acceptable to other donors. The United States can currently work with the governments in Iraq, Egypt, Nigeria, and Afghanistan. But the challenges in Syria and Libya, which lack legitimate governments, are more serious.

In the former category of states, the United States should work with other donors, whose overall contribution is likely to be larger than the American commitment. The international financial institutions—the World Bank, the regional development banks, and the International Monetary Fund—can make important contributions. Establishing common priorities for international assistance will greatly increase the impact of anything the United States can do on its own.

To widen the pool of donors, the Iraqi government needs to improve its relations with the Gulf states, which requires reducing its dependency on Iran. Egypt already receives substantial support from the Gulf. Europe is likely to be the principal source of humanitarian and development assistance for Nigeria and its affected neighbors.

There is already a well-developed donor community for Afghanistan, which has pledged nearly $4 billion in annual economic assistance through 2020.

Until national governments recognized as legitimate domestically and internationally can be restored in Syria and Libya, assistance to these countries will be largely limited to humanitarian aid. In Syria, the United States should also provide limited stabilization-type aid to areas liberated by partner forces and should seek to encourage other donors to do likewise. This will be difficult to do unless Turkey can be encouraged to open its borders to the flow of such aid.

Like George W. Bush and even Barack Obama, President Donald Trump has expressed an aversion to "nation-building."[18] The costs and disappointing results of the American efforts in Afghanistan and Iraq have led most Americans to the same conclusion. Yet the military campaign against the Islamic State, which we recommend here, will be of little enduring value unless the quality of governance is improved in all the affected states.

Funding Rollback

The United States should sufficiently resource its campaign against the Islamic State. We estimated costs in three categories: the deployment of military forces, security assistance, and economic and humanitarian assistance. We did not analyze the costs to physically rebuild cities and infrastructure destroyed by the fighting in Iraq and Syria. Some of these costs will ultimately be borne by the local authorities and much of the costs by the broader international community, including the relevant multinational institutions. But the United States will be expected to make a significant contribution. Our estimates are necessarily rough, as outlined in Appendixes A and B. It is not possible to determine precisely what programs and activities may be necessary in

---

[18] See, for example, Donald Trump, "Transcript: Donald Trump's Foreign Policy Speech," *New York Times*, April 27, 2016.

the future. Rather, we have extrapolated from current costs, indicating where these are likely to increase or decline and why.

We assess that total annual military deployment costs and the security, economic, and humanitarian aid costs could range from $18 billion to $77 billion. This breakdown includes between $12 billion and $40 billion annually for the deployment of 7,900 to 31,050 U.S. military forces, respectively; between $4 billion and $16 billion for security assistance to key allies; and between $2 billion and $21 billion for economic and humanitarian assistance to key allies.

The Islamic State is not the only threat coming out of these countries that the United States faces, and defeating it is not the only American interest in this region. These costs must therefore be applied across a wider range of threats and interests, of which combating the Islamic State is currently the most prominent. While these costs may seem large, they are significantly smaller than the cost of the wars in Afghanistan (Operation Enduring Freedom [OEF]) and Iraq (Operation Iraqi Freedom [OIF]). These wars cost U.S. taxpayers roughly $1.5 trillion between 2001 and 2013, which translated into $115 billion per year for only the two countries.[19]

Long-Term Prospects

Because the Islamic State relies on an image of success to attract recruits, its leaders will continue to conduct and incite external attacks even while they lose territory. Advances against the core group in Iraq and Syria may lead to more terrorism in the West, at least temporarily. In the long term, shrinking and eventually ending the Islamic State's base will have a significant payoff. Nevertheless, success against the Islamic State may lead some affiliates and potential recruits to switch to al-Qa'ida or other terrorist groups. Because terrorism is likely to continue, efforts to promote domestic resilience in the United States are

---

[19] Amy Belasco, *The Cost of Iraq, Afghanistan, and Other Global War on Terror Operations Since 9/11*, Washington, D.C.: Congressional Research Service, RL33110, December 8, 2014.

vital. In the wake of recent attacks in Europe and the United States, polling has found that Americans feel more unsafe than they did in September 2002, in the aftermath of the 9/11 attacks. This may be surprising to some, given that terrorism on U.S. soil has been relatively low by modern historical standards.[20] Similarly, terrorism concerns in Europe are high.

Finally, when considering new areas into which the Islamic State might expand, the United States should recognize the risks of creating new enemies and of overstretch. Some regions, such as Central Asia, may not reach a threat level worthy of significant U.S. attention. Still, intelligence monitoring and cooperation with regional services are worthwhile for contingency planning in case the threat changes. Diminishing the Islamic State's global appeal is difficult, demands cooperation with allies and partners, and will require a range of instruments. But a comprehensive rollback strategy that targets both the hard and soft power of the Islamic State can tarnish the group's image, hinder its operations, and contribute to its eventual demise.

---

[20] Murray, 2014.

Per-Troop Rollback Cost Methodology

As noted in Chapter Eleven, our costing efforts were rough approximations. It is not possible to determine precisely what programs and activities may be necessary in the future, and more-precise figures cannot be established without that information. Rather, we have extrapolated from current and historical costs and assumed that future costs will be of the magnitude of previous programs.

To estimate the cost per year of deploying U.S. military forces as part of light rollback, we first used estimates for military deployment costs. We then provided rough estimates for deploying U.S. military forces to the countries in which the Islamic State controls territory: Iraq, Syria, Libya, Nigeria, Egypt, and Afghanistan.[1] We also added several miscellaneous countries to which the U.S. could deploy forces to support local partners against the Islamic State and other jihadist groups, such as Tunisia, Yemen, Jordan, the Philippines, and Somalia. As Table A.1 shows, the cost of military deployments for rollback could range from $12 billion to $41 billion per year, depending on such factors as the number of forces deployed.

In deriving these cost estimates of direct military operations to counter the Islamic State, we first considered the annual per-troop cost estimates for recent military engagements available in the academic literature. These estimates varied significantly (see Table A.2). On a per-troop basis, the costs of the wars in Iraq and Afghanistan seem to

---

[1] A U.S. deployment to Afghanistan would likely be sufficient to deal with the Islamic State–Khorasan Province because the Islamic State holds territory only on the Afghan side of the border.

Table A.1
Projected Estimated Cost of U.S. Military Deployment, Per Year

Country	Low		High	
	Number of U.S. Soldiers	Cost ($M)	Number of U.S. Soldiers	Cost ($M)
Iraq	2,500	3,860	10,000	15,440
Syria	200	62	2,000	622
Libya	50	16	2,000	622
Nigeria	50	16	1,000	311
Egypt[a]	0	0	50	16
Afghanistan	5,000	7,720	15,000	23,160
Miscellaneous countries[b]	100	31	1,000	311
Total	7,900	11,705	31,050	40,482

[a] For Egypt, we exclude forces operating under the Multinational Force and Observers mission.

[b] Examples are Tunisia, Yemen, Jordan, Somalia, and the Philippines.

have been trending upward since 2002. While the precise cause of this trend is unclear, many factors could be at work besides the size of the force, such as cost increases associated with higher operational tempos, the need for force protection, support facility and infrastructure investment costs, command-and-control requirements, intelligence support requirements, and equipment depreciation.[2]

The per-troop cost for a special operations forces–centric operation with a small footprint and limited infrastructure might be considerably different from that for a heavy operational footprint with a host of infrastructure, sustainment, and logistics costs. We therefore looked at several historical cases, ranging from small train-and-assist operations, such as those employed during OEF–Philippines (OEF-P) and OEF–Trans-Sahara (OEF-TS), to the massive force levels deployed at the height of the surges during OEF-Afghanistan and OIF-Iraq. We

---

[2] Belasco, 2014.

Table A.2
Rising Estimated Per-Troop Costs in Iraq and Afghanistan

Fiscal Year	Annual Cost per Troop ($000)	Country	Source
2003	320	Iraq and Afghanistan	Belasco, 2009
2004	340	Iraq and Afghanistan	Belasco, 2009
2005	350	Iraq and Afghanistan	Belasco, 2009
2005	490	Iraq	Belasco, 2014
2005	580	Afghanistan	Belasco, 2014
2006	390	Iraq and Afghanistan	Belasco, 2009
2008	800	Iraq	Belasco, 2014
2008	820	Afghanistan	Belasco, 2014
2011	900	Afghanistan	Belasco, 2014
2011	1,000	Afghanistan	Hanrahan, 2011
2012	850	Afghanistan	Hale, 2012
2012	1,600	Iraq	Belasco, 2014
2013	1,300	Afghanistan	Harrison, 2013
2014	1,000	Iraq and the Levant	Shabad, 2014
2014	2,100	Afghanistan	Harrison, 2013

SOURCES: Amy Belasco, *The Cost of Iraq, Afghanistan, and Other Global War on Terror Operations Since 9/11*, Washington, D.C.: Congressional Research Service, RL33110, September 28, 2009; Belasco, 2014; John Hanrahan, "A Cold Calculation: How Much Is Too Much to Spend on Afghanistan?" Cambridge, Mass.: Nieman Foundation for Journalism, Harvard University, June 15, 2011; Robert F. Hale, U.S. Department of Defense Comptroller, "Defense Department Fiscal Year 2013 Budget," testimony before the Senate Budget Committee, February 28, 2012; Rebecca Shabad, "Costs Rack Up In ISIS Fight," *The Hill*, September 25, 2014; Todd Harrison, *Chaos and Uncertainty: The FY 2014 Defense Budget and Beyond*, Washington, D.C.: Center for Strategic and Budgetary Assessments, October 2013.

calculated annual average per-troop costs by dividing best estimates of total war-related costs by in-country boots on the ground.

Where available, we derived annual war-related cost estimates and personnel data from the latest overseas contingency operations (OCO) funding requests from U.S. Department of Defense's Comptroller. For smaller operations, such as OEF-P, OEF-TS, and OEF–Horn of Africa (HOA),[3] we relied on cost and personnel estimates from Congressional Research Service reports, U.S. Department of Defense's Defense Manpower Data Center, and *The Military Balance*. The war-related costs in the OCO funding requests included appropriations for operations and force protection (including personnel special pays and subsistence for deployed force, ground vehicles and equipment, combat aviation, special operations forces, communications, deployment and redeployment of combat and support forces, and life support and sustainment), in-theater support, equipment reset and readiness, and classified programs.[4] The estimates in this section exclude OCO obligations earmarked for the Afghan Security Forces Fund, Iraq Security Forces Fund, Iraq Train and Equip Fund, and Syria Train and Equip Fund. These costs are considered instead in Appendix B.

As Table A.3 shows, we estimate that the cost per troop of relatively small, special operations forces–centric footprints (similar to those of OEF-Ps, OEF-TS, and/or OEF-HOA) would be substantially less—$100,000 to $300,000 annually—than that of a heavier footprint (such as those employed in OEF-Afghanistan, OIF-Iraq, Operation New Dawn–Iraq, or OIR-Iraq and Syria—$1 million to $1.6 million annually). Additionally, according to our analysis of the U.S.

---

[3] Note that, after OEF formally ended in December 2014, OEF-TS and OEF-HOA continued under Operation Freedom's Sentinel (OFS). OEF-TS supports the Commander, U.S. Africa Command in the execution of the National Military Strategy in ten partner nations (Algeria, Burkina Faso, Chad, Mali, Mauritania, Morocco, Niger, Nigeria, Senegal, and Tunisia). OEF-HOA supports the U.S. Navy's Combat Command Support Activity at Camp Lemonnier, Djibouti, and includes special operations forces to conduct operations, civil affairs, and military information support operations in HOA, including operations in Burundi, Djibouti, Eritrea, Ethiopia, Kenya, Rwanda, Seychelles, Somalia, Tanzania, and Uganda. The broader Combined Joint Task Force HOA area of interest includes the Central African Republic, Chad, Comoros, the Democratic Republic of the Congo, Egypt, Mauritius, Madagascar, Mozambique, Sudan, South Sudan, and Yemen. See Combined Joint Task Force HOA website, "About the Command," undated.

[4] U.S. Department of Defense, "FY2017 Amended Budget Request to Congress," Washington, D.C.: Office of the Under Secretary of Defense (Comptroller), November 2016c, pp. 5-7.

Department of Defense Comptroller's November 2016 budget amendment request for fiscal year 2017 (which updates the original February 2016 budget request), the current marginal cost of an additional troop in Iraq, Syria, or Afghanistan is about $1,050,000. For the estimates in Table A.1, we used $311,000 per soldier per year for the smaller operations, based on the cost of OEF-HOA. We also used the estimate of $1,544,000 per soldier per year for Iraq and Afghanistan operations, based on the 2017 Iraq and Syria OIR costs.

Table A.3
Average Annual Cost Estimates for Selected Military Operations Since 9/11

Country or Area	Operation	FY	Average Annual Force Levels	Estimated Annual Funding ($B)	Average Annual Cost per U.S. Troop ($000)	Marginal Cost per Additional U.S. Troop ($000)[a]
Iraq	OIF	2008	154,000[b]	143.6[c, d, e]	932	—
Iraq	New Dawn	2011	47,000[b]	44.0[c, e, f]	936	—
Iraq and Syria	OIR	2017	5,600[e]	8.7[e, g]	1,554	1,052
Afghanistan	OEF	2011	98,000[b]	104.1[c, e, h]	1,062	—
Philippines	OEF-P	2007	500[i]	0.05[j]	100	—
Northwest Africa	OEF-TS	2017	550[k]	0.08[l]	145	—
Horn of Africa	OEF-HOA	2017	3,900[m]	1.21[l]	311	—

NOTES: Numbers may not add due to rounding.

[a] In November 2016, the U.S. Department of Defense released an amended OCO budget request for FY 2017 updating its original request released in February 2016. These estimated marginal costs per additional soldier are based on the changes in the November 2016 budget, which boosted the number of troops in Afghanistan for OFS by 2,457 at a requested cost of $2.5 billion and in Iraq and the Levant by 2,012 at a requested cost of $2.1 billion. See U.S. Department of Defense, 2016c, pp. 1–2. The November 2016 OCO amendment also included an additional $290 million for support to the Kurdish Peshmerga under OIR-OCO funds and $814.5 million for Afghan aviation modernization under OFS-OCO funds, but our marginal cost estimates for an additional U.S. troop for OIR and OFS (2017) exclude these requests.

[b] U.S. Department of Defense, "FY2017 Budget Request to Congress," Washington, D.C.: Office of the Under Secretary of Defense (Comptroller), February 2016b, Sec. 7-5.

[c] USAID, 2014.

Table A.3—Continued

d We have subtracted $4.4 billion appropriated for Iraq Security Forces Fund from the topline OCO funding level of $148 billion for Iraq in 2008.

e U.S. Department of Defense, 2016c, pp. 1–5.

f We subtracted $0.96 billion appropriated for the Iraq Security Forces Fund from the top-line OCO funding of $45 billion for Iraq in 2011.

g We subtracted $1.2 billion appropriated for the Iraq Train and Equip Fund and the Syria Train and Equip Fund from the top-line OCO funding of $9.9 billion for Iraq and Syria in 2017.

h We subtracted $9.9 billion appropriated for the Afghan Security Forces Fund from the top-line OCO funding of $114 billion for Afghanistan in 2011.

i Thomas Lum and Ben Dolven, The Republic of the Philippines and U.S. Interests: 2014, Washington, D.C.: Congressional Research Service, R43498, May 15, 2014, p. 14, which states that Joint Special Operations Task Force–Philippines (part of OEF-P) averaged 500 to 600 members annually between 2004 and 2014 (down from nearly 2,000 in 2003).

j Lum and Dolven, 2014, p. 14, which states that operating Joint Special Operations Task Force–Philippines cost an average of about $50 million annually between 2004 and 2014. This figure presumably excluded interagency program funds, such as the International Criminal Investigative Training Assistance Program, and contract lift support from private firms, such as Evergreen International.

k A total of 160 U.S. personnel were deployed in OEF-TS's area of operational responsibility according to the Defense Manpower Data Center's monthly personnel location database of active duty, reserve, and AFP civilian forces deployed abroad (as of September 30, 2016) (Defense Manpower Data Center, "DoD Personnel, Workforce Reports & Publications," various dates). However, other open-source reporting of U.S. deployments in the Trans-Sahara region suggests that this is low. For instance, the United States currently has approximately 250 personnel in Niger and 300 in Cameroon (International Institute for Strategic Studies, The Military Balance 2017, Vol. 117, 2017; Craig Whitlock, "Pentagon Setting Up Drone Base in Africa to Track Boko Haram Fighters," Washington Post, October 14, 2015).

l Susan Epstein and Lynn Williams, Overseas Contingency Operations Funding: Background and Status, Washington, D.C.: Congressional Research Service, June 13, 2016, p. 37; these figures include funds appropriated in both U.S. Department of Defense's FY 2017 Base Budget Request and FY 2017 OCO Request (see Office of the Secretary of Defense, Fiscal Year 2017 President's Budget: Justification for Base Funded Contingency Operations and the Overseas Contingency Operation Transfer Fund (OCOTF), February

Table A.3—Continued

2016). The current request for $80 million annually for OEF-TS is slightly higher than in recent years; between FY 2010 and FY 2012, it ranged from $46 million to $50 million. On historical funding levels, see Lauren Ploch, *Africa Command: U.S. Strategic Interests and the Role of the U.S. Military in Africa*, Washington, D.C.: Congressional Research Service, RL34003, July 22, 2011.

[m] Summed totals of U.S. personnel deployed in the countries under OEF-HOA's area of operational responsibility, as published by the Defense Manpower Data Center's monthly personnel location database of active duty, reserve, and AFP civilian forces deployed abroad (as of September 30, 2016). Because many of the personnel deployed at Camp Lemonnier in Djibouti may not directly support OEF-HOA, this estimate may be high. Indeed, according to Ploch, 2011, p. 21, an estimated 2,000–2,500 short-term rotational U.S. military and civilian personnel made up Combined Joint Task Force HOA.

Security, Economic, and Humanitarian Assistance Cost Methodology

To estimate security assistance costs, we first compiled and analyzed U.S. security assistance between 2001 and 2016 to countries and regions important for rolling back the Islamic State and other Salafi-jihadist groups and examined the associated trends. The data came from USAID's Greenbook.[1] We broke the programs into several regions: Near East (including Iraq, Syria, Turkey, and Jordan); South Asia (including Afghanistan, Pakistan, and Bangladesh); Lake Chad Basin (Nigeria, Cameroon, and Chad); the Sahel and Maghreb including (Libya, Tunisia, and Mali); East Africa (including Somalia, Kenya, and Ethiopia); and the Pacific (including the Philippines, Thailand, and Indonesia). We looked at a range of U.S. security assistance packages from the U.S. Department of Defense, including the following:

- International Military Education and Training
- U.S. Code, Title 10, §2282. Authority to Build the Capacity of Foreign Security Forces
- Public Law 108-375 §1208
- the Combating Terrorism Fellowship Program
- defense institution-building programs, such as the Defense Institution Reform Initiative, foreign military sales, and excess defense articles.

---

[1] USAID, 2014.

We also examined U.S. Department of State security assistance programs. Finally, we examined programs from other U.S. agencies, such as the Department of Homeland Security and Department of Justice.

Next, we estimated the costs for specific security assistance packages. For each set of countries, the high estimate represents the upper bound of what we assess could be necessary to counter the Islamic State and other Salafi-jihadist groups by improving local security. The smaller estimate represents the lower bound. We based both estimates on historical trends and qualitative judgments about such factors as the local government's security capabilities, capacity to utilize assistance, needs, and terrorist threats. As Table B.1 shows, we assessed that the costs for U.S. security assistance could range from roughly $4 billion to $16 billion per year. Current U.S. security assistance to these countries totals $9 billion. To be clear, U.S. security assistance does not need to be used by state and nonstate actors *only* to combat the Islamic State and other terrorist groups. U.S. assistance can also have second- and

Table B.1
Cost Ranges for U.S. Security Assistance Options

Country or Region	Current ($M)[a]	Low ($M)	High ($M)[b]
Iraq, Syria, and select Near Eastern countries	3,597	2,683.00	8,949
Afghanistan, Pakistan, and select South Asian countries	5,139	1,487.00	5,783
Nigeria and select Lake Chad Basin countries	38	0.40	54
Libya and select Sahel and Maghreb countries	51	8.00	658
Select Pacific countries	81	9.00	123
Select East African countries	214	0.30	442
Total	9,120	4,188.00	16,009

SOURCE: USAID, 2014.

NOTE: Totals might not sum due to rounding.

[a] FY 2014 is the most recent year for which complete data are available.

[b] Because security assistance to Iraq and Afghanistan were such outliers at the height of the wars, we have substituted the average annual amount of security assistance to these countries since the start of the wars for the highest annual amount in these calculations. For Iraq, the average annual amount was $2.2 billion, compared to a high of $6.2 billion in 2006. For Afghanistan, the average annual amount was $4.8 billion, compared to a high of $10.8 billion in 2011.

third-order affects by helping states deal more effectively with criminal organizations and establish fair justice systems. But this assistance should be targeted to countries that can play a critical role in countering the Islamic State and its allies in the region.

To estimate economic and humanitarian assistance costs, we first compiled and analyzed the costs of U.S. economic and humanitarian assistance between 2001 and 2016 to countries and regions important for rolling back the Islamic State and other Salafi-jihadist groups and examined the associated trends. The data came from the U.S. Overseas Loans and Grants database. We broke the programs into the same regions as for security assistance. We looked at a range of U.S. assistance from the U.S. Department of State, such as from the democracy fund, refugee and migration, and global health and child survival programs. We also examined USAID programs, such as from the Office of U.S. Foreign Disaster Assistance and Office of Food for Peace. Finally, we compiled economic and humanitarian aid packages from several other U.S. government organizations.[2]

Next, as for security assistance, we estimated the costs for economic and humanitarian assistance packages (see Table B.2). We assessed that U.S. economic and humanitarian assistance could range from roughly $1.9 billion to $21 billion per year, with current U.S. assistance to these countries totaling $11 billion. Much as with U.S. security assistance, U.S. economic and humanitarian aid to these countries and regions goes beyond counterterrorism and can support human rights, democracy, education, global health, and the environment.

Tables B.1 and B.2 provide aggregated information. Tables B.3 and B.4 break out the assistance the United States provided country by country for security assistance and economic and humanitarian assistance, respectively.

---

[2] These organizations were the Department of Agriculture, Department of Commerce, Department of Energy, Department of Health and Human Services, Department of Homeland Security, Department of Justice, Department of Labor, Department of the Treasury, Department of Transportation, Department of the Interior, the U.S. Trade and Development Agency, Peace Corps, Millennium Challenge Corporation, the Federal Trade Commission, the Overseas Private Investment Corporation, the African Development Foundation, and the Environment Protection Agency.

Table B.2
Cost Ranges for U.S. Economic and Humanitarian Assistance Options

Country or Region	Current ($M)[a]	Low ($M)	High ($M)[b]
Iraq, Syria, and select Near Eastern countries	2,820	416	8,854
Afghanistan, Pakistan, and select South Asian countries	3,481	492	4,663
Nigeria and select Lake Chad Basin countries	901	129	1,009
Libya and select Sahel and Maghreb countries	541	139	2,162
Select Pacific countries	522	271	1,450
Select East African countries	2,400	408	2,817
Total	10,665	1,855	20,955

SOURCE USAID, 2014.

[a] FY2014 is the most recent year for which complete data are available.

[b] Because economic and humanitarian assistance to Iraq and Afghanistan were such outliers at the height of the wars, we have substituted the average annual amount of economic and humanitarian assistance to these countries since the start of the wars for the highest annual amount in these calculations. For Iraq, the average annual amount was $3.4 billion, compared to a high of $9.2 billion in 2004. For Afghanistan, the average annual amount was $2.2 billion, compared to a high of $4.4 billion in 2010.

Table B.3
Current, High, Low, and Average Annual Security Assistance, by Country, 2001–2014

Country	Current[a] ($M)	High ($M)	Low ($M)	Average ($M)
Near East				
Iraq	22	6,236	0.0	2,182.0
Syria	0	39	0.0	4.0
Lebanon	87	101	0.7	36.0
Jordan	346	803	99.0	315.0
Turkey	10	91	2.0	22.0
Egypt	0.3	1,684	0.3	1,375.0
Yemen	21	68	0.3	20.0
Israel	3,100	3,864	2,576.0	2,877.0
Bahrain	11	118	5.0	26.0
Total	3,597	8,949	2,683.0	6,544.0

Table B.3—Continued

Country	Current[a] ($M)	High ($M)	Low ($M)	Average ($M)
South Asia				
Afghanistan	4,864	10,786	0.0	4,753.0
Pakistan	264	994	0.2	338.0
Bangladesh	6	26	0.7	5.0
India	5	10	0.6	3.0
Total	5,139	5,783	1.0	4,760.0
Lake Chad Basin				
Nigeria	8	21	0.0	6.0
Cameroon	3	3	0.2	1.0
Chad	17	17	0.2	2.0
Niger	10	13	0.0	3.0
Total	38	54	0.4	12.0
Sahel and Maghreb				
Libya	1	32	0.0	5.0
Tunisia	44	44	8.0	19.0
Mali	3	133	0.0	12.0
Mauritania	1	34	0.0	5.0
Sudan	0	413	0.0	80.0
Algeria	2	2	0.1	1.0
Eritrea	0	0.5	0.0	0.1
Total	51	658	8.0	122.0
Pacific				
Philippines	61	72	6.0	43.0
Thailand	3	21	3.0	9.0
Indonesia	16	29	0.0	12.0
Total	81	122	9.0	65.0
East Africa				
Somalia	136	291	0.0	82.0
Kenya	31	62	0.0	12.0
Ethiopia	6	9	0.0	3.0
Djibouti	11	17	0.3	5.0

Table B.3—Continued

Country	Current[a] ($M)	High ($M)	Low ($M)	Average ($M)
Uganda	31	62	0.0	12.0
Total	214	442	0.3	114.0

SOURCE: USAID, 2014.

NOTE: Totals might not sum due to rounding.

[a] FY2014 is the most recent year for which complete data are available.

Table B.4
Current, High, Low, and Average Annual Economic and Humanitarian Assistance, by Country, 2001–2014

Country	Current[a] (U.S. $M)	High (U.S. $M)	Low (U.S. $M)	Average (U.S. $M)
Near East				
Iraq	388	9,205	0	3,420
Syria	795	795	0	128
Lebanon	347	347	19	148
Jordan	791	1,338	205	557
Turkey	102	260	6	42
Egypt	179	1,334	165	551
Yemen	192	256	2	84
Israel	23	1,102	18	347
Bahrain	1	2	0	1
Total	2,820	8,854	416	4,789
South Asia				
Afghanistan	2,396	4,360	110	2,245
Pakistan	717	1,878	229	767
Bangladesh	232	302	66	154
India	137	238	86	168
Total	3,481	4,663	492	3,181
Lake Chad Basin				
Nigeria	585	585	105	325
Cameroon	63	63	7	21

Table B.4—Continued

Country	Current[a] (U.S. $M)	High (U.S. $M)	Low (U.S. $M)	Average (U.S. $M)
Chad	130	227	5	105
Niger	123	133	11	56
Total	901	1,009	129	506
Sahel and Maghreb				
Libya	49	92	0	22
Tunisia	27	133	0	19
Mali	166	587	44	136
Mauritania	25	31	7	17
Sudan	264	1,207	89	593
Algeria	11	16	2	8
Eritrea	-1	97	–2	29
Total	541	2,162	139	826
Pacific				
Philippines	268	598	103	188
Thailand	74	84	15	54
Indonesia	180	768	153	283
Total	522	1,450	271	525
East Africa				
Somalia	266	301	27	131
Kenya	860	1,029	118	522
Ethiopia	737	913	153	589
Djibouti	10	25	2	11
Uganda	527	548	107	335
Total	2,400	2,817	408	1,589

SOURCE: USAID, 2014.

NOTE: Totals might not sum due to rounding.

[a] FY2014 is the most recent year for which complete data are available.

Abbreviations

AQI	al-Qa'ida in Iraq
CAPMAS	Central Agency for Public Mobilization and Statistics
CIA	Central Intelligence Agency
CIFG	Counter ISIL Finance Group
CJTF	civilian joint task force
EU	European Union
FATA	Federally Administered Tribal Areas (Pakistan)
GCC	Gulf Cooperation Council
GPW	Gridded Population of the World
HOA	Horn of Africa
HVE	homegrown violent extremist
IDP	internally displace person
IED	improvised explosive device
ISIL	Islamic State of Iraq and the Levant
ISIS	Islamic State of Iraq and al-Sham (Syria)
JaN	Jabhat al-Nusrah
JIC	Joint Intelligence Committee

MNJTF	Multinational Joint Task Force
NATO	North Atlantic Treaty Organization
NSC	National Security Council
OCO	overseas contingency operations
OEF	Operation Enduring Freedom
OFS	Operation Freedom's Sentinel
OIF	Operation Iraqi Freedom
OIR	Operation Inherent Resolve
PKK	Kurdistan Workers' Party
PPG	Presidential planning guidance
PYD	Democratic Union Party
SDF	Syrian Defence Forces
SEDAC	NASA Socioeconomic Data and Applications Center
TTP	Tehreek-e-Taliban Pakistan
UK	United Kingdom
UN	United Nations
USAID	U.S. Agency for International Development
YPG	People's Protection Units

References

Abdelaty, Ali, and Ahmed Aboulenein, "Islamic State Extending Attacks Beyond Sinai to Egyptian Heartland" Reuters, January 25, 2017.

Abdo, Geneive, *Salafists and Sectarianism: Twitter and Communal Conflict in the Middle East*, Washington, D.C.: Brookings Institution, 2015. As of February 13, 2017:
https://www.brookings.edu/research/
salafists-and-sectarianism-twitter-and-communal-conflict-in-the-middle-east/

Adili, Ali Yawar, and Martine van Bijlert, "Pushing the Parliament to Accept a Decree: Another Election Without Reform," Afghanistan Analysts Network website, June 10, 2016. As of February 9, 2017:
https://www.afghanistan-analysts.org/
pushing-the-parliament-to-accept-a-decree-another-election-without-reform/

al-Adnani, Abu Muhammad, "Hadha wa'd Allah," Al-Battar Media Foundation, June 29, 2014.

"Afghan Air Strike Against Islamic State Kills 40," *Dawn* (Pakistan), April 15, 2016.

"Afghan Official: IS Group Present in at Least 3 Provinces," Associated Press, June 28, 2015. February 9, 2017:
http://www.cnsnews.com/news/article/
afghan-official-group-present-least-3-provinces

"Afghanistan Mourns Protest Blast Victims," Al Jazeera, July 23, 2016.

Ahmad, Jibran, and Yeganeh Torbati, "U.S. Drone Kills Islamic State Leader for Afghanistan, Pakistan: Officials," Reuters, August 13, 2016.

Ahmed, Farouk, "Sons of Iraq and Awakening Forces," Washington, D.C.: Institute for the Study of War, February 21, 2008.

Akinola, Olabanji, "Boko Haram Insurgency in Nigeria: Between Islamic Fundamentalism, Politics, and Poverty," *African Security*, Vol. 8, No. 1, March 2015.

Alaaldin, Ranj, "Iran's Weak Grip: How Much Control Does Tehran Have over Shia Militias in Iraq?" *Foreign Affairs*, February 11, 2016. As of 29 July 2016: https://www.foreignaffairs.com/articles/iran/2016-02-11/irans-weak-grip

Albayrak, Ayla, and Dana Ballout, "U.S., Turkey Step Up Border Campaign Against Islamic State," *Wall Street Journal*, April 26, 2016.

Ali, Shafqat, "70 Dead as Taliban Bomb Protest over Lawyer's Killing in Quetta," *Nation* (Pakistan), August 8, 2016.

Alokozay, Khalid, and Mujib Mashal, "ISIS Claims Assault that Killed 7 Near Pakistani Consulate in Afghanistan," *New York Times*, January 13, 2016.

Amos, Deborah, "30 Years Later, Photos Emerge from Killings in Syria," National Public Radio, February 2, 2012. As of August 3, 2016: http://www.npr.org/2012/02/01/146235292/30-years-later-photos-emerge-from-killings-in-syria#

el Amrani, Issandr, "How Much of Libya Does the Islamic State Control?" *Foreign Policy*, February 18, 2016. As of February 9, 2017: http://foreignpolicy.com/2016/02/18/how-much-of-libya-does-the-islamic-state-control/

Ansary, Abdullah F., "Combating Extremism: A Brief Overview of Saudi Arabia's Approach," *Middle East Policy*, Vol. 15, No. 2, Summer 2008, pp. 111–142. As of February 13, 2017: http://onlinelibrary.wiley.com/doi/10.1111/j.1475-4967.2008.00353.x/abstract

Arab Center for Research and Policy Studies, *The Military Campaign Against the Islamic State in Iraq and the Levant: Arab Public Opinion*, Doha, November 26, 2014.

Arango, Tim, "Dozens Killed in Battles Across Iraq as Sunnis Escalate Protests Against Government," *New York Times*, April 23, 2013. As of 26 July 2016: http://www.nytimes.com/2013/04/24/world/middleeast/clashes-at-sunni-protest-site-in-iraq.html

Arreguín-Toft, Ivan, *How the Weak Win Wars: A Theory of Asymmetric Conflict*, New York: Cambridge University Press, 2005.

ASDA'A Burson-Marsteller, "Inside the Hearts and Minds of Arab Youth: Arab Youth Survey 2016," Dubai, 2016. As of February 8, 2016: http://www.arabyouthsurvey.com/en/home

Ashour, Omar, "Sinai's Stubborn Insurgency," *Foreign Affairs*, November 8, 2015.

Assanvo, William, Jeannine Ella A. Abatan, and Wendyam Aristide Sawadogo, "Assessing the Multinational Joint Task Force Against Boko Haram," Pretoria, South Africa: Institute for Security Studies, West Africa Report No. 19, September 2016.

Awad, Mokhtar, and Samuel Tadros, "Bay`a Remorse? Wilayat Sinai and the Nile Valley," *CTC Sentinel*, Vol. 8, No. 8, August 2015. As of February 9, 2017: https://www.ctc.usma.edu/posts/baya-remorse-wilayat-sinai-and-the-nile-valley

al-Baghdadi, Abu Bakr, "Allah Will Not Allow Except that His Light Should Be Perfected," Fursan Al-Balagh Media, July 2012.

———, "Baqiya fi al-'Iraq wa-l-Sham," audio recording, June 2014a.

———, "A Message to the Mujahideen and the Muslim Ummah in the Month of Ramadan," Fursan Al-Balagh Media, July 1, 2014b.

Bahney, Benjamin, Howard J. Shatz, Carroll Ganier, Renny McPherson, and Barbara Sude, *An Economic Analysis of the Financial Records of Al-Qa'ida in Iraq*, Santa Monica, Calif.: RAND Corporation, MG-1026-OSD, 2010. As of February 8, 2017: http://www.rand.org/pubs/monographs/MG1026.html

Barr, Nathaniel, and David Greenberg, "Libya's Political Turmoil Allows Islamic State to Thrive," *Terrorism Monitor*, Vol. 14, No. 7, April 1, 2016. As of February 9, 2017: https://jamestown.org/program/libyas-political-turmoil-allows-islamic-state-to-thrive/

Bassiuni, Mohamed 'Abd al-Halim, "al-Hurūb al-Hajīna: Dalālāt Imtilāk al-Irhābīyīn lil Sawārīkh Mahmūla fi al-Sharq al-Awsat [Hybrid Wars: Evidence of Terrorist Acquisition of Portable Missiles in the Middle East]," Cairo: Regional Center for Strategic Studies, April 26, 2016.

Becker, Michael, "Explaining Lone Wolf Target Selection in the United States," *Studies in Conflict and Terrorism*, Vol. 37, No. 11, November 2014.

Belasco, Amy, *The Cost of Iraq, Afghanistan, and Other Global War on Terror Operations Since 9/11*, Washington, D.C.: Congressional Research Service, RL33110, September 28, 2009.

———, *The Cost of Iraq, Afghanistan, and Other Global War on Terror Operations Since 9/11*, Washington, D.C.: Congressional Research Service, RL33110, December 8, 2014.

Benraad, Myriam, "Iraq's Tribal 'Sahwa': Its Rise and Fall," *Middle East Policy Council Journal*, Vol. 18, No. 1, Spring 2011. As of July 24, 2016: http://www.mepc.org/journal/middle-east-policy-archives/iraqs-tribal-sahwa-its-rise-and-fall

Bergen, Peter, "Jihad 2.0: Social Media in the Next Evolution of Terrorist Recruitment," testimony before the U.S. Senate Committee on Homeland Security and Governmental Affairs, May 7, 2015.

Berger, J. M., "Tailored Online Interventions: The Islamic State's Recruitment Strategy," *CTC Sentinel*, October 23, 2015. As of February 13, 2017:
https://www.ctc.usma.edu/posts/
tailored-online-interventions-the-islamic-states-recruitment-strategy

———, "Making CVE Work: A Focused Approach Based on Process Disruption," The Hague: International Centre for Counter-Terrorism, May 2016. As of February 13, 2017:
https://www.icct.nl/wp-content/uploads/2016/05/J.-M.-Berger-Making-CVE-Work-A-Focused-Approach-Based-on-Process-Disruption-.pdf

Berger, J. M., and Jonathon Morgan, *The ISIS Twitter Census: Defining and Describing the Population of ISIS Supporters on Twitter*, Washington, D.C.: Brookings Institution, 2015. As of February 13, 2017:
https://www.brookings.edu/wp-content/uploads/2016/06/isis_twitter_census_berger_morgan.pdf

Berger, J. M., and Heather Perez, "The Islamic State's Diminishing Returns on Twitter: How Suspensions Are Limiting the Social Networks of English-Speaking ISIS Supports," Washington, D.C.: George Washington University Program on Extremism, February 2016. As of February 13, 2017:
https://cchs.gwu.edu/sites/cchs.gwu.edu/files/downloads/Berger_Occasional%20 Paper.pdf

Berger, Samuel R., Stephen J. Hadley, James F. Jeffrey, Dennis Ross, and Robert Satloff, *Key Elements of a Strategy for the United States in the Middle East*, Washington, D.C.: Washington Institute for Near East Policy, 2015.

Biddle, Stephen, and Jacob Shapiro, "America Can't Do Much About ISIS," *Atlantic*, April 20, 2016a.

———, "The Problem with Vows to 'Defeat' the Islamic State," *Atlantic*, August 21, 2016b.

bin Laden, Osama, "Jihad Against Jews and Crusaders," Federation of American Scientists website, February 23, 1998. As of March 20, 2017:
https://fas.org/irp/world/para/docs/980223-fatwa.htm

Blanchard, Lauren Ploch, "Nigeria's Boko Haram: Frequently Asked Questions," Washington, D.C., Congressional Research Service, R43558, March 29, 2016. As of February 9, 2017:
https://fas.org/sgp/crs/row/R43558.pdf

Blinken, Antony J., "To Defeat ISIS, Arm the Syrian Kurds," *New York Times*, January 31, 2017.

Bodine-Baron, Elizabeth, Todd Helmus, Madeline Magnuson, and Zev Winkelman, *Examining ISIS Support and Opposition Networks on Twitter*, Santa Monica, Calif.: RAND Corporation, RR-1328-RC, 2016. February 8, 2017:
http://www.rand.org/pubs/research_reports/RR1328.html

Boghardt, Lori Plotkin, "Saudi Funding of ISIS," Washington, D.C.: Washington Institute for Near East Policy, June 23, 2014. As of 29 July 2016:
http://www.washingtoninstitute.org/policy-analysis/view/saudi-funding-of-isis

"Boko Haram Attacks Jere, Borno State," NTA News (Nigeria), May 27, 2016. As of February 9, 2017:
http://www.nta.ng/news/20160527-boko-haram-attacks-jere-borno-state/

Boot, Max, "Maliki's Actions, and Obama's Inaction, Threaten an Iraq Democracy," Los Angeles Times, May 9, 2010. As of 29 July 2016:
http://articles.latimes.com/2010/may/09/opinion/la-oe-boot-20100509.

Borhi, László, "Containment, Rollback, Liberation or Inaction? The United States and Hungary in the 1950s," Journal of Cold War Studies, Vol. 1, No. 3, 1999, pp. 67–108.

Brandon, Heather, "Will Obama's Targeted Killing Policy Say What 'Areas of Active Hostilities' Means?" Lawfare, May 5, 2016.

Brands, Hal, and Peter Feaver, "Trump and Terrorism: U.S. Strategy After ISIS," Foreign Affairs, Vol. 96, No. 2, March/April 2017, pp. 28–36.

Brandt, Patrick T., T. David Mason, Mehmet Gurses, Nicolai Petrovsky, and Dagmar Radin, "When and How the Fighting Stops: Explaining the Duration and Outcome of Civil Wars," Defence and Peace Economics, Vol. 19, No. 6, December 2008, pp. 415–434.

Brennan, Rick, Jr., Charles P. Ries, Larry Hanauer, Ben Connable, Terrence K. Kelly, Michael J. McNerney, Stephanie Young, Jason H. Campbell, and K. Scott McMahon, Ending the U.S. War in Iraq: The Final Transition, Operational Maneuver, and Disestablishment of the United States Forces–Iraq, Santa Monica, Calif.: RAND Corporation, RR-232-USFI, 2013. As of February 8, 2017:
http://www.rand.org/pubs/research_reports/RR232.html

Byman, Daniel L., Going to War with the Allies You Have: Allies, Counterinsurgency, and the War on Terrorism, Carlisle, Pa.: U.S. Army War College, November 2005.

———, "Friends Like These: Counterinsurgency and the War on Terrorism," International Security, Vol. 31, No. 2, Fall 2006, pp. 79–115.

———, A High Price: The Triumphs & Failures of Israeli Counterterrorism, New York: Oxford University Press, 2011.

———, "The Homecomings: What Happens when Arab Foreign Fighters in Iraq and Syria Return?" Studies in Conflict and Terrorism, Vol. 38, No. 8, 2015, pp. 581–602.

———, Al-Qaeda, the Islamic State, and the Global Jihadist Movement: What Everyone Needs to Know, New York: Oxford University Press, 2015.

———, "Six Bad Options for Syria," Washington Quarterly, Vol. 38, No. 4, Winter 2016a, pp. 171–186.

————, "ISIS Goes Global: Fight the Islamic State by Targeting Its Affiliates," *Foreign Affairs*, Vol. 95, No. 2, March/April 2016b, pp. 76–85.

Cafiero, Girgio, and Daniel Wagner, "The UAE and Qatar Wage a Proxy War in Libya," *Huffington Post*, December 14, 2015. As of February 9, 2017: http://www.huffingtonpost.com/giorgio-cafiero/the-uae-and-qatar-wage-a-_b_8801602.html

Callimachi, Rukmini, "ISIS and the Lonely Young American," *New York Times*, June 27, 2015. As of February 13, 2017: https://www.nytimes.com/2015/06/28/world/americas/isis-online-recruiting-american.html

————, "How a Secretive Branch of ISIS Built a Global Network of Killers," *New York Times*, August 3, 2016. As of February 13, 2017: https://www.nytimes.com/2016/08/04/world/middleeast/isis-german-recruit-interview.html

"Camp Speicher Massacre Trial Begins in Iraq," Al Jazeera, December 27, 2015. As of 26 July 2016: http://www.aljazeera.com/news/2015/12/trial-starts-suspects-isil-massacre-iraq-151227144148919.html

CAPMAS—*See* Central Agency for Public Mobilization and Statistics.

Carpenter, Ted Galen, "How the West Should Respond to a Divided Iraq—And Not Intervene Again," *Aspenia*, August 27, 2014. As of 29 July 2016: https://www.aspeninstitute.it/aspenia-online/article/how-west-should-respond-divided-iraq-and-not-intervene-again

Carter, Ashton B., and John F. Kerry, "Section 1222 Report: Strategy for the Middle East and to Counter Violent Extremism," report submitted to Congress in response to NDAA for Fiscal Year 2016 requirement under Section 1222, undated but written and posted in May 2016. As of June 21, 2016: https://armedservices.house.gov/sites/republicans.armedservices.house.gov/files/wysiwyg_uploaded/Section%201222%20Report.pdf

Carter, Joseph, Shiraz Maher, and Peter Neumann, "#Greenbirds: Measuring Importance and Influence in Syrian Foreign Fighter Networks," London: International Centre for the Study of Radicalization and Political Violence, 2014.

Centanni, Evan, "War in Nigeria: Map of Boko Haram Control, September 2014)," *Political Geography Now*, September 29, 2014. As of February 9, 2017: http://www.polgeonow.com/2014/09/war-in-nigeria-map-of-boko-haram.html

Center for the Analysis of Terrorism, *ISIS Financing 2015*, Paris, May 2016.

Central Agency for Public Mobilization and Statistics, "Statistical Yearbook—Labor," 2015. As of February 9, 2017: http://www.capmas.gov.eg/Pages/Publications.aspx?page_id=5106&YearID=16603

————, website, undated. As of March 8, 2017:
http://www.capmas.gov.eg/

Central Intelligence Agency, *Guide to the Analysis of Insurgency*, Washington, D.C., 2012.

Chaliand, Gérard, *Guerrilla Strategies: An Historical Anthology from the Long March to Afghanistan*, Berkeley: University of California Press, 1982.

Chandrasekaran, Rajiv, "Key General Criticizes April Attack in Fallujah," *Washington Post*, September 13, 2004. As of 23 July 2016:
http://www.washingtonpost.com/wp-dyn/articles/A16309-2004Sep12.html.

Chivvis, Christopher S., *The French War on Al Qa'ida in Africa*, New York: Cambridge University Press, 2015.

Chivvis, Christopher S., and Andrew M. Liepman, *Authorities for Military Operations Against Terrorist Groups: The State of the Debate and Options for Congress*, Santa Monica, Calif.: RAND Corporation, RR-1145-1-OSD, 2016. As of February 8, 2016:
http://www.rand.org/pubs/research_reports/RR1145-1.html

CIA—*See* Central Intelligence Agency.

Clapper, James R., "Statement for the Record: Worldwide Threat Assessment of the US Intelligence Community," testimony before Senate Select Committee on Intelligence, February 9, 2016.

Clark, Kate, and Borhan Osman, "First Wave of IS attacks? Claim and Denial over the Jalalabad Bombs," Afghanistan Analysts Network website, April 22, 2015. As of February 9, 2017:
https://www.afghanistan-analysts.org/
first-wave-of-is-attacks-claim-and-denial-over-the-jalalabad-bombs/

Clausewitz, Carl von, *On War*, trans. J. J. Graham, New York: Penguin, 1968.

CNN/ORC International, poll, May 5, 2016. Available at:
http://i2.cdn.turner.com/cnn/2016/images/05/05/rel6c.-.isis.pdf

Coll, Steve, *Ghost Wars: The Secret History of the CIA, Afghanistan, and Bin Laden, from the Soviet Invasion to September 10, 2001*, New York: Penguin Press, 2004.

Combined Joint Task Force–Horn of Africa, website, "About the Command," undated. As of February 16, 2017:
https://www.hoa.africom.mil/about

Combined Joint Task Force, "Operation Inherent Resolve Fact Sheet," undated. As of March 9, 2017, available at:
http://www.inherentresolve.mil/Portals/14/Documents/Mission/History.
pdf?ver=2016-03-23-065243-743

Comolli, Virginia, "The Regional Problem of Boko Haram," *Survival*, Vol. 57, No. 4, August–September 2015.

Connable, Ben, "Defeating the Islamic State in Iraq," testimony presented before the Senate Foreign Relations Committee, Santa Monica, Calif.: RAND Corporation, CT-418, 2014. As of 23 July 2016:
http://www.rand.org/pubs/testimonies/CT418.html

Connable, Ben, and Martin C. Libicki, *How Insurgencies End*, Santa Monica, Calif.: RAND Corporation, MG-965-MCIA, 2010. As of February 8, 2017:
http://www.rand.org/pubs/monographs/MG965.html

Cook, Steven A., "Is Turkey Really at the Table," *Politico*, November 42, 2015. As of February 13, 2017:
http://www.politico.com/magazine/story/2015/11/isil-strategy-turkey-213392

Cooper, Helene, "Saudi's Role in Iraq Frustrates U.S. Officials," *New York Times*, July 27, 2007. As of July 29, 2016:
http://www.nytimes.com/2007/07/27/world/middleeast/27saudi.html

Cronin, Audrey Kurth, "Behind the Curve: Globalization and International Terrorism," *International Security*, Vol. 27, No. 3, Winter 2002/03, pp. 30–58.

———, *How Terrorism Ends: Understanding the Decline and Demise of Terrorist Campaigns*, Princeton, N.J.: Princeton University Press, 2009.

———, "ISIS Is Not a Terrorist Group," *Foreign Affairs,* March/April 2015a.

———, "Why Counterterrorism Won't Stop the Latest Jihadist Threat," *Foreign Affairs*, March/April 2015b.

Cronin, Conor, and Phuong Nguyen, "Recalibrating the Islamic State Threat in Southeast Asia," commentary, Washington, D.C.: Center for Strategic and International Studies, July 7, 2016. As of February 13, 2017:
https://www.csis.org/analysis/recalibrating-islamic-state-threat-southeast-asia

Crowcroft, Orlando, and Arij Liman, "ISIS: Foreign Fighters 'Live Like Kings' in Syrian Raqqa Stronghold of Islamic State," *International Business Times*, March 12, 2015. As of August 8, 2016:
http://www.ibtimes.co.uk/
isis-foreign-fighters-live-like-kings-syrian-raqqa-stronghold-islamic-state-1491683

Crowley, Michael, "How the Fate of One Holy Site Could Plunge Iraq Back into Civil War," *Time*, June 26, 2014. As of July 24, 2016:
http://time.com/2920692/iraq-isis-samarra-al-askari-mosque/

Dagher, Munqith M., "Public Opinion Towards Terrorist Organizations in Iraq, Syria, Yemen, and Libya: A Special Focus on Dai'sh in Iraq," briefing presented at the Center for Strategic and International Studies (CSIS), Washington, D.C., March 4, 2015.

Dalrymple, William, *Return of a King: The Battle for Afghanistan, 1839–42*, New York: Alfred A. Knopf, 2013.

Decamme, Guillaume, and Salam Faraj, "Patience Wears Thin in Fallujah, 6 Months after IS Ouster," Agence France Presse, January 18, 2017.

Defense Manpower Data Center, "DoD Personnel, Workforce Reports & Publications," various dates. As of March 17, 2017:
https://www.dmdc.osd.mil/appj/dwp/dwp_reports.jsp

Destrijcker, Lucas, "Boko Haram Refugees in Niger Find Safety, But Lack Aid," Al Jazeera, September 27, 2016.

Dietrich, Kyle, "'When the Enemy Can't See the Enemy, Civilians Become the Enemy': Living through Nigeria's Six-Year Insurgency," Washington, D.C.: Center for Civilians in Conflict, 2015.

Dobbins, James, Seth G. Jones, Benjamin Runkle, and Siddharth Mohandas, *Occupying Iraq: A History of the Coalition Provisional Authority*, Santa Monica, Calif.: RAND Corporation Corporation, MG-847-CC, 2009. As of February 8, 2017:
http://www.rand.org/pubs/monographs/MG847.html

Dodwell, Brian, Daniel Milton, and Don Rassler, *The Caliphate's Global Workforce: An Inside Look at the Islamic State's Foreign Fighter Paper Trail*, West Point, N.Y.: Combating Terrorism Center, 2016. As of February 13, 2017:
https://www.ctc.usma.edu/v2/wp-content/uploads/2016/04/CTC_Caliphates-Global-Workforce-Report.pdf

Donati, Jessica, and Habib Khan Totakhil, "Afghan Spy Agency Enlists Villagers to Hold Off Islamic State," *Wall Street Journal*, April 5, 2016. As of February 9, 2017:
http://www.wsj.com/articles/
afghan-spy-agency-arms-villagers-to-hold-off-islamic-state-1459848602

Doyle, Michael W., and Nicholas Sambanis, *Making War and Building Peace*, Princeton, N.J.: Princeton University Press, 2006.

Drake, Bruce, and Carroll Doherty, *Key Findings on How Americans View the U.S. Role in the World*, Washington, D.C.: Pew Research Center, May 5, 2016.

Ehrlich, Paul, "Islamic State's Asian Offensive," *Politico*, August 16, 2016. As of February 13, 2017:
http://www.politico.eu/article/the-islamic-states-isil-asian-offensive-operations-thailand-malaysia-southeast-asia-muslim-sharia-law/

Einhorn, Jessica, "The World Bank's Mission Creep," *Foreign Affairs*, Vol. 80, No. 5, 2001, pp. 22–35.

Epstein, Susan, and Lynn Williams, *Overseas Contingency Operations Funding: Background and Status*, Washington, D.C.: Congressional Research Service, June 13, 2016

Even, Yair, "Syria's 1956 Request for Soviet Military Intervention," Washington, D.C.: Wilson Center, February 2, 2016. As of August 3, 2016: https://www.wilsoncenter.org/publication/syrias-1956-request-for-soviet-military-intervention

Faruki, Yasmin, Jenna Gowell, and Laura Hoffman, "ISIS's Wilayat Sinai Launches Largest Offensive in Sheikh Zuweid," Washington, D.C.: Institute for the Study of War, July 2, 2015. As of February 9, 2017: http://www.understandingwar.org/backgrounder/isis%E2%80%99s-wilayat-sinai-launches-largest-offensive-sheikh-zuweid

Faucon, Benoit, and Margaret Coker, "The Rise and Deadly Fall of Islamic State's Oil Tycoon," *Wall Street Journal*, April 24, 2016. As of June 16, 2016: http://www.wsj.com/articles/the-rise-and-deadly-fall-of-islamic-states-oil-tycoon-1461522313

Faucon, Benoit, and Ahmed Al Omran, "Terror Group Boosts Sales of Oil, Gas to Assad Regime," *Wall Street Journal*, January 20, 2017.

Faux, Jeff, Muhammad Idrees Ahmad, Phyllis Bennis, and Sherle R. Schwenniger, "Is it Time for the U.S. to Pull out of Iraq and Syria?" *Nation*, January 14, 2016.

Fearon, James D., and David D. Laitin, "Ethnicity, Insurgency, and Civil War," *American Political Science Review*, Vol. 97, No. 1, February 2003, pp. 75–90. As of February 13, 2017: http://fsi.stanford.edu/publications/ethnicity_insurgency_and_civil_war

Felter, Joseph, and Brian Fishman, *Al-Qa'ida's Foreign Fighters in Iraq: A First Look at the Sinjar Records*, West Point, N.Y.: Combatting Terrorism Center, 2007.

Filkins, Dexter, "The Fight of Their Lives," *New Yorker*, September 29, 2014. As of July 29, 2016: http://www.newyorker.com/magazine/2014/09/29/fight-lives

Financial Action Task Force, "FATF-CIFG Communiqué," February 2016. As of February 8, 2017: http://www.fatf-gafi.org/publications/fatfgeneral/documents/fatf-cifg-communique-feb-2016.html

Fishman, Brian H., *The Master Plan: ISIS, al-Qaeda, and the Jihadi Strategy for Final Victory*, New Haven, Conn.: Yale University Press, 2016.

Flournoy, Michèle, and Richard Fontaine, *An Intensified Approach to Combatting the Islamic State*, Washington, D.C.: Center for a New American Security, 2015a.

———, "To Defeat the Islamic State, the U.S. Will Have to Go Big," *Washington Post*, June 24, 2015b.

Forrest, Caitlin, "ISIS Sanctuary Map: July 1, 2016," Washington, D.C.: Institute for the Study of War, July 1, 2016. As of July 26, 2016: http://www.understandingwar.org/backgrounder/isis-sanctuary-map-july-1-2016

Freedman, Lawrence, *Strategy: A History*, New York: Oxford University Press, 2013.

Frej, Willa, "How 70,000 Muslim Clerics Are Standing Up to Terrorism," *World Post*, December 11, 2015. As of February 13, 2017:
http://www.huffingtonpost.com/entry/
muslim-clerics-condemn-terrorism_us_566adfa1e4b009377b249dea

Fromson, James, and Steven Simon, "ISIS: The Dubious Paradis of Apocalypse Now," *Survival*, Vol. 57, No. 3, June–July 2015, pp. 7–56.

Fulannasrullah, "Fulan's SITREP," blog, August 5, 2015. As of February 9, 2017:
http://fulansitrep.com/2015/08/05/august-5th-2015-sitrep/

Gaddis, John Lewis, *Strategies of Containment: A Critical Appraisal of Postwar American National Security Policy*, New York: Oxford University Press, 1982.

———, *We Now Know: Rethinking Cold War History*, New York: Oxford University Press, 1997.

Gall, Carlotta, "How Kosovo Was Turned into Fertile Ground for ISIS," *New York Times*, May 21, 2016. As of February 13, 2017:
https://www.nytimes.com/2016/05/22/world/europe/how-the-saudis-turned-kosovo-into-fertile-ground-for-isis.html

Gallup, "Islamophobia: Understanding Anti-Muslim Sentiment in the West," webpage, undated. As of February 13, 2017:
http://www.gallup.com/poll/157082/islamophobia-understanding-anti-muslim-sentiment-west.aspx

Gambhir, Harleen, "ISIS in Afghanistan," Washington, D.C.: Institute for the Study of War, December 3, 2015. As of February 9, 2017:
http://www.understandingwar.org/sites/default/files/ISIS%20in%20Afghanistan_2.pdf

Gambill, Gary, "Abu Musab al-Zarqawi: A Biographical Sketch," *Terrorism Monitor*, Vol. 2, No. 24, 15 December 2004. As of July 23, 2016:
http://www.jamestown.org/single/?tx_ttnews%5Btt_news%5D=27304#.V5NtLGUzPzI

Garnett, Jantzen W., "An Islamic State in the Sinai," *Journal of International Security Affairs*, No. 28, Spring/Summer 2015. As of February 8, 2017:
http://www.securityaffairs.org/issues/number-28/islamic-state-sinai

Ghazi, Yasir, and Tim Arango, "Iraq Fighters, Qaeda Allies, Claim Falluja as New State," *New York Times*, January 3, 2014. As of 26 July 2016:
http://www.nytimes.com/2014/01/04/world/middleeast/fighting-in-falluja-and-ramadi.html?_r=0

al-Ghobashy, Tamer, "U.S.-Backed Plan for Iraqi National Guard Falters," *Wall Street Journal*, October 16, 2014. As of July 26, 2016:
http://www.wsj.com/articles/u-s-backed-plan-for-iraqi-national-guard-unraveling-1413493028

Gibbons-Neff, Thomas, "Number of Foreign Fighters Entering Iraq and Syria Drops by 90 Percent," *Washington Post*, April 26, 2016. As of February 13, 2017:
https://www.washingtonpost.com/news/checkpoint/wp/2016/04/26/number-of-foreign-fighters-entering-iraq-and-syria-drops-by-90-percent-pentagon-says/?utm_term=.94dafaa2dcc3

Gilsinan, Kathy, "How ISIS Territory Has Changed Since the U.S. Bombing Campaign Began," *Atlantic*, September 11, 2015. As of 26 July 2016:
http://www.theatlantic.com/international/archive/2015/09/isis-territory-map-us-campaign/404776/

Giustozzi, Antonio, "The Islamic State in 'Khorasan': A Nuanced View," London: Royal United Services Institute, February 5, 2016. As of February 13, 2017:
https://rusi.org/commentary/islamic-state-khorasan-nuanced-view

Gladstone, Rick, "Iraqis Take Eastern Mosul from Islamic State," *New York Times*, January 19, 2017.

Glaser, Daniel L., "Remarks by Assistant Secretary for Terrorist Financing Daniel Glaser at Chatham House," U.S. Department of the Treasury, February 8, 2016.

———, "Testimony of A\S for Terrorist Financing Daniel L. Glaser Before the House Committee on Foreign Affair's Subcommittee on Terrorism, Nonproliferation, and Trade, and House Committee on Armed Services' Subcommittee on Emerging Threats and Capabilities," June 9, 2016. As of June 13, 2016:
https://www.treasury.gov/press-center/press-releases/Pages/jl0486.aspx

Global Terrorism Database, website, undated. As of February 13, 2017:
https://www.start.umd.edu/gtd/

Gold, Zack, "Salafi Jihadist Violence in Egypt's North Sinai: From Local Insurgency to Islamic State Province," The Hague: International Centre for Counter-Terrorism, April 2016.

Gold, Zack, and Elissa Miller, "Egypt's Theory of Terrorism," *Foreign Affairs*, June 16, 2016.

Goldman, Adam, "'I Am Fed Up with This Evil': How an American Went from Ivy League Student to Disillusioned ISIS Fighter," *Washington Post*, June 30, 2016. As of February 13, 2017:
https://www.washingtonpost.com/world/national-security/i-am-fed-up-with-this-evil-how-an-american-went-from-ivy-league-student-to-disillusioned-isis-fighter/2016/06/29/155e777e-3e07-11e6-80bc-d06711fd2125_story.html?utm_term=.7ea3549a6281

Goldstein, Joseph, "In ISIS, the Taliban Face an Insurgent Threat of Their Own," *New York Times,* June 4, 2015. As of February 9, 2017: http://www.nytimes.com/2015/06/05/world/asia/afghanistan-taliban-face-insurgent-threat-from-isis.html?_r=0

Gordon, Michael, and Bernard E. Trainor, *Endgame: The Inside Story of the Struggle for Iraq, from George W. Bush to Barack Obama*, New York: Pantheon Press, 2012.

Graham, Robert, "How Terrorists Use Encryption," *CTC Sentinel*, June 16, 2016. As of February 13, 2017: https://www.ctc.usma.edu/posts/how-terrorists-use-encryption

Gray, Simon, and Ibikunle Adeakin, "The Evolution of Boko Haram: From Missionary Activism to Transnational Jihad and the Failure of the Nigerian Security Intelligence Agencies," *African Security*, Vol. 8, No. 3, September 2015.

Grignard, Alain, "La Littérature Politique du GIA, des Origines à Djamal Zitoun—Esquisse d'Une Analyse," in F. Dassetto, ed., *Facettes de l'Islam Belge*, Louvain-la-Neuve: Academia-Bruylant, 2001.

Grose, Peter, *Operation Rollback: America's Secret War Behind the Iron Curtain*, New York: Houghton Mifflin Co., 2000.

Guevara, Ernesto (Che), *Guerrilla Warfare*, Lincoln, Neb.: University of Nebraska Press, 1998.

Guibert, Nathalie, "La France Mène des Opérations Secrètes en Libie," *Le Monde*, February 24, 2016.

Gurr, Ted Robert, *Peoples Versus States: Minorities at Risk in the New Century*, Washington, D.C.: U.S. Institute of Peace, 2000.

Haddad, Fanar, "Reinventing Sunni Identity in Iraq After 2003," Current Trends in Islamist Ideology, Vol. 17, 2014, pp. 70-101.

Hanrahan, John, "A Cold Calculation: How Much Is Too Much to Spend on Afghanistan?" Cambridge, Mass.: Nieman Foundation for Journalism, Harvard University, June 15, 2011

Hale, Robert F., U.S. Department of Defense Comptroller, "Defense Department Fiscal Year 2013 Budget," testimony before the Senate Budget Committee, February 28, 2012. As of March 17, 2017: https://www.c-span.org/video/?c2127434/clip-defense-department-fiscal-year-2013-budget

Harrison, Todd, *Chaos and Uncertainty: The FY 2014 Defense Budget and Beyond*, Washington, D.C.: Center for Strategic and Budgetary Assessments, October 2013.

Hart, B. H. Liddell, *Strategy: The Indirect Approach*, London: Faber, 1967.

Hartig, Luke, "U.S. at Crossroads on Drone Ops," CNN, August 21, 2016.

Hashim, Ahmad S., "Iraq's Numerous Insurgent Groups," National Public Radio, June 8, 2006. As of July 23, 2016:
http://www.npr.org/templates/story/story.php?storyId=5468486

Hassan, Hassan, "Is the Islamic State Unstoppable?" *New York Times*, July 9, 2016. As of 23 July 2016:
http://www.nytimes.com/2016/07/10/opinion/is-the-islamic-state-unstoppable.html?_r=0

Al Hayat, "The End of Sykes-Picot," LiveLeak.com, video, Islamic State in Iraq and Syria, undated. As of July 23, 2016:
http://www.liveleak.com/view?i=d43_1404046312

Hegghammer, Thomas, "Resources," webpage, undated. As of February 13, 2017:
http://hegghammer.com/text.cfm?path=2176

———, "Should I Stay or Should I Go? Explaining Variation in Western Jihadists' Choice Between Domestic and Foreign Fighting," American Political Science Review, Vol. 107, No. 1, February 2013, pp. 1–14.

Hern, Alex, "Facebook, YouTube, Twitter, and Microsoft Sign EU Hate Speech Code," *Guardian* (UK), May 31, 2016.

Herszenhorn, David, "For Syria, Reliant on Russia for Weapons and Food, Old Bonds Run Deep," *New York Times*, February 18, 2012. As of August 3, 2016:
http://www.nytimes.com/2012/02/19/world/middleeast/for-russia-and-syria-bonds-are-old-and-deep.html?_r=0

Hironaka, Ann, *Neverending Wars: The International Community, Weak States, and the Perpetuation of Civil War*, Cambridge, Mass.: Harvard University Press, 2008.

Hoffman, Bruce, *Inside Terrorism*, 2nd ed., New York: Columbia University Press, 2006.

Hokayem, Emile, *Syria's Uprising and the Fracturing of the Levant*, London: International Institute for Strategic Studies, 2013.

Holliday, Joseph, "Syria Update 13-01: Iraq-Syria Overland Supply Routes," Washington, D.C.: Institute for the Study of War, May 8, 2013. As of August 3, 2016:
http://www.understandingwar.org/backgrounder/syria-update-13-01-iraq-syria-overland-supply-routes

Holman, Timothy, "'Gonna Get Myself Connected': The Role of Facilitation in Foreign Fighter Mobilizations," *Perspectives on Terrorism*, Vol. 10, No. 2, 2016. As of February 13, 2017:
http://www.terrorismanalysts.com/pt/index.php/pot/article/view/497

Horgan, John, and Jessica Stern, "Terrorism Research Has Not Stagnated," *Chronicle of Higher Education*, May 8, 2013.

Hudson, John, "FBI Director: For Would Be Terrorists, Twitter Is the 'Devil on Their Shoulder,'" *Foreign Policy,* July 8, 2015. As of March 20, 2017:
http://foreignpolicy.com/2015/07/08/
fbi-director-for-would-be-terrorists-twitter-is-the-devil-on-their-shoulder/

Hughes, Seamus, "Countering the Virtual Caliphate," testimony before the House Committee on Foreign Affairs, June 23, 2016.

Ignatius, David, "Southeast Asia Could Be a Haven for Displaced Islamic State Fighters," *Washington Post*, August 18, 2016. As of February 13, 2017:
https://www.washingtonpost.com/opinions/southeast-asia-could-be-a-haven-for-displaced-islamic-state-fighters/2016/08/18/c2213b28-6566-11e6-96c0-37533479f3f5_story.html?utm_term=.c384006b309e

IHS Janes, "Terrorism and Insurgency Database," 2017. As of March 28, 2017:
http://janes.ihs.com/TerrorismInsurgencyCentre/Home

International Committee of the Red Cross, "How Is the Term 'Armed Conflict' Defined in International Humanitarian Law," opinion paper, March 2008. As of February 13, 2017:
https://www.icrc.org/eng/assets/files/other/opinion-paper-armed-conflict.pdf

International Crisis Group, "Nigeria: The Challenge of Military Reform," June 6, 2016. As of February 9, 2017:
https://www.crisisgroup.org/africa/west-africa/nigeria/
nigeria-challenge-military-reform

International Institute for Strategic Studies, *The Military Balance 2017*, Vol. 117, 2017. As of February 14, 2016:
http://www.iiss.org/en/publications/military-s-balance

"Iraq Cleric Issues Call to Arms Against ISIL," Al Jazeera, June 13, 2014. As of July 26, 2016:
http://www.aljazeera.com/news/middleeast/2014/06/iraq-cleric-issues-call-arms-against-isil-2014613125518278210.html

"Iraqi Sunni Protest Clashes in Hawija Leave Many Dead," British Broadcasting Corporation, April 23, 2013. As of July 26, 2016:
http://www.bbc.com/news/world-middle-east-22261422

Iron, Richard, "Charge of the Knights," *RUSI Journal*, Vol. 158, No. 1, 2013, pp. 54-62.

"IS Fighters Run Training Centre, Find Foothold in Farah," *Pajhwok Afghan News*, January 14, 2015. As of February 9, 2017:
http://www.pajhwok.com/en/2015/03/10/
fighters-run-training-centre-find-foothold-farah

"ISIS Claims Deadly Car Bomb in Libya's Benghazi," Al Arabiya, February 27, 2016. As of February 9, 2017:
https://english.alarabiya.net/en/News/middle-east/2016/02/27/
ISIS-claims-deadly-car-bomb-in-Libya-s-Benghazi-.html

"ISIS Launches Dari-Language Program on 'Voice of the Caliphate' in Nangarhar," *Nation* (Pakistan), January 28, 2016.

"ISIS Militants Seize University in Libya's Sirte," Al Arabiya, February 19, 2016. As of February 9, 2017:
http://english.alarabiya.net/en/News/middle-east/2015/02/19/-ISIS-jihadists-occupy-university-in-libya-s-Sirte-professor-.html

"'IS Khorasan' Chief Dies in Afghan Drone Strike," *Dawn* (Pakistan), July 12, 2015.

"Islamic State a Serious Threat to Pakistan, Foreign Secretary Admits," *Dawn* (Pakistan), February 23, 2015.

Islamic State, "Documenting the Crimes of the Alliance of the Jews and Army of Apostasy Against Our People in the Sinai #4—Wilāyat Sīnāʾ (Sinai)," February 9, 2015 (with links to earlier videos in the series). February 13, 2017:
http://jihadology.net/2015/02/09/new-video-message-from-the-islamic-state-documenting-the-crimes-of-the-alliance-of-the-jews-and-army-of-apostasy-against-our-people-in-the-sinai-4-wilayat-sina-sinai/

al-Jarid, Usamah, "ISIL: The Road to Sirte Emirate," *Al-Wasat*, December 14, 2015.

Jenkins, Brian Michael, *Stray Dogs and Virtual Armies: Radicalization and Recruitment to Jihadist Terrorism in the United States Since 9/11*, Santa Monica, Calif.: RAND Corporation, OP-343-RC, 2011. As of February 8, 2017:
http://www.rand.org/pubs/occasional_papers/OP343.html

Jensen, Sterling, *Iraqi Narratives of the Anbar Awakening*, doctoral thesis, London: King's College, 2014.

JIC—*See* Joint Intelligence Committee.

"Jihadi Preacher Latest to Condemn ISIS' Methods," Associated Press (via CBS News), February 6, 2015. As of February 13, 2017:
http://www.cbsnews.com/news/jihadi-preacher-abu-mohammed-al-maqdesi-blasts-isis-methods-jordan-pilot-burned/

Johnson, David E., "Fighting the 'Islamic State': The Case for US Ground Forces," *Parameters*, Vol. 45, No. 1, Spring 2015. As of February 13, 2017:
http://www.strategicstudiesinstitute.army.mil/pubs/parameters/Issues/
Spring_2015/4_Special-Commentary_Johnson.pdf

Johnston, Patrick, "Islamic State's Money Problems," *USA Today*, March 4, 2016.

Johnston, Patrick B., Jacob N. Shapiro, Howard J. Shatz, Benjamin Bahney, Danielle F. Jung, Patrick K. Ryan, and Jonathan Wallace, *Foundations of the Islamic State: Management, Money, and Terror in Iraq, 2005–2010*, Santa Monica, Calif.: RAND Corporation, RR-1192-DARPA, 2016. As of February 8, 2017: http://www.rand.org/pubs/research_reports/RR1192.html

Joint Intelligence Committee, "Iraq: Sunni Arab Opposition," September 30, 2004a. As of 24 July 2016: http://www.iraqinquiry.org.uk/media/225294/2004-09-30-jic-assessment-iraq-sunni-arab-opposition.pdf#search=iraq%20sunni%20arab%20opposition

———, "Iraq Security: External Support for Insurgents," October 7, 2004b. As of August 3, 2016: http://www.iraqinquiry.org.uk/media/225299/2004-10-07-jic-assessment-iraq-security-external-support-for-insurgents.pdf#search=syria%20finance

———, "Iraq: How Is the Sunni Insurgency Evolving?" May 10, 2006a. As of 24 July 2016: http://www.iraqinquiry.org.uk/media/211441/2006-05-10-jic-assessment-how-is-the-sunni-insurgency-evolving.pdf#search=jic%20iraq%202006

———, "Iraq: Insurgency, Sectarianism, and Violence," July 19, 2006b. As of 24 July 2016: http://www.iraqinquiry.org.uk/media/211241/2006-07-19-jic-assessment-iraq-insurgency-sectarianism-and-violence.pdf#search=jic%20sunni%20insurgency%202006

Joint Publication 1-02, *Department of Defense Dictionary of Military and Associated Terms*, Washington, D.C.: Joint Staff, February 15, 2016.

Jones, Seth G., *Hunting in the Shadows: The Pursuit of Al-Qa'ida Since 9/11*, New York: W.W. Norton, 2012.

———, "Expanding the Caliphate: ISIS' South Asia Strategy," *Foreign Affairs*, June 11, 2015. As of February 8, 2016: https://www.foreignaffairs.com/articles/afghanistan/2015-06-11/expanding-caliphate

———, *Waging Insurgent Warfare*, New York: Oxford University Press, 2016.

Jonsson, Michael, "Following the Money: Financing the Territorial Expansion of Islamist Insurgents in Syria," Swedish Defense Research Agency, FOI Memo #4947, May 2014.

Jordan, Jenna, and Lawrence Rubin, "An ISIS Containment Doctrine," *National Interest*, June 14, 2016.

Joscelyn, Thomas, "Al-Qa'ida in the Islamic Maghreb Backs Jihadists Fighting Islamic State in Derna, Libya" *Long War Journal*, July 9, 2015a. As of February 9, 2017:
http://www.longwarjournal.org/archives/2015/07/al-qaeda-in-the-islamic-maghreb-backs-jihadists-fighting-islamic-state-in-derna-libya.php

———, "In Dabiq Magazine, Islamic State Complains About Jihadist Rivals in Libya," *Long War Journal*, September 13, 2015b. As of February 9, 2017:
http://www.longwarjournal.org/archives/2015/09/in-dabiq-magazine-islamic-state-complains-about-jihadist-rivals-in-libya.php

———, "Islamic State's Safe Haven in Sirte, Libya Shrinks to a 'Single Neighborhood,'" *Long War Journal*, September 22, 2016. As of February 9, 2017:
http://www.longwarjournal.org/archives/2016/09/islamic-states-safe-haven-in-sirte-libya-shrinks-to-a-single-neighborhood.php

Kagan, Kimberly, Frederick W. Kagan, and Jessica D. Lewis, *A Strategy to Defeat the Islamic State*, Washington, D.C.: Institute for the Study of War, September 2014.

Kalyvas, Stathis N., *The Logic of Violence in Civil War*, New York: Cambridge University Press, 2006.

Kalyvas, Stathis N., and Laia Balcells, "International System and Technologies of Rebellion: How the End of the Cold War Shaped Internal Conflict," *American Political Science Review*, Vol. 104, No. 3, August 2010, pp. 415–429.

Keatinge, Tom, "How the Islamic State Sustains Itself: The Importance of the War Economy in Syria and Iraq," London: Royal United Services Institute, August 29, 2014.

Kemp, Robert, "Counterinsurgency in Nangarhar Province, Eastern Afghanistan, 2004–2008," *Military Review*, November–December 2010, pp. 34–42.

Kepel, Gilles, *Muslim Extremism in Egypt: The Prophet and the Pharaoh*, trans. John Rothschild, Berkeley: University of California Press, 1993.

———, *Jihad: The Trail of Political Islam*, Cambridge, Mass.: Harvard University Press, 2002.

Kerry, John, "Certification Pursuant to Section 7041(a)(6)(c) of the Department of State, Foreign Operations, and Related Programs Appropriation Act, 2015," May 12, 2015. As of February 9, 2017:
http://graphics8.nytimes.com/packages/pdf/international/2015/egyptwaiver.pdf

Khan, Iftikhar A., "IS Emerging as a Threat, Warns IB Chief," *Dawn* (Pakistan), February 11, 2016.

Khan, Ismail, "ISIS Leaders Reported Killed in Drone Strikes in Afghanistan," *New York Times*, July 9, 2015.

Khatib, Lina, "The Islamic State's Strategy: Lasting and Expanding," paper, Washington, D.C.: Carnegie Middle East Center, June 29, 2015. As of February 13, 2017:
http://carnegie-mec.org/2015/06/29/
islamic-state-s-strategy-lasting-and-expanding-pub-60511

Khedery, Ali, "Why We Stuck with Maliki—And Lost Iraq," *Washington Post*, July 3, 2014. As of July 24, 2016:
https://www.washingtonpost.com/opinions/why-we-stuck-with-maliki--and-lost-iraq/2014/07/03/0dd6a8a4-f7ec-11e3-a606-946fd632f9f1_story.html

Kilcullen, David, *Blood Year: The Unraveling of Western Counterterrorism,* New York: Oxford University Press, 2016.

Kirdar, M. J., "Al-Qa'ida in Iraq," Washington, D.C.: Center for Strategic and International Studies, June 2011. As of 21 July 2016:
https://csis-prod.s3.amazonaws.com/s3fs-public/legacy_files/files/
publication/110614_Kirdar_AlQaedaIraq_Web.pdf

Kirkpatrick, David D., "Libya Democracy Clashes with Fervor for Jihad" *New York Times*, June 23, 2012, p. A1.

———, "Leaked Emirati Emails Could Threaten Peace Negotiations in Libya" *New York Times*, November 13, 2015, p. A10.
http://www.nytimes.com/2015/11/13/world/middleeast/leaked-emirati-emails-could-threaten-peace-talks-in-libya.html

Lang, Hardin, and Muath Al Wari, "The Flow of Foreign Fighters to the Islamic State: Assessing the Challenge and the Response," Washington, D.C.: Center for American Progress, March 2016.

Leverett, Flynt, *Inheriting Syria: Bashar's Trial by Fire*, Washington, D.C.: Brookings Institution, 2005.

Lewis, Aidan, "Islamic State: How It Is Run," British Broadcasting Corporation, May 22, 2015.

Lewis, Jessica, "Al-Qa'ida in Iraq Resurgent: Breaking the Walls Campaign, Part 1," Washington, D.C.: Institute for the Study of War, September 2013. As of July 29, 2016:
http://www.understandingwar.org/sites/default/files/AQI-Resurgent-10Sept_0.pdf

Lister, Charles, *Profiling the Islamic State*, Washington, D.C.: Brookings Institution, November 2014. As of August 2, 2016:
https://www.brookings.edu/wp-content/uploads/2014/12/en_web_lister.pdf

———, *The Syrian Jihad: Al-Qaida, the Islamic State and the Evolution of an Insurgency*, New York: Oxford University Press, 2016a.

———, *Jihadi Rivalry, The Islamic State Challenges al-Qaida*, Washington, D.C.: Brookings Institution, January 27, 2016b. As of February 13, 2017:
https://www.brookings.edu/wp-content/uploads/2016/07/en-jihadi-rivalry-2.pdf

Lister, Tim, "ISIS Rides Wave of Attacks as Its Core Territory Shrinks," CNN, June 14, 2016. As of February 13, 2017:
http://www.cnn.com/2016/06/14/middleeast/isis-territory-attacks-lister

Long, Austin, Stephanie Pezard, Bryce Loidolt, and Todd C. Helmus, *Locals Rule: Historical Lessons for Creating Local Defense Forces for Afghanistan and Beyond*, Santa Monica, Calif.: RAND Corporation, MG-1232-CFSOCC-A, 2012. As of February 9, 2017:
http://www.rand.org/pubs/monographs/MG1232.html

Lostumbo, Michael J., Michael J. McNerney, Eric Peltz, Derek Eaton, David R. Frelinger, Victoria A. Greenfield, John Halliday, Patrick Mills, Bruce R. Nardulli, Stacie L. Pettyjohn, Jerry M. Sollinger, and Stephen M. Worman, *Overseas Basing of U.S. Military Forces: An Assessment of Relative Costs and Strategic Benefits*, Santa Monica, Calif.: RAND Corporation, RR-201-OSD, 2013. As of February 8, 2017:
http://www.rand.org/pubs/research_reports/RR201.html

Lubold, Gordon, "U.S. Clears Path to Target Islamic State in Afghanistan," *Wall Street Journal*, January 19, 2016.

Luck, Taylor, "ISIS, Losing Territory in Syria, Signals Strategic Shift," *Christian Science Monitor*, May 27, 2016. As of July 23, 2016:
http://www.csmonitor.com/World/Middle-East/2016/0527/ISIS-losing-territory-in-Syria-signals-strategic-shift

Lum, Thomas, and Ben Dolven, *The Republic of the Philippines and U.S. Interests: 2014*, Washington, D.C.: Congressional Research Service, R43498, May 15, 2014. As of February 13, 2017:
https://fas.org/sgp/crs/row/R43498.pdf

Lyall, Jason, and Isaiah Wilson III, "Rage Against the Machines: Explaining Outcomes in Counterinsurgency Wars," *International Organization*, No. 63, No. 1, Winter 2009, pp. 67–106.

Lynch, Marc, *The Tourniquet: A Strategy for Defeating the Islamic State and Saving Iraq and Syria*, Washington, D.C.: Center for a New American Security, 2014.

Ma'oz, Moshe, *The "Shi'i Crescent": Myth and Reality*, Washington, D.C.: Brookings Institution, November 15, 2007. As of August 3, 2016:
https://www.brookings.edu/wp-content/uploads/2016/06/11_middle_east_maoz.pdf

Mao Tse-Tung, *On Guerrilla Warfare*, Urbana and Chicago: University of Illinois Press, [1937] 2000.

Mansfield, David, "The Devil Is in the Details: Nangarhar's Continued Decline Into Insurgency, Violence and Widespread Drug Production," brief, Kabul: Afghan Research and Evaluation Unit, February 2016.

Marmocchi, Francesca, "Come Funziona il Califfato di Sirte" *L'Espresso*, December 4, 2015. As of February 9, 2017:
http://espresso.repubblica.it/plus/articoli/2015/12/03/news/
come-funziona-il-califfato-di-sirte-1.242043

Marty, Franz J., "On the Trail of the Islamic State in Afghanistan," *Foreign Policy*, April 5, 2016. As of February 9, 2017:
http://foreignpolicy.com/2016/04/05/afghanistan-islamic-state-taliban/

Mason, David, Joseph P. Weingarten, Jr., and Patrick J. Fett, "Win, Lose, or Draw: Predicting the Outcome of Civil Wars," *Political Research Quarterly*, Vol. 52, No. 2, June 1999, pp. 239–268.

McCants, William, *The ISIS Apocalypse: The History, Strategy, and Doomsday Vision of the Islamic State*, New York: St. Martin's Press, 2015.

McCants, William, and Charlie Winter, "Experts Weigh in (Part 4): Can the United States Counter ISIS Propaganda?" Washington, D.C.: Brookings Institution, July 1, 2015. As of February 8, 2016:
https://www.brookings.edu/blog/markaz/2015/07/01/
experts-weigh-in-part-4-can-the-united-states-counter-isis-propaganda/

McLaughlin, John, "How the Islamic State Could Win," *Washington Post*, May 17, 2015.

McWilliams, Timothy S., and Curtis P. Wheeler, eds., *Al-Anbar Awakening*, Vol. I: *American Perspectives, U.S. Marines and Counterinsurgency in Iraq, 2004–2009*, Quantico, Va.: Marine Corps University Press, 2009.

Mearsheimer, John J., *Conventional Deterrence*, Ithaca, N.Y.: Cornell University Press, 1983.

———, "America Unhinged," *National Interest*, January-February 2014, pp. 9–30.

Media Office of Ninawa Province, "Isqāt al-Tā'ira al-Rūsīya Thā'ran li Ahalina fī Bilād al-Shām [Downing of the Russian Plane Is Revenge for Our People in the Levant]," November 2015. As of March 28, 2017:
https://archive.org/details/nenwa_201511

Media Office of Sinai State, "Min Wilayat Sayna' ila Bayt al-Maqdis [From Sinai State to Jerusalem]," November 2015.

Meijer, Roel, ed., *Counterterrorism Strategies in Indonesia, Saudi Arabia, and Algeria*, The Hague, Netherlands: Clingendael, 2012.

Meir Amit Intelligence and Terrorism Information Center, "ISIS in Libya: A Major Regional and International Threat," January 2016. As of February 13, 2017:
http://www.terrorism-info.org.il/Data/articles/
Art_20943/E_209_15_1076923854.pdf

"Message from the Soldiers," video message from Boko Haram fighters loyal to Aboubakar Shekau, August 7, 2016. As of February 9, 2017: http://jihadology.net/category/the-islamic-state/wilayat-gharb-ifriqiyyah/

Michaels, Jim, "Air Campaign Shifts to ISIL's Cash and Oil," *USA Today*, April 17, 2016.

"Misr: Lajna Barlamānīya Tuqirr Barnāmaj Khādim al-Haramayn li Tanmīya Sīnā' [Egypt: A Parliamentary Committee Approves the Program of the Custodian of the Two Holy Shrines for the Development of the Sinai]," *Al-Hayat*, June 13, 2016.

Moghadam, Assaf, "The Salafi-Jihad as a Religious Ideology," *CTC Sentinel*, Vol. 1, No. 3, February 2008, pp. 14–16.

———, "Motives for Martyrdom: Al-Qaida, Salafi Jihad, and the Spread of Suicide Attacks," *International Security*, Vol. 33, No. 3, Winter 2008/09, pp. 46–78.

Mogherini, Federica, EU High Representative/Vice-President of the Commission; Neven Mimica, EU Commissioner for International Cooperation and Development; and Smail Chergui, AU Commissioner for Peace and Security, "Joint Communiqué," August, 1, 2016. As of February 9, 2017: http://europa.eu/rapid/press-release_STATEMENT-16-2702_en.htm

Montgomery, Gary W., and Timothy S. McWilliams, eds., *Al-Anbar Awakening*, Vol. II: *Iraqi Perspectives From Insurgency to Counterinsurgency in Iraq, 2004–2009*, Quantico, Va.: Marine Corps University Press, 2009.

"Most IS Men in Afghanistan Are TTP Fighters," *Dawn* (Pakistan), August 1, 2016.

Mueller, John, "Why the ISIS Threat Is Totally Overblown," *The Week*, July 23, 2015.

Mueller, John, and Mark G. Stewart, "Hardly Existential: Thinking Rationally About Terrorism," *Foreign Affairs*, April 2, 2010.

———, *Terror, Security, and Money: Balancing the Risks, Benefits, and Costs of Homeland Security*, New York: Oxford University Press, 2011.

———, *Chasing Ghosts: The Policing of Terrorism*, New York: Oxford University Press, 2015.

Muir, Jim, "Fears of Shia Muscle in Iraq's Sunni Heartland," British Broadcasting Corporation, May 18, 2015. As of July 26, 2016: http://www.bbc.com/news/world-middle-east-32786138

Multinational Forces West, *State of the Insurgency in al-Anbar*, Multinational Forces Iraq, August 17, 2006.

Murray, Mark, "ISIS Threat: Fear of Terror Attack Soars to 9/11 High, NBC News/WSJ Poll Finds," NBC News, September 9, 2014. As of February 13, 2017: http://www.nbcnews.com/politics/first-read/ isis-threat-fear-terror-attack-soars-9-11-high-nbc-n199496

Musa, Njadvara, "No Progress Until Sambisa Forest Is Cleared of Boko Haram," *Guardian* (Nigeria), November 21, 2016. As of February 9, 2017: http://guardian.ng/news/ no-progress-until-sambisa-forest-is-cleared-of-boko-haram/

NASA Socioeconomic Data and Applications Center, "Gridded Population of the World (GPW), v4," undated. As of February 13, 2017: http://beta.sedac.ciesin.columbia.edu/data/collection/gpw-v4

National Directorate of Security, written statement, Afghanistan, February 9, 2015.

National Security Council, "A Report to the National Security Council by the Executive Secretary on United States Objectives and Programs for National Security," NSC 68, April 14, 1950. As of February 17, 2017: http://digitalarchive.wilsoncenter.org/document/116191

———, "United States Policy Toward the Soviet Satellites in Eastern Europe," draft, Washington, D.C., NSC 174, December 11, 1953. As of February 13, 2017: http://digitalarchive.wilsoncenter.org/document/112620

———, *National Strategy for Victory in Iraq*, Washington, D.C.: The White House, November 2005. As of February 13, 2017: http://www.washingtonpost.com/wp-srv/nation/documents/ Iraqnationalstrategy11-30-05.pdf

National Security Decision Directive 75, "U.S. Relations with the USSR," January 17, 1983. Available in Executive Secretariat, NSC: Records [NSDDs], NSDD 75 [U.S. Relations with the USSR], Box 91287, Ronald Reagan Presidential Library.

Nesser, Petter, *Islamist Terrorism in Europe: A History*, London: Hurst Publishers, 2014.

Neumann, Peter, "Countering the Virtual Caliphate," testimony before the Committee on Foreign Affairs, U.S. House of Representatives, 114th Cong., 2nd Sess., June 23, 2016.

Nichols, Robert, *The Frontier Crimes Regulation: A History in Documents*, New York: Oxford University Press, 2013.

Nordland, Rod, "Iraqi Premier Places Unity Second to Fighting ISIS," *New York Times*, July 2, 2014. As of 26 July 2016: http://www.nytimes.com/2014/07/03/world/middleeast/maliki-says-fight-against-isis-is-iraqs-top-priority.html

North Sinai Governorate, website, undated. As of February 9, 2017: http://www.northsinai.gov.eg/home.aspx

NSC—*See* National Security Council.

Obama, Barack, "Statement by the President on the End of the Combat Mission in Afghanistan," Washington, D.C.: The White House, December 28, 2014. As of February 8, 2017:
https://obamawhitehouse.archives.gov/the-press-office/2014/12/28/
statement-president-end-combat-mission-afghanistan

O'Neill, Bard E., "Insurgency and Terrorism: From Revolution to Apocalypse, 2nd ed. rev., Washington, D.C.: Potomac Books, 2005.

Office of the Secretary of Defense, *Fiscal Year 2017 President's Budget: Justification for Base Funded Contingency Operations and the Overseas Contingency Operation Transfer Fund (OCOTF)*, February 2016.

Olorunyomi, Ladi, "U.S. General Counters Buhari, Says Boko Haram Still Holds Territory in Nigeria," *Premium Times Nigeria*, March 10, 2016. As of February 13, 2017:
http://www.premiumtimesng.com/news/headlines/199950-u-s-general-counters-buhari-says-boko-haram-still-holds-territory-nigeria.html

Operation Inherent Resolve website, undated. As of January 10, 2017:
http://www.inherentresolve.mil

Osman, Borhan, "The Shadows of 'Islamic State' in Afghanistan: What Threat Does it Hold?" Afghanistan Analysts Network website, February 12, 2015. As of February 9, 2017:
https://www.afghanistan-analysts.org/
the-shadows-of-islamic-state-in-afghanistan-what-threat-does-it-hold/

———, "The Islamic State in 'Khorasan': How It Began and Where it Stands Now in Nangarhar," Afghanistan Analysts Network website, July 27, 2016a. As of February 9, 2017:
https://www.afghanistan-analysts.org/
the-islamic-state-in-khorasan-how-it-began-and-where-it-stands-now-in-nangarhar/

———, "Descent into Chaos: Why Did Nangarhar Turn into an IS Hub?" Afghanistan Analysts Network website, September 27, 2016b. As of February 9, 2017:
https://www.afghanistan-analysts.org/
descent-into-chaos-why-did-nangarhar-turn-into-an-is-hub/

"Pakistan Taliban Vow Support for ISIS Fighters," Al Arabiya, October 5, 2014.

"Pakistani Taliban Splinter Group Again Pledges Allegiance to Islamic State," *Long War Journal*, January 13, 2015.

Pape, Robert A., *Dying to Win: The Strategic Logic of Suicide Terrorism*, New York: Random House, 2005.

Pape, Robert A., and James K. Feldman, *Cutting the Fuse: The Explosion of Global Suicide Terrorism and How to Stop It*, Chicago: University of Chicago Press, 2010.

Parvez, Tariq, "The Islamic State in Pakistan," Washington, D.C.: U.S. Institute of Peace, Peace Brief 213, September 2016.

Perlez, Jane, "Philippines' Deal with China Pokes a Hole in U.S. Strategy," *New York Times*, November, 2, 2016.

Perthes, Volker, *The Political Economy of Syria Under Asad*, New York: I.B. Tauris and Company, Ltd., 1995.

Pew Research Center, "Articles of Faith," in *The World's Muslims: Unity and Diversity*, Washington, D.C., August 9, 2012. As of March 20, 2017:
http://www.pewforum.org/2012/08/09/
the-worlds-muslims-unity-and-diversity-3-articles-of-faith/

———, "The World Facing Trump: Public Sees ISIS, Cyberattacks, North Korea as Top Threats," Washington, D.C., January 12, 2017.

Pieri, Zacharias, and Jacob Zenn, "The Boko Haram Paradox: Ethnicity, Religion, and Historical Memory in Pursuit of a Caliphate," *African Security*, Vol. 9, No. 1, March 2016.

Ploch, Lauren, *Africa Command: U.S. Strategic Interests and the Role of the U.S. Military in Africa*, Washington, D.C.: Congressional Research Service, RL34003, July 22, 2011. As of February 13, 2017:
https://fas.org/sgp/crs/natsec/RL34003.pdf

Pollock, David, "ISIS Has Almost No Support in Egypt, Saudi Arabia, or Lebanon—But America Has Little More," *Fikra Forum*, October 14, 2015.

Posen, Barry R., "Contain ISIS," *Atlantic*, November 20, 2015.

Posen, Barry R., and Andrew L. Ross, "Competing Visions for U.S. Grand Strategy," *International Security*, Vol. 21, No. 3, Winter 1996/1997, pp. 5–53.

Poushter, Jacob, "In Nations with Significant Muslim Populations, Much Disdain for ISIS," Washington, D.C.: Pew Research Center, November 17, 2015.

Preston, Diana, *The Dark Defile: Britain's Catastrophic Invasion of Afghanistan 1838–1842*, New York: Walker & Company, 2012.

Prince, S. J., "Read: Taliban Writes Letter to ISIS Leader Baghdadi," Heavy website, June 16, 2015. As of February 9, 2017:
http://heavy.com/news/2015/06/taliban-letter-to-isis-islamic-state-online-pdf-text/

Price, Bryan, Dan Milton, Muhammad al-'Ubaydi, and Nelly Lahoud, *The Group That Calls Itself a State: Understanding the Evolution and Challenges of the Islamic State*, West Point, N.Y.: Combatting Terrorism Center, December 16, 2014. As of August 2, 2016:
https://www.ctc.usma.edu/posts/the-group-that-calls-itself-a-state-understanding-the-evolution-and-challenges-of-the-islamic-state

Public Law 108-375 §1208, October 28, 2004. As of March 21, 2017:
http://www.gpo.gov/fdsys/pkg/PLAW-108publ375/pdf/PLAW-108publ375.pdf

Pursley, Sara, "'Lines Drawn on an Empty Map': Iraq's Borders and the Legend of the Artificial State (Part 1)," *Jadaliyyah*, June 2, 2015. As of July 23, 2016:
http://www.jadaliyya.com/pages/index/21759/
lines-drawn-on-an-empty-map_iraq's-borders-and-the

"Qabā'il Sīnā' Tatlub Mawāfaqat al-Jaysh 'ala Qitāl Ibnā'iha li Dā'sh [Sinai Tribes Ask for the Army's Agreement That Their Sons Fight ISIL]," Al Arabiya, April 28, 2015.

Qutb, Sayyid, *Ma'alim fi al-Tariq [Milestones]*, reprint, New Delhi: Islamic Book Service, 2007.

Rago, Joseph, "How Algorithms Can Help Beat the Islamic State," *Wall Street Journal*, March 11, 2017.

Rasmussen, Nicholas J., "Worldwide Threats to the Homeland: ISIS and the New Wave of Terror," testimony before the House Homeland Security Committee, July 14, 2016.

Rasmussen, Sune Engel, "ISIS in Afghanistan: 'Their Peak Is Over, But They Are Not Finished,'" *Guardian*, November 18, 2016. As of X:
https://www.theguardian.com/world/2016/nov/18/
isis-in-afghanistan-their-peak-is-over-but-they-are-not-finished

Razoux, Pierre, *The Iran-Iraq War*, trans. Nicholas Elliot, Cambridge, Mass.: Harvard University Press, 2015.

"Remaining and Expanding," *Dabiq*, No. 5, 1436 Muharram [2014], p. 22.

Reuter, Christoph, "Secret Files Reveal the Structure of Islamic State," *Der Spiegel*, April 18, 2015.

Robinson, Linda, Patrick B. Johnston, and Gillian S. Oak, *U.S. Special Operations Forces in the Philippines, 2001–2014*, Santa Monica, Calif.: RAND Corporation, RR-1236-OSD, 2016. As of February 8, 2017:
http://www.rand.org/pubs/research_reports/RR1236.html

Roggio, Bill, "Islamic State Strikes Egyptian Naval Vessel off Sinai Coast," *Long War Journal*, July 16, 2015.

Rosand, Eric, "Taking the Off-Ramp: A Path to Preventing Terrorism," War on the Rocks website, July 1, 2016. As of February 13, 2017:
https://warontherocks.com/2016/07/
taking-the-off-ramp-a-path-to-preventing-terrorism/

Ross, Dennis, "A Strategy for Beating the Islamic State," *Politico*, September 2, 2014.

Roy, Olivier, *Islam and Resistance in Afghanistan*, 2nd ed., New York: Cambridge University Press, 1990.

———, *Globalized Islam: The Search for a New Ummah*, New York: Columbia University Press, 2004.

Rubin, Barnett R., *The Fragmentation of Afghanistan: State Formation and Collapse in the International System*, New Haven, Conn.: Yale University Press, 1995.

Rugh, Bill, "Syria: The Hama Massacre," Washington, D.C.: Middle East Policy Council, February 26, 2015. As of August 3, 2016:
http://www.mepc.org/articles-commentary/commentary/syria-hama-massacre

Ryan, Missy, "U.S. Officials: Chief of the Islamic State in Libya Thought to be Killed in Airstrike" *Washington Post*, November 14, 2015. As of February 9, 2017:
https://www.washingtonpost.com/world/national-security/us-officials-leader-of-islamic-state-in-libya-believed-killed-in-us-airstrike/2015/11/14/b42cb714-8af0-11e5-be39-0034bb576eee_story.html

Sabry, Mohannad, *Sinai: Egypt's Linchpin, Gaza's Lifeline, Israel's Nightmare*, Cairo: American University in Cairo Press, October 2015.

Sageman, Marc, "The Stagnation of Research on Terrorism," *Chronicle of Higher Education*, April 30, 2013.

Sanders, Bernie, "Bernie Sanders on ISIS," February 2015. As of February 8, 2017:
http://feelthebern.org/bernie-sanders-on-isis/

Savage, Charlie, "U.S. Removes Libya from List of Zones with Looser Rules for Drone Strikes," *New York Times*, January 20, 2017.

Schaller, Christian, "Using Force Against Terrorists 'Outside Areas of Active Hostilities'—The Obama Approach and the Bin Laden Raid Revisited," Journal of Conflict Security Law, Vol. 20, No. 2, February 2, 2015, pp. 195–227.

Schanzer, Jonathan, "Turkey's Secret Proxy War in Libya?" *National Interest*, March 17, 2015. As of February 9, 2017:
http://nationalinterest.org/feature/turkeys-secret-proxy-war-libya-12430?page=2

Schenker, David, "How the Israeli Drone Strike in the Sinai Might Backfire," *Atlantic*, August 13, 2013.

———, "Security Challenges in Egypt Two Years After Morsi," testimony before the House Foreign Affairs Subcommittee on the Middle East and North Africa, December 16, 2015.

Schmidt, Michael, and Eric Schmitt, "As ISIS Loosens Grip, U.S. and Iraq Prepare for Grinding Insurgency," *New York Times*, July 25, 2016. As of 25 July 2016:
http://www.nytimes.com/2016/07/26/world/middleeast/isis-iraq-insurgency.html?_r=0

Schmitt, Eric, and Helene Cooper, "U.S. and Allies Weigh Military Action Against ISIS in Libya," *New York Times*, January 22, 2016.

Schmitt, Eric, and Dionne Searcey, "U.S. Plans to Put Advisers on Front Lines of Nigeria's War on Boko Haram," *New York Times*, February 25, 2016.

Searcey, Dionne, "Nigerian Jet Mistakenly Bombs Refugee Camp, Killing Scores," *New York Times*, January 17, 2017.

SEDAC—*See* NASA Socioeconomic Data and Applications Center.

Shabad, Rebecca, "Costs Rack Up in ISIS Fight," *The Hill*, September 25, 2014.

Shah, Syed Ali, "14 Injured as Roadside Bomb Targets Judge's Police Escort in Quetta," *Dawn* (Pakistan), August 11, 2016.

Shahid, Kunwar Khuldune, "What Quetta Bombing Reveals About Islamic State and Pakistani Taliban," *Diplomat*, August 9, 2016.

Shalizi, Hamid, "Exclusive: In Turf War with Afghan Taliban, Islamic State Loyalists Gain Ground," Reuters, June 29, 2015. As of February 9, 2017:
http://www.reuters.com/article/
us-afghanistan-islamic-state-idUSKCN0P91EN20150629

ash-Shamali, Abu Jarir, "Al-Qa'idah of Waziristan," *Dabiq*, No. 6, December 2014 (1436 Rabi' Al-Awwal), pp. 40–55.

ash-Shāmī, Mujāhid Shaykh Abū Muhammad al-'Adnānī ,"Say, 'Die in Your Rage!" video message, January 2015.

Sharp, Jeremy, "Egypt: Background and U.S. Relations," Washington, D.C.: Congressional Research Service, RL33003, February 25, 2016. As of February 9, 2017:
https://fas.org/sgp/crs/mideast/RL33003.pdf

Shatz, Howard J., and Erin-Elizabeth Johnson, *The Islamic State We Knew: Insights Before the Resurgence and Their Implications*, Santa Monica, Calif.: RAND Corporation, RR-1257-OSD, 2015. As of February 8, 2017:
http://www.rand.org/pubs/research_reports/RR1267.html

Sherazi, Zahir Shah, "Six Top TTP Commanders Announce Allegiance to Islamic State's Baghdadi," *Dawn* (Pakistan), October 14, 2014.

———, "Islamic State Footprints Surface in Parts of Bannu," *Dawn* (Pakistan), November 14, 2014.

Sherlock, Ruth, "Why Business Is Booming Under Islamic State One Year On," *Telegraph*, June 8, 2015. Available:
http://www.telegraph.co.uk/news/worldnews/islamic-state/11657918/Why-business-is-booming-under-Islamic-State-one-year-on.html

Shoman, Mohamed, "Kayfa Nantasir 'ala al-Irhāb fī Sīnā'? [How Can We Be Victorious over Terrorism in Sinai?]," *Al-Hayat*, November 5, 2014.

"Sinai Province: Egypt's Most Dangerous Group," British Broadcasting Corporation, May 12, 2016. As of February 9, 2017:
http://www.bbc.com/news/world-middle-east-25882504

Sinai State, "Tahdhīr wa wa'īd li min a'ān junūd ar-ridda wa at-tandīd [Warning and threat to anyone who helps the condemned soldiers of apostasy]," communiqué, March 26, 2015.

Small Arms Survey, "The Online Trade of Light Weapons in Libya," Security Assessment, No. 6, April 2016. As of February 9, 2017: http://www.smallarmssurvey.org/about-us/highlights/2016/highlight-sana-dispatch6.html

Smith, Niel, and Sean MacFarland, "Anbar Awakens: The Tipping Point," *Military Review*, August 2008, pp. 65–76. As of July 24, 2016: http://www.mccdc.marines.mil/Portals/172/Docs/SWCIWID/COIN/Recent%20 US%20ARMY%20Counterinsurgency%20History/Military%20Review%20 Magazine%20-%20Counterinsurgency%20Reader%20II%20(Aug2008).pdf

Smith, Scott, and Colin Cookman, eds., *State Strengthening in Afghanistan: Lessons Learned, 2001–2014*, Washington, D.C.: U.S. Institute of Peace, May 2016.

Somanader, Tanya, "President Obama Provides an Update on Our Strategy to Degrade and Destroy ISIL, July 6, 2015. As of February 13, 2017: https://obamawhitehouse.archives.gov/blog/2015/07/06/ president-obama-provides-update-our-strategy-degrade-and-destroy-isil

Soufan Group, *Foreign Fighters: An Updated Assessment of the Flow of Foreign Fighters into Syria and Iraq*, New York, December 2015. As of February 13, 2017: http://soufangroup.com/wp-content/uploads/2015/12/TSG_ ForeignFightersUpdate3.pdf

Soufan, Ali H., *The Black Banners: The Inside Story of 9/11 and the War Against al-Qaeda*, New York: W.W. Norton, 2011.

Spaaij, Ramón, "The Enigma of Lone Wolf Terrorism: An Assessment," *Studies in Conflict & Terrorism*, Vol. 33, No. 9, 2010. As of February 13, 2017: http://www.tandfonline.com/doi/abs/10.1080/1057610X.2010.501426

Speckhard, Anne, and Ahmet S. Yayla, *ISIS Defectors: Inside Stories of the Terrorist Caliphate*, McLean, Va.: Advances Press, 2016.

Stern, Jessica, "Containing ISIS: What Would George Kennan Do?" *Atlantic*, December 9, 2015.

Stern, Jessica, and J. M. Berger, *ISIS: The State of Terror*, New York: HarperCollins, 2015.

Stevens, Tim, and Peter R. Neumann, *Countering Online Radicalisation: A Strategy for Action*, London: International Centre for the Study of Radicalisation and Political Violence, 2009. As of February 13, 2017: http://icsr.info/wp-content/uploads/2012/10/1236768491ICSROnlineRadicalisati onReport.pdf

Stromseth, Jane, David Wippman, and Rosa Brooks, *Can Might Make Rights? Building the Rule of Law after Military Interventions*, New York: Cambridge University Press, 2006.

Sullivan, Marisa, *Hezbollah in Syria*, Washington, D.C.: Institute for the Study of War, April 2014. As of August 3, 2016:
http://www.understandingwar.org/sites/default/files/Hezbollah_Sullivan_FINAL.pdf

Szubin, Adam, "Remarks of Acting Under Secretary Adam Szubin on Countering the Financing of Terrorism at the Paul H. Nitze School of Advanced International Studies," October 20, 2016. As of February 13, 2017:
https://www.treasury.gov/press-center/press-releases/Pages/jl0590.aspx

Taber, Robert, *War of the Flea: The Classic Study of Guerrilla Warfare*, Washington, D.C.: Potomac Books, 2002.

Tabler, Andrew J., Soner Cagaptay, David Pollock, and James F. Jeffrey, "The Syrian Kurds: Whose Ally?" Washington, D.C.: Washington Institute for Near East Policy, March 29, 2016. As of August 3, 2016:
http://www.washingtoninstitute.org/policy-analysis/view/the-syrian-kurds-whose-ally

Tahrir Institute for Middle East Policy, "Wilayat Sinai," undated. As of February 9, 2017:
http://timep.org/esw/profiles/terror-groups/wilayat-sinai/

al-Tamimi, Aymenn, "The Evolution in Islamic State Administration: The Documentary Evidence," *Perspectives on Terrorism*, Vol. 9, No. 4, 2015.

Tastekin, Fahim, "Turkey's War in Libya" *Al-Monitor*, December 4, 2014. As of February 9, 2017:
http://www.al-monitor.com/pulse/originals/2014/12/turkey-libya-muslim-brotherhood.html#

Thorne, John, "What's in the Internet Videos Posted by Tamerlan Tsarnaev," *Christian Science Monitor*, April 28, 2013.

Thurston, Alex, "'The Disease Is Unbelief': Boko Haram's Religious and Political Worldview," Washington, D.C.: Brookings Institution, Analysis Paper No. 22, January 2016. As of February 9, 2017:
https://www.brookings.edu/research/the-disease-is-unbelief-boko-harams-religious-and-political-worldview/

Tinker, Jerry M., ed., *Strategies of Revolutionary Warfare*, New Delhi: S. Chand & Co., 1969.

Toft, Monica Duffy, *Securing the Peace: The Durable Settlement of Civil Wars*, Princeton, N.J.: Princeton University Press, 2009.

Torbati, Yeganeh, "Islamic State Yearly Oil Revenue Halved to $250 Million: U.S. Official," Reuters, May 11, 2016, as of June 16, 2016:
http://www.reuters.com/article/us-mideast-crisis-islamic-state-revenue-idUSKCN0Y22CW

Trager, Eric, and Marina Shalabi, "Egypt's Muslim Brotherhood Gets a Facelift: The Movement's Young Leaders Turn Revolutionary to Stay Relevant," *Foreign Affairs*, May 20, 2015.

Trump, Donald, "Transcript: Donald Trump's Foreign Policy Speech," *New York Times*, April 27, 2016. As of February 13, 2017:
https://www.nytimes.com/2016/04/28/us/politics/
transcript-trump-foreign-policy.html

"Two Locals Were Core of Fallujah Insurgency," Associated Press, November 24, 2004. As of July 23, 2016:
http://www.nbcnews.com/id/6578062/ns/world_news-mideast_n_africa/t/two-locals-were-core-fallujah-insurgency/#.V5OzBGUzPzI

UN—*See* United Nations.

U.S. Code, Title 10, §2282, Authority to Build the Capacity of Foreign Security Forces, undated. As of March 20, 2017:
https://www.law.cornell.edu/uscode/text/10/2282

"U.S. Cross-Border Raid Highlights Syria's Role in Islamist Militancy," *CTC Sentinel*, November 15, 2008. As of August 3, 2016:
https://www.ctc.usma.edu/
posts/u-s-cross-border-raid-highlights-syria's-role-in-islamist-militancy

U.S. Department of Defense, "Iraq and Syria: ISIL's Areas of Influence, August 2014 through April 2016," Washington, D.C., 2016a. As of February 13, 2017:
http://www.defense.gov/Portals/1/features/2014/0814_iraq/docs/20160512_
ISIL%20Areas%20of%20Influence_Aug%202014%20through%20Apr%20
2016%20Map.pdf

———, "FY2017 Budget Request to Congress," Washington, D.C.: Office of the Under Secretary of Defense (Comptroller), February 2016b.

———, "FY2017 Amended Budget Request to Congress," Washington, D.C.: Office of the Under Secretary of Defense (Comptroller), November 2016c.

U.S. Department of State, "Global Coalition to Counter ISIL," webpage, undated. As of January 10, 2017:
http://www.state.gov/s/seci/

———, *Country Reports on Terrorism 2005*, Washington, D.C.: Office of the Coordinator for Counterterrorism, April 2006.

———, "Nigeria 2015 Human Rights Report," *Country Reports on Human Rights Practices for 2015*, Washington, D.C.: Bureau of Democracy, Human Rights, Labor, 2015a. As of February 13, 2017:
https://www.state.gov/documents/organization/252927.pdf

———, "Establishment of the Counter-ISIL Finance Group in Rome, Italy," media note, Washington, D.C.: Office of the Spokesperson, March 20, 2015b.

————, *Country Reports on Terrorism 2015*, Washington, D.C.: Bureau of Counterterrorism and Countering Violent Extremism, June 2016.

U.S. Department of the Treasury, "Treasury Sanctions Networks Providing Support to the Government of Syria, Including for Facilitating Syrian Government Oil Purchases from ISIL," Washington, D.C., November 25, 2015.

United Nations, "Preliminary Findings by the United Nations Working Group on the Use of Mercenaries on Its Official Visit to Tunisia," July 2015. As of February 9, 2017:
http://www.ohchr.org/EN/NewsEvents/Pages/DisplayNews.aspx?NewsID=16219&LangID=E

United Nations High Commissioner for Refugees, "Facts and Figures About Refugees," Geneva, 2016a. As of February 9, 2016:
http://www.unhcr.ie/about-unhcr/facts-and-figures-about-refugees

————, "Lake Chad Basin Emergency Response," Geneva, July 2016b.

USAID—See Agency for International Development.

U.S. Agency for International Development, *U.S. Overseas Loans and Grants: Obligations and Loan Authorizations, July 1, 1945–September 30, 2014* ("Greenbook"), Washington, D.C., 2014.

Vidino, Lorenzo, and Seamus Hughes, "ISIS in America: From Retweets to Raqqa," Washington, D.C.: George Washington University Program on Extremism, December 2015. As of February 13, 2017:
https://cchs.gwu.edu/sites/cchs.gwu.edu/files/downloads/ISIS%20in%20America%20-%20Full%20Report_0.pdf

Vissar, Reidar, "Iraq's New Government and the Question of Sunni Inclusion," *CTC Sentinel*, September 29, 2014. As of July 24, 2016:
https://www.ctc.usma.edu/posts/iraqs-new-government-and-the-question-of-sunni-inclusion.

"Wālī Gharb Ifrīqīya: Al-Shaykh Abu Musa'b al-Barnawi," *An Naba'*, No. 41, August 2016.

Walsh, Declan, Ben Hubbard, and Eric Schmidt, "U.S. Bombing in Libya Reveals Limits of Strategy Against ISIS," *New York Times*, February 20, 2016, p. A1.

Walt, Stephen M., "What Should We Do if the Islamic State Wins? Live with It," *Foreign Policy*, June 10, 2015a.

————, "ISIS as a Revolutionary State," *Foreign Affairs*, Vol. 94, No. 6, November/December 2015b, pp. 42–51.

Warrick, Joby, *Black Flags: The Rise of ISIS*, New York: Doubleday, 2015.

————, "New Poll Finds Young Arabs Are Less Swayed by the Islamic State," *Washington Post*, April 12, 2016a.

————, "In Albania—NATO Member and U.S. Ally—Worries About the Emergence of ISIS," *Washington Post*, June 11, 2016b. As of February 8, 2016: https://www.washingtonpost.com/world/national-security/in-albania--nato-member-and-us-ally--the-worrying-emergence-of-isis/2016/06/11/1c56c4f6-2f47-11e6-9b37-42985f6a265c_story.html?utm_term=.7c421de891e6

Warrick, Joby, and Souad Mekhennet, "Inside ISIS: Quietly Preparing for the Loss of the 'Caliphate,'" *Washington Post*, July 12, 2016. As of February 8, 2016: https://www.washingtonpost.com/world/national-security/inside-isis-quietly-preparing-for-the-loss-of-the-caliphate/2016/07/12/9a1a8a02-454b-11e6-8856-f26de2537a9d_story.html?utm_term=.b8f2c4723f93

Watts, Clint, "Foreign Fighters: How Are They Being Recruited? Two imperfect Recruitment Models," *Small Wars Journal*, June 22, 2008.

————, "Let Them Rot: The Challenges and Opportunities of Containing Rather Than Countering the Islamic State," *Perspectives on Terrorism*, Vol. 9, No. 4, August 2015, pp. 156–164.

————, "When the Caliphate Crumbles: The Future of the Islamic State's Affiliates," War on the Rocks Website, June 13, 2016. As of February 13, 2017: https://warontherocks.com/2016/06/when-the-caliphate-crumbles-the-future-of-the-islamic-states-affiliates/

Weaver, Mary Anne, "The Short, Violent Life of Abu Musab al-Zarqawi," *Atlantic*, July/August 2006. As of July 22, 2016: http://www.theatlantic.com/magazine/archive/2006/07/the-short-violent-life-of-abu-musab-al-zarqawi/304983/

Weber, Max, "Politics as a Vocation," in H. H. Gerth and C. Wright Mills, eds., *From Max Weber: Essays in Sociology*, New York: Oxford University Press, 1958.

Wehrey, Fred, *The Struggle for Security in Eastern Libya*, Washington, D.C.: Carnegie Endowment for International Peace, 2012.

Weiss, Michael, and Hassan Hassan, *ISIS: Inside the Army of Terror*, New York: Regan Arts, 2015.

White House, "Procedures for Approving Direct Action Against Terrorist Targets Located Outside the United States and Areas of Active Hostilities," Washington, D.C., May 22, 2013. As of February 13, 2017: https://fas.org/irp/offdocs/ppd/ppg-procedures.pdf

————, "The Administration's Strategy to Counter the Islamic State of Iraq and the Levant (ISIL) and the Updated FY 2015 Overseas Contingency Operations Request," fact sheet, November 7, 2014. As of February 13, 2017: https://obamawhitehouse.archives.gov/the-press-office/2014/11/07/fact-sheet-administration-s-strategy-counter-islamic-state-iraq-and-leva

————, "Our Strategy to Defeat and Ultimately Destroy ISIL," strategy pocket card, November 20, 2015.

Whitlock, Craig, "Pentagon Setting Up Drone Base in Africa to Track Boko Haram Fighters," *Washington Post*, October 14, 2015.

Whiteside, Craig Andrew, "The Smiling, Scented Men: The Political Worldview of the Islamic State of Iraq, 2003–2013," dissertation, Pullman: Washington State University, December 2014. As of February 8, 2017: https://research.libraries.wsu.edu/xmlui/bitstream/handle/2376/5421/Whiteside_wsu_0251E_11248.pdf?sequence=1&isAllowed=y

————, *Lighting the Path: The Evolution of the Islamic State Media Enterprise, 2003–2016*, Hague: International Centre for Counter-Terrorism, November 2016.

Wicken, Stephen, *Iraq's Sunnis in Crisis*, Washington, D.C.: Institute for the Study of War, 2012. As of 24 July 2016: http://www.understandingwar.org/sites/default/files/Wicken-Sunni-In-Iraq.pdf

Wickham-Crowley, Timothy P., *Guerrillas and Revolution in Latin America: A Comparative Study of Insurgents and Regimes Since 1956*, Princeton, N.J.: Princeton University Press, 1992.

Wikas, Seth, *Battling the Lion of Damascus: Syria's Domestic Opposition and the Asad Regime*, Washington, D.C.: Washington Institute for Near East Policy, May 2007. As of August 3, 2016: https://www.washingtoninstitute.org/uploads/Documents/pubs/PolicyFocus69.pdf

Williams, Rob, "Syrian Refugees Will cost Ten Times More to Care for In Europe than in Neighboring Countries," *Independent*, 2016. As of February 13, 2017: http://www.independent.co.uk/voices/syrian-refugees-will-cost-ten-times-more-to-care-for-in-europe-than-in-neighboring-countries-a6928676.html

Williams, Lynn M., and Susan B. Epstein, *Overseas Contingency Operations Funding: Background and Status*, Washington, D.C.: Congressional Research Service, R44519, February 7, 2017. As of February 13, 2017 https://fas.org/sgp/crs/natsec/R44519.pdf

Winter, Charlie, *Documenting the "Virtual Caliphate,"* London: Quilliam Foundation, October 2015. As of August 2, 2016: http://www.quilliaminternational.com/wp-content/uploads/2015/10/FINAL-documenting-the-virtual-caliphate.pdf

————, "ISIS Is Using the Media Against Itself," *Atlantic*, March 23, 2016. As of February 13, 2017: https://www.theatlantic.com/international/archive/2016/03/isis-propaganda-brussels/475002/

Wood, Graeme, "What ISIS Really Wants," *Atlantic*, March 2015. As of August 2, 2016: http://www.theatlantic.com/magazine/archive/2015/03/what-isis-really-wants/384980/

World Bank, *Reforming Public Institutions and Strengthening Governance*, Washington D.C., 2000.

———, *Governance Matters 2006: Worldwide Governance Indicators*, Washington, D.C., 2006.

———, Worldwide Governance Indicators, database, 2017. As of February 14, 2017:
http://www.govindicators.org

X, "The Sources of Soviet Conduct," *Foreign Affairs*, Vol. 25, No. 4, 1947, pp. 566–582.

Yapp, M. E., *The Near East Since the First World War: A History to 1995*, London: Addison Wesley Longman, Ltd., 1996.

"Young Libyans Head to Join ISIS in Syria and Iraq," *Libya Herald*, September 8, 2014.

Zahid, Farhan, "Islamic State in Afghanistan Ready to Capitalize on Mullah Omar's Death," *Terrorism Monitor*, Vol. 13, No. 18, September 3, 2015.

Zahran, Mustafa, "al-Tanzhīmāt al-Musallaha fi Saynā' wa Imkānīyāt at-Tamadud Dākhilīan [Armed Groups in the Sinai and their Potential to Spread Internally]," Istanbul: Egyptian Institute for Political and Strategic Studies, December 20, 2015.

Zakheim, Dov S., "The Only ISIS Strategy Left for America: Containment," *National Interest*, May 23, 2015.

Zelin, Aaron Y., "The Islamic State's Burgeoning Capital in Sirte, Libya" Washington, D.C.: Washington Institute for Near East Policy, Policywatch 2462, February 19, 2015. As of February 13, 2017:
http://www.washingtoninstitute.org/policy-analysis/view/the-islamic-states-burgeoning-capital-in-sirte-libya

———, "The Islamic State's Territorial Methodology," Washington, D.C.: Washington Institute for Near East Policy, No. 29, January 2016. As of August 2, 2016:
http://www.washingtoninstitute.org/uploads/Documents/pubs/ResearchNote29-Zelin.pdf

Zenn, Jacob, "A Biography of Boko Haram and the Bay'a to al-Baghdadi," *CTC Sentinel*, Vol. 8, No. 3, March 2015a. As of February 9, 2017:
https://www.ctc.usma.edu/posts/a-biography-of-boko-haram-and-the-baya-to-al-baghdadi

———, "Wilayat West Africa Reboots for the Caliphate," *CTC Sentinel*, Vol. 8, No. 8, August 2015b. As of February 9, 2017:
https://www.ctc.usma.edu/posts/wilayat-west-africa-reboots-for-the-caliphate

Zogby Research Services, "Today's Middle East: Pressures and Challenges," November 2014.

El-Zoghby, Salwa, "15 Ma'lūma 'an Hisham 'Ashmawi, al-'Aql al-Mudabbir li Ightiyāl al-Nā'ib al-'Amm [15 Facts About Hisham 'Ashmawi, the Mastermind of the Assassination of the Prosecutor General]," *al-Watan*, July 2, 2015.